Latina Realities

New Directions in Theory and Psychology

Series Editors
Rachel T. Hare-Mustin and Jeanne Marecek

Focusing on emerging theory in psychology and related fields, this scholarly/trade series examines contemporary ideas broadly associated with postmodernism, social constructionism, feminist theory, and other critical reformulations of psychology. We seek manuscripts that propose or exemplify new ways of doing psychology, that reconsider foundational assumptions of psychological inquiry and practice, and that offer new approaches to therapy theory and practice. Among the topics considered are the social construction of such categories of difference/hierarchy as gender, race and ethnicity, class, and sexuality; and the politics of knowledge. Of interest as well are works that examine ways in which psychology—as a body of knowledge and a cultural institution—replicates or challenges arrangements of power and privilege in society.

Rachel T. Hare-Mustin, Villanova University, and **Jeanne Marecek,** Swarthmore College, coauthored *Making a Difference: Psychology and the Construction of Gender.*

Books in This Series

Latina Realities: Essays on Healing, Migration, and Sexuality, Oliva M. Espín

Through the Looking Glass:
Women and Borderline Personality Disorder, Dana Becker

Men's Ways of Being,
edited by Christopher McLean, Maggie Carey, and Cheryl White

Sex Is Not a Natural Act and Other Essays, Leonore Tiefer

Celebrating the Other: A Dialogic Account of Human Nature,
Edward E. Sampson

LATINA
REALITIES

*Essays on Healing,
Migration, and Sexuality*

Oliva M. Espín

WestviewPress
A Division of HarperCollinsPublishers

New Directions in Theory and Psychology

Copyright © 1997 by Westview Press, A Division of HarperCollins Publishers, Inc.

Published in 1997 in the United States of America by Westview Press, 5500 Central Avenue, Boulder,
Colorado 80301-2877, and in the United Kingdom by Westview Press, 12 Hid's Copse Road, Cumnor
Hill, Oxford OX2 9JJ

A CIP catalog record of this book is available from the Library of Congress.
ISBN 0-8133-3233-8   ISBN 0-8133-3234-6 (pbk.)

The paper used in this publication meets the requirements of the American National Standard for Perma-
nence of Paper for Printed Library Materials Z39.48-1984.

10   9   8   7   6   5   4   3   2   1

Contents

Foreword:
The Enigma of Arrival—
Journey and
Transformation

Lillian Comas-Díaz

Latina Realities is a remarkable tapestry depicting women's lives. Oliva Espín's inspiring weaving reveals an extraordinarily rich and diverse portrait of women that emphasizes themes of loss, migration, grief, adaptation, oppression, healing, creativity, and identity. *Journey* is an apt metaphor for the process by which we come to understand the situated knowledge of Latinas. The author shares with us her expert account of Latinas' journeys as well as her own odyssey. Emphasizing a narrative approach to women's lives, Oliva Espín documents not only that the personal is political but also that the distinctly personal touches us all.

Latina Realities is a compilation of essays based on Dr. Espín's extraordinary work over a sustained period. Her own scholastic journey, influenced by her personal migrations, provides a map for understanding the psychology of women. In her journey, Espín transforms herself into a witness, storyteller, subversive, alchemist, and sibyl. As a witness, she encourages Latinas to break their silence by listening to their testimonies. As a *cantadora* (storyteller), she inspires women to compose their lives. As a psychologist, she subversively challenges mainstream theory. Aiming at empowerment, her work transforms victims into victors. She rescues traditional wisdom and restores women's sense of dignity. And as an alchemist, Espín searches for the transforming source of knowledge, a search that culminates in the crafting of a multicultural feminist psychology. Along the way, she examines the arcane knowledge of Latina healers, including *espiritistas, santeras,* and *curanderas,* such that Latina ways of knowing transform her into a sibyl. Her scholastic prophecies are conjugated with her superb ability to examine, understand, and translate Latinas' realities.

Latina Realities acknowledges oppression as a psychological force. It documents a collaborative method of empowering women that is culturally congruent. Aided by the Latino tradition of storytelling, Espín's therapeutic stories affirm women's fluid identities. She confronts taboo topics. She reminds us that the sexual behavior of women serves a function beyond the personal, thus addressing the paradox of Latina sexuality as a source of both oppression and power. This collection restores to the self both power and agency, making the unknown known. It is revolutionary as it challenges the rigid patriarchal knowledge that bans women into the otherland. Espín's feminist tools help to effectively dismantle the master's house. Indeed, she is one of the true architects of the psychology of liberation.

Please join me in celebrating the publication of this book. *Latina Realities* significantly advances our knowledge not only of Latinas and women of color but of all women. It offers a model for addressing women's realities. Underlying it is the belief that those who differ from the mainstream have important knowledge to impart: *Firsthand knowledge of multiple distinct realities sharpens our perspective and makes us see ourselves and others in a new and creative light.* *Latina Realities* provides insightful wisdom to those who reside in the margins of society as well as to those who enjoy the privilege of being insiders. This book solves the enigma of the arrival; our journeys end in transformation. *Latina Realities* is about finding ourselves.

Preface

This book is a collection of selected pieces of my previously published work. The essays chosen for inclusion address a range of topics crucial to contemporary debates in psychology. The main purpose of this book is to contribute to ongoing debates on the impact of social forces on individual psychological development. These essays emphasize psychology's role "as a means of human welfare," focusing on the complexities of the psychological development of immigrant women, Latinas, and other women of color and issues relevant to providing psychological services to them. The essays cover issues of method, sexuality, therapy with Latinas and other women of color, immigrant and refugee women, ethnic-minority and immigrant women of diverse sexual orientations, and theoretical perspectives on feminist psychology and diversity.

During most of my professional career I have been both a faculty member engaged in the training of psychotherapists at the graduate level and a practicing feminist therapist. Since 1990, this combination, which had been central to my professional identity and development, has changed: I have been immersed in the world of women's studies with continuing involvement in psychology. This deeper involvement in women's studies has stimulated my thinking and intellectual growth, yet I remain deeply committed to psychology. In these essays, I speak as a feminist psychologist who has learned as much from practice and teaching as from purely intellectual and research endeavors.

The essays—written between 1984 and 1996—have been collected in this volume with the intention of making readily accessible pieces otherwise scattered in journals, edited books, and conference proceedings. In selecting pieces for inclusion, I have attempted to avoid overlaps while providing representativeness and breadth. I have emphasized those essays that have been most frequently cited by others through the years and those for which I consistently receive reprint requests.

I believe this book will contribute to the increased dialogue on epistemology and method in psychology. Many of these pieces illustrate the use of personal narratives as a source of knowledge in psychology. In this collection, I add my voice to those who have invited and encouraged psychology to embrace a fresh perspective by incorporating the study of narratives at its core. I hope this book helps to "make clear that story making, storytelling, and story comprehension are fundamental conceptions for a revived psychology" (Sarbin, 1986, p.vii). Presently, there is a renewed interest among psychologists in the role of narrative in establishing personal identity. This is based on the premise that a self needs a story in order to be. This collection of research studies and clinical experiences shows how cultures provide specific plots for lives and how social prescriptions become individually appropriated as one constructs a life story and a sense of self.

When people tell life stories, they do so through commonly understood models specific to their culture. Not only acceptable behavior but also acceptable *accounts* of behavior are socialized. Alongside acceptable behavior, we learn how to tell our stories in accordance with cultural "scripts." Stories/lives develop through compromises; the individual's desire and society's stabilizing power balance each other or push each other's limits (Rosenwald & Ochberg, 1992). The culture speaks through the individual narrator's "voice" and the culture provides the individual with the needed support to live, develop, and feel "normal." Indeed, even models of "craziness" have to meet standards on which the culture has agreed. Explanations of the etiology of psychological disturbance vary cross-culturally and include such dissimilar theoretical perspectives as attributing their causes to spirit possession, the chemicals in the brain, or events in one's past.

Other social sciences have used narratives and sought cultural explanations to understand human life, but in psychology perceptions of the value of narratives and of the importance of cultural factors on behavior have been contradictory. On the one hand, there is a tradition of using narrative for research in psychology, particularly in the field of personality psychology (e.g., such classic works in the field as Murray's 1938 *Explorations in Personality* and Allport's 1942 *The Use of Personal Documents in Psychological Science*). Feminist and cultural psychologists have stressed the impact of cultural forces on the individual. On the other hand, psychological research has been dominated by formal research methods that isolate characteristics and behaviors for study through experimental and statistical procedures. This perspective, which has dominated psychology since the 1950s, perceives the use of narrative for research as "soft" and "unscientific." And for the most part, psychology has persisted in using intrapsychic individual explanatory models.

Paradoxically, the whole field of psychotherapy is based on the use of narrative. Psychotherapy is a reconstruction of the life story, the telling of one's story to a sympathetic listener. In the process of being listened to and responded to in a different way, one finds that one's story and one's habitual modes of reaction take on reinterpreted meaning and become incorporated in a different way. Diagnosis is nothing but a way of organizing a narrative and making sense of disparate symptoms and experiences.

When I started writing the pieces included in this book, I did not make a conscious decision to focus my research through narrative approaches. But as I read these pieces collectively, I saw that they emphasize a narrative approach to women's lives. The essays collectively offer an answer to questions about life narratives and life transformations. For example: What happens to the individual life, sense of self, and life story when the cultural narrative changes abruptly through migration? Although "the story about life is open to editing and revision" (Polkinghorne 1988, p.154), some stories may require more work than others. "Re-writing one's story involves major life changes" (Polkinghorne, 1988, p.182). What happens when events that are not "personal events" in the usual way "invade" the life story? These essays present my firm conviction that "external" events are both "social" and "psychological." Some of these events (such as revolutions, war, migration, peace accords, and earthquakes or other natural phenomena) disrupt individual lives for days and weeks; others irrevocably alter one's life course. These events transform the "plots" provided by the culture and social context. At times, they transform the culture itself. In other instances, individuals find themselves in new cultural contexts that allow a different kind of story. Some classical studies of life history have their source in these cataclysms (e.g., Thomas & Znaniecki, 1918–1920/1927). As psychologists, we devise answers for these questions about the effect of sociohistorical dislocation on personal development that have profound implications for the lives of our clients and the theoretical basis of our profession.

In addition to this preface, in which I provide a context for the essays en masse, I include in each section a short introduction to its specific essays. These introductions frame the papers and position them in their historical context: The introductions and the chapters reflect both the development of my thinking and the development of feminist psychology. The introductory comments illuminate each chapter's special qualities and contributions to my thinking. These comments will, I hope, contribute to sharpening the reader's interpretive and critical skills. They also signal that all work is ongoing and no piece of work is ever perfect. These comments ideally will spur further conversation on gender issues in a multicultural context—while bringing psychological understandings to the development of feminist theory. In rereading these essays, I have once again rethought my own interpretations of these issues. I encourage the reader to assume a spirit of authorial kinship with me.

In my introductions to the five different sections, I have aimed to bring the material up to date by (1) critically discussing omissions and silences in each article and (2) providing a brief historical context for each essay. The essays themselves were geared toward different audiences. Some are easily accessible to all readers, regardless of their professional background. Others are more demanding and complex; these require knowledge of the psychotherapeutic process or theories in psychology and feminism. Although I have attempted to avoid repetitions and overlaps among the essays selected for inclusion in this anthology, some are inevitable. When ideas are repeated in several essays, they are presented in the context of different arguments. Each paper's perspective develops through the presentation of a set of arguments that may be needed for the development of a different set of ideas in another paper. Abridgement was not an option; it would create an incomplete and stunted version of the essays. I hope the inevitable repetitions serve to hone and clarify my thoughts anew.

Rereading these essays, some after many years, has refamiliarized me with my development as a scholar. Taken together, several basic threads run throughout. Although I did not intentionally focus on women immigrants in some of my early projects, the studies highlighted them nonetheless. For example, the Latina lesbians and the Latina healers of my early research all "happened" to be immigrants. Similarly, I see in retrospect that in the articles focused on feminist therapy with women of color I used two clinical examples of Latin American immigrant women. Likewise, during my years as a practicing feminist therapist my clientele consisted almost exclusively of women of color, immigrant and refugee women, and many Latinas. For a quarter of a century, I have done research, taught, and practiced therapy with and about women from diverse countries (particularly Latin American). Through my clinical practice and writing, I sought to understand how these women formed a comfortable identity and a sense of well-being amid turmoil and contradictory role expectations. Through these therapeutic relationships and observations of bilingual/bicultural experiences, I learned to understand the science and practice of psychology in a much richer way than was portrayed to me in textbooks. Since the late 1960s, feminist psychologist researchers, practitioners, and writers have proffered a new vision of gender studies in psychology. My contribution to that process, alongside the work of many others, has been to distill the significance of gender in the psychological development of women who are twice or sometimes three times "othered" by "mainstream" psychology. Through my teaching, writing, and practice of therapy, I hope I have given voice to those other realities. The intermingling of the personal, the political, and the theoretical that I believe so vital to good psychology has been present in my writing and therapeutic work.

A few words about the use of terms in the context of these essays and in the title of the book are in order. The title of this anthology refers to Latinas, who are the focus of most of the articles in the book. *Latina* is the term generally preferred by members of this population to designate themselves and I use it in most of the essays; in some of the essays, I use *Hispanic* interchangeably with *Latina* or *Latino,* reflecting the term current at the time these particular essays were written. Similarly, issues of sexuality and the immigrant experience resound through these essays. And although only one chapter focuses on healing in the traditional sense, all psychotherapy in fact aspires to healing. Thus, the inclusion of the word in the title is merited.

When I refer to psychotherapy in these essays, I usually have in mind a psychodynamic approach. I am obviously cognizant that there are many other varieties and theoretical approaches to therapy, but psychodynamic theoretical perspectives were central to my training and at the time, for me, synonymous with therapy. In the age of managed care, this may not be the predominant or preferred form of therapy, but it was the perspective from which I practiced and thus is implied in my references to psychotherapy. By psychodynamic psychotherapy, I do not mean orthodox Freudian psychoanalysis, but rather an approach that despite its Freudian origins incorporates radically different perspectives—in both theory and practice—from traditional psychoanalysis. From this perspective—nourished by feminist theoretical perspectives, object relations theory, and Kohut's self-psychology—the therapeutic relationship is central to the healing process. Rogerian person-centered theory has also been influential in forming my belief that the possibility of transforming psychological pain and learning new behaviors is dependent on the quality of the therapeutic relationship. In addition, I have focused equally on the effects of unconscious processes and on the importance of social forces in shaping individual psychology. In fact, I believe that the power of social forces to shape lives resides in their unconscious assimilation by individuals and societies. But my particular theoretical perspective on practice does not preclude the possibility of extrapolating clinical implications from these essays that could be valuable to practitioners of other psychotherapeutic approaches.

This collection of essays provides relevant information for students, instructors, practitioners, and researchers wishing to study the psychology of women from a multicultural approach. It also provides examples of contemporary approaches in the field. For those within the therapeutic and organizational consulting realm, I hope these essays clarify and promote the uses of narratives, collaborative interactive processes, and issues of diversity. Needless to say, I am not the only—or necessarily the best—representative of a diverse feminist perspective in psychology. No one scholar has the total picture. We all search to produce a piece of the truth and hope for transformation accordingly. My hope is that this collection contributes to the thinking of others and to the development of more accurate conceptions of psychology from a multicultural feminist point of view.

Oliva M. Espín
San Diego, California

References

Allport, G. (1942). *The use of personal documents in psychological science*. New York: Social Science Research Council.

Murray, H. (1938). *Explorations in personality*. New York: Oxford University Press.

Polkinghorne, D.E. (1988). *Narrative knowing and the human sciences*. Albany: State University of New York Press.

Rosenwald, G.C., & Ochberg, R.L. (Eds.). (1992). *Storied lives: The cultural politics of self-understanding*. New Haven, CT: Yale University Press.

Sarbin, T. (Ed.). (1986). *Narrative psychology: The storied nature of human conduct*. New York: Praeger.

Thomas, W.I., & Znaniecki, F. (1927). *The Polish peasant in Europe and America*. Boston: Richard C. Badger/New York: Knopf. (Original work published in 1918–1920)

Acknowledgments

No book is ever the work of one person alone. This book, which expands work produced over many years and contexts, owes debts to many people. Friends and colleagues who were influential in my life as these essays were being produced challenged my thinking. The questions I asked ten or fifteen years ago, like the questions I ask today, were often inspired through conversations and spirited discussions with them. Many friends and colleagues have read and offered detailed comments on the pieces contained in this book. Their generous sharing has no doubt improved the quality of my thinking through the years. Although our relationships have changed over time, their inspiration has been profound. There are too many to be mentioned adequately—I trust they know my debt to them.

Mary Ann Gawelek, my coauthor in one included essay, has been for over twenty years a trusted friend, inspiring colleague, and source of questions, ideas, and support. She was present while all these articles were written, and more than anyone else she has witnessed my personal and professional development. Her friendship, as well as that of Raquel Matas and Virginia Aponte, has provided sustenance to my emotional and intellectual life for most of my professional career. Doralba Muñoz and Lourdes Rodríguez-Nogués were present and supportive at different points in my career. They too inspired my thinking. In recent years, the feminist psychologists Esther Rothblum, Laura Brown, Carol Goodenow, Beverly Greene, Lillian Comas-Díaz, Ellyn Kaschak, Doris Howard, Gail Wyatt, and many others have provided me with support and inspiration through their friendship and writings.

I have the good fortune to have been a member of the faculty of the Department of Women's Studies at San Diego State University for the past six years. I owe a very large debt of thanks to all of my colleagues in the department for being a source of support and encouragement. This context has nourished and strengthened me considerably. Without these colleagues and the rich intellectual environment they have provided for me, this book would have never seen the light of day. Susan E. Cayleff in particular is a supportive colleague, trusted friend, and skilled editor. She has the ability to help me say what I am trying to say with new clarity and accessible prose. Pat Huckle, first as associate dean and now as a colleague, has encouraged and supported me and provided wise advice. She has also opened her home on the other side of the border to me, where I rest and think undisturbed. Bonnie Zimmerman, our department chair for many years, has supported every intellectual pursuit and worked hard to provide for all of us structures in which we can develop and flourish.

Kathy Jones has always challenged me to think deeper about significant issues in women's studies. Barbara Watson's work inspired new possibilities and understanding. Janet Kohen, as well as several of the lecturers in the department, has given me collegial support.

My colleagues at the California School of Professional Psychology in San Diego, particularly Michael Pittenger, Ray Trybus, Donald Viglione, Adele Rabin, Billy Vaughn, Bernando Ferdman, and Sharon Foster, have also provided support and encouragement.

The ideas in this book (and the book itself) developed in the context of feminist thought and action. The pieces included in this book were born of the feminist movement. All the psychotherapy clients I worked with through the years while practicing feminist therapy were a source of learning. The questions they posed challenged my thinking and my skills in various directions. My respect for women and their strengths was corroborated through my work with these women. My students in psychology and in women's studies courses have challenged and questioned my positions through the last quarter of a century. Their inquiring minds stimulated new levels of analysis and sharing. The editors and publishers of the books and journals in which these pieces first appeared made possible the initial presentation of these ideas. Their generous permission to reprint these articles and chapters have made this book possible. Abigail Stewart and Cynthia Gómez, my collaborators in one study, graciously agreed to reprinting it in this book.

Rachel Hare-Mustin and Jeanne Marecek, the editors of this book series, encouraged me and supported the idea of this book. At different points in time, Gordon Massman, Michelle Baxter, Cathy Pusateri, Ruth Tobias, and Jennifer Chen have helped in its production. Anna Sanchez's careful typing, proofreading, and tying together of all the different pieces has been an invaluable help in the production of this manuscript.

To all of them, my heartfelt thanks. Any shortcomings in this book are my doing, not theirs.

O.M.E.

Latina Realities

Part One

Experience as a Source of Theory and Method

Feminist epistemology starts with the conviction that "the personal is political." Translating the phrase into academic language, I understand it to mean that "the personal is theoretical." The essays included in this section present significant aspects of the development of my thinking about the theory and practice of psychology. Chapter 1, "Giving Voice to Silence," summarizes the most significant turning points of my professional development. This chapter offers the reader insights that illuminate most of the other essays in the book. In Chapter 1, originally written as the acceptance speech for the 1991 Award for Distinguished Professional Contribution to Public Service from the American Psychological Association, I reflect on the connections between theory and experience. These reflections illuminate how my personal experiences have affected my theoretical perspectives and also have implications for the theory and practice of psychology.

Chapter 1 identifies the challenges and frustrations that eventually produced professional insights despite the difficulty of questioning traditional ideas of what constitutes knowledge in psychology. My training emphasized the need to be "objective" rather than "subjective" in research. The issues I wanted to explore professionally were already deemed less than deserving of professional attention because they focused on women who belonged to nondominant social groups. In the past decade, however, I have become convinced of the value of subjectivity in the development of knowledge—and less fearful of being judged by pseudoscientific "objective" standards. The notion that personal experience is not objective and thus always suspect represented a barrier to my professional development. But the climate of the scientific world is changing, albeit rather slowly. It is now possible to admit to subjective experiences as a source of valid study. That change in climate, inspired largely by feminist theory, is transforming the academic disciplines—psychology included. This chapter is a plea for acknowledging the situated nature of knowledge in psychology and the relevance of this understanding for research and practice.

As a feminist and a psychologist, I strive to understand personal experiences not only as interesting events in one's life or individual exercises in consciousness raising but also as sources of theory. This understanding provides practical guidelines for working with others in therapy or in teaching. In both of the chapters in this section, my personal experience serves as a source of theory to better understand the lives of other women.

Obviously, experience is always subject to revision and reinterpretation. Experience is not transparent. Because I am trained as a psychologist, I am a feminist, and I am writing in what is for me a second language, I interpret my experience from a certain perspective and present it accordingly. These pieces were written several years ago and my interpretation of some of the experiences I describe is different now from when I originally wrote about them. Of necessity, the pieces describe only brief aspects of experience. And experience—my own and others'—is always filtered through a myriad of factors. Even the decision as to which experiences to focus on and which to ignore is determined by circumstances. A multiplicity of factors affected my choice of my experience of return to my country of origin to focus a discussion on the theoretical importance of experience in Chapter 2.

My first serious attempt to make personal experience the source of theory, research, and practice is represented in Chapter 2. "Roots Uprooted" was a long time in the making; I needed to discover what professional and personal events held a kernel of ideas that could inform the development of feminist theory and practice in psychology. And above all, I had to unlearn rigid notions about what constituted scholarly writing.

The first version of the chapter was written for a presentation in 1985 at the Women's Theological Center in Boston for the series "Historical Dislocation and Uprootedness." Except for an abridged version in the Boston feminist monthly *Sojourner,* the piece long remained unpublished. Finally, after several revisions, it was published in 1992, but not in a psychology journal. Rather, it was published by an interdisciplinary journal focused on writing by Latinos. Shortly thereafter (as the credit note states), a slightly modified version of the same piece served as the basis for my introductory chapter in a coedited book on the mental health of refugee women, simultaneously published as a volume of the journal *Women and Therapy.* The chapter represents the first time I dared present the interconnections I saw between personal and scholarly pursuits. When I reread this piece now, I see my defensiveness about the approach I used. I felt the need to insist that the information provided really had "scientific" implications. I was trying to convince my scholarly audience of the validity and "seriousness" of this source of data. In the past few years, the increased acceptance of other approaches to constructing psychological knowledge makes that defensiveness less necessary. But when this piece was initially written in the mid-1980s, that acceptance was not readily forthcoming. In fact, many small individual efforts contributed to this transformation in psychology. When I wrote this piece, I hesitated to take the risk; yet I had the strong intuition that there was value in my approach. Then, I knew very few others who shared my conviction. Over time, I realized many psychologists shared this profound conviction about the need to transform the nature of psychological knowledge through a feminist perspective and methods.

Regrettably, the research project I mention briefly at the end of Chapter 2 was never done. Instead, I focused my attention on an absorbing and substantial project on the sexuality of immigrant women. That work is described in the final chapters of this book and soon will appear as a separate book. There remains important psychological information to be discovered from the experiences of women who return to their countries of origin after living most of their lives elsewhere. Whether it is me or another scholar who pursues these questions is unimportant. The investigation will contribute valuable insights to the field of immigration studies.

Considered together, the chapters in this book argue for the validity of the personal as a source of theoretical knowledge. They do this in two ways. First, the simple progression of my own thinking is revealed, from the timid comments in "Roots Uprooted" (Chapter 2) to the bolder and riskier statements in "On Knowing You Are the Unknown" (Chapter 5), penned more recently and included in the next section of the book. But more important is the historical progression explained in Chapter 1, "Giving Voice to Silence," a description of personal and professional development that runs parallel to, intermingles with, and profits from the awareness brought about by the feminist movement—in and out of psychology— and by the paradigm shift occurring in psychology.

My attempts to create knowledge and theoretical understandings on the basis of the information provided by my experience and that of my therapy clients and psychology and women's studies students over twenty years is significant because it can constitute one vital thread in the tapestry of a renewed psychology. This renewed psychology will be truly feminist and encompass all of human experience.

1

Giving Voice to Silence: The Psychologist as Witness

Since new experiences to some extent change the meaning of the life history, and the single items of the life course gain in turn a different significance within the new whole, we may rightly say that the past of the person is in continuous change.

—Angyal, 1965, p.63

Paraphrasing these words from Andras Angyal, I can truly say that receiving an APA Distinguished Professional Contribution Award has changed the meaning of my professional past.

It would sound elegant and perhaps convincing to say that I knew all along where my professional choices and circumstances were leading me. But that is simply not the truth. A web of historical events beyond my control, personal experiences, ideas, feelings, decisions, indecision, chance, and people have brought me here. Sometimes I was consciously choosing, sometimes life was choosing for me. As the Beatles say, "Life is what happens to you when you are making other plans." Or, to use a more scholarly source, according to Bandura (1982), "chance encounters play a prominent role in shaping the course of human lives" (p.747). While "most developmental models of human behavior presuppose a developmental determinism in which childhood experiences set the course of later development" (Bandura, 1982, p.747), other factors such as the impact of sociocultural change, unpredictable occurrences in the physical world, and chance encounters can and do become determinants of life paths (Bandura, 1982).

What I would like to describe in the present article are some of those events, decisions, and chance encounters that have shaped my professional life and, through that process, present you with some of my thoughts about psychology. I would like to describe for you some of the "silences" I have observed in psychology and some of the ways in which I have sought to "give witness" to the experience of women who have entrusted me with knowledge about their lives in therapy, teaching, or research.

In order to do this it is essential for you to understand my own personal history. I was born in Cuba. My family, although not rich, was stable and placed great value on education. During my high school years, I was sure that I would have finished my college education and had a doctorate by the time I reached 25. But then, the final years of the Batista government, during which the universities were closed, and, later, the advent of the Cuban Revolution completely disrupted my life plans and adolescent dreams of achievement. Survival became the primary concern, particularly after I left Cuba.

As a young woman in my early twenties, I lived in four countries and three different continents in the course of three years. I felt rootless (Espín, 1991b). I felt I had lost my incipient sense of identity. The painful sense of being different was forever associated with my sense of self. The work I was doing, teaching and mentoring young women, demanded a level of responsibility and maturity beyond my years. Despite many obstacles, I completed my baccalaureate degree, and this accomplishment tethered me to my earlier and more stable identity. My own learning and teaching experiences provided me with a deep sense of accomplishment, purpose, and solidity.

After I finished my bachelor's degree in Costa Rica I received a fellowship to pursue doctoral studies in psychology in Belgium. I was by then 30 and experiencing the pressures of female socialization, the expectation of marriage and children. It had never occurred to me to question that the heterosexual path was the only one available to fulfill my emotional needs. I entered and soon left a disastrous marriage, the flight from which brought me to the United States.

In this country I quickly entered and finished a doctoral program in counseling psychology. This transition forced me into a minority person's experience, for in the United States being a Hispanic person has very specific emotional, social, and identity implications that I had never confronted before. During these years I fell in love with a woman and went through a coming-out process as a lesbian. Although two separate processes, these experiences deeply altered my adult identity and forever placed me at the margin.

I offered you this brief sketch of my life so that you might understand how and why I am compelled to listen to the experiences of marginal people. My own experience of not being heard, seen, or understood created in me a passion to give voice to others' experiences.

"Like many of those who have 'discovered' the idea of cultural psychology, I found my thinking was enormously influenced by the experience of going to a radically different culture" (Cole, 1990, p.291). Although I did not go, as is the usual case for psychologists in a cross-cultural context, "with the assignment of figuring out how growing up in cultural circumstances markedly different from my own influenced the mental processes of the local people" (Cole, 1990, p.291), my working and studying in different countries made me aware of the different "mental processes of the local people."

I had personally experienced the ever-presence of human variability. Even among the peoples of the Western countries where I had lived, differences were noticeable. It was clear to me that there were many valid ways of being human and that human development had many different healthy courses. Most important, experiencing myself in different countries and different languages taught me things about who I was that I would have never had access to had I not experienced myself in these cultural and linguistic contexts.

It seemed obvious to me, then as now, that since "the self of the observer is always implicated, it should be converted into an invaluable tool" (Reinharz, 1979, p.241). However, my professional training had taught me to remain detached and objective. All my training "defined the self as a source of error rather than as a source of knowledge, or as an impediment rather than a conduit for discovery" (Reinharz, 1979, p.252). I was taught to suspect the validity of the knowledge I already had and encouraged to do research that "objectively" portrayed some experiences while completely discarding others. In my earliest research I felt frustrated by the fact that I did not have categories to classify and quantify some of the most interesting data provided by the research participants (Espín, 1980).

My training had not prepared me for working with most of my clients. My bilingual clients were switching languages in the course of the therapy hour and changing topics and mood with these language switches. Women from different Latin American countries were talking about the influence of their cultural background in their expression of gender and sexuality (Espín, 1984, 1987a). Immigrant women were talking about the losses and gains brought about by the acculturation process (Espín, 1987b). Basically, we were talking together in the therapy hour about processes which were not "psychological" according to traditional theory. My gut reaction told me that such issues were at the core of these women's emotional lives as they had been at the core of mine.

When a prospective client called me saying she wanted a Spanish-speaking therapist because "her problems were in Spanish," I knew there was a silence about the importance of language in therapy that needed to be broken. When a student of mine was told that he needed to compare his data about the identity development of Latino boys with a comparable group of Anglo boys in order to make his research valid, I knew there was a silence about biases in research that needed to be broken. When the sexuality of both lesbian and heterosexual Latinas was either omitted or misinterpreted by well-intentioned writers, I knew there was a silence that needed to be broken. When the traumatic experiences of refugee and immigrant women were described as individual pathology, I knew there was a silence to be broken. Traditional psychology could not "hear" the fundamental experiences of the people I encountered in my practice and research. Neither scientific inquiry nor clinical practice provided a means for me to more fully respond to my clients' experiences, my students' need, and my research "subjects." "Scientific knowledge" had to be detached from any suspicion of "political activism." Clinical practice that did not conform to traditional methods was probably an expression of dangerous countertransference. And many of my students thought that a professor who spoke with an accent probably could not think without one.

The students I was training could not work with clients who did not "believe" in therapy, whose values and life experiences did not fit their own. Whatever literature there was at the time concerning ethnic minority populations, with rare exceptions, referred only to "the culturally disadvantaged" with a focus on ways of making those people "catch up" with "mainstream" American society by letting go of their "culture of poverty." Bilingualism was mentioned only as a difficulty in treatment. Homosexuality was, of course, mental illness, and women were not really healthy adults. People who did not fit traditional models of treatment were defective. They needed to adjust to these models or else go untreated. This is the case of square pegs not fitting round holes, the equivalent of asking people to catch only the illness we know how to cure, rather than developing the cure needed for the illness. Many of the researchers who are now known in the field of cultural and feminist psychology had barely started doing their work. At times I felt professionally alone in a world where I was being confronted with questions, doubts, and frustrations.

In spite of the lack of literature and the lack of research data (Sue, 1992), I began teaching a course, first on therapy with bilinguals and later on cross-cultural issues in counseling and psychotherapy. The literature I had available at the time consisted basically of the ideas of Karen Horney in *The Neurotic Personality of Our Time* (1937); Frieda Fromm-Reichmann's (1950) comments on cultural styles in therapy and on the impact of the clinician's accent on the treatment; Edith Buxbaum's (1949) article on therapy with bilinguals and a few other German immigrant clinicians of the 1940s; some of the initial work of Wallace Lambert (see Lambert, 1992), Derald Wing Sue (e.g., 1973) and Stanley Sue (see Sue, 1992), and Amado Padilla (e.g., Padilla & Aranda, 1974), Grier and Cobbs's *Black Rage* (1968), Thomas and Sillen's, *Racism and Psychiatry* (1972), and some of the work of Argentinian psychoanalysts (e.g., Krapf, 1955). Paulo Freire's (1970) insight into the psychological effects of oppression was for me an invaluable tool to make sense of the experience of ethnic minority individuals. Freire's ideas, together with the more recent writing on the topic of psychological oppression by the late Ignacio Martín-Baró (1994), continue to be an important influence on my thinking.

To my disappointment, very few students from the department believed that the course had any relevance to their training. Some of my colleagues believed that cultural issues were just "my pet issue" and actively discouraged their advisees from taking a course that was "political" rather than "scholarly." Addressing diversity concerns is now an expectation of the American Psychological Association accreditation of programs. However, many students and faculty continue to fail to understand their relevance and continue to frame the topic as "political" or relevant only for those who are themselves "minorities." The scholarly significance and importance of these issues for the knowledge base of psychology still escapes some people.

My interest in cultural and ethnic issues in psychology has always been intertwined with my commitment to women's issues. My years as a student of psychology coincided with the beginnings of the second wave of feminism. The ideals of the Women's Movement resonated deeply within my own experience. Luckily, in a department where all professors were male, my dissertation advisor gave me the opportunity to co-teach a course on counseling women while I was still a student and suggested I take this topic as my subject of specialization for my doctoral qualifying exams. Not knowing how extraordinary this was, because of my limited knowledge of the norms of the American academy, I enjoyed opportunities then that some feminist doctoral students do not yet have.

However, the beginning feminist perspective on psychological theory that provided me with an intellectual home once again presented the usual Anglo, white, middle-class, heterosexual, mainstream perspective that characterizes American psychology. Over and over, I was confronted with perspectives in which culture, race, class, and ethnicity did not seem to exist in the lives of women. This was happening while I was also struggling with perspectives in which the issues relevant to women did not seem important to my male colleagues working in cultural psychology. The prototype of woman was white, middle-class, and North American. The prototype of ethnic minority person was Black, male, and heterosexual. Yet, I knew from experience that there is no being who is only a woman or only a person of color. We are men and women of a certain race, culture, and class and we are persons of color as women or as men. This is true for all human beings, not only those of us who are "different." But I learned early that those of us who combine in our experiences several categories of oppression are more often than not confined to the margin and need to construct our understandings from the perspective of that margin (hooks, 1984).

My firsthand knowledge of the interlocking nature of oppression presented me with a challenge as a psychologist. Whatever research I have done has been an attempt to shed some light on this interlocking of gender, ethnicity, race, class, and sexual orientation. I did not set out to study unique experiences with unique methods; I set out to study and understand what I needed to know to serve my clients and train my students. In the process, I encountered some interesting issues and found myself using somewhat unorthodox methods. I did what I felt was needed while all along doubting my professional competence. And yet, I could not do anything else. Doing traditional research felt empty and devoid of meaning. My experience confirms that "the ability of feminists to transform the situation at hand into a research opportunity may be a survival mechanism" (Fonow & Cook, 1991, p.13).

For example, I did a study of letters written by an immigrant adolescent over a span of 10 years, trying to determine the impact of traumatic historical events on her psychological development and trying to determine if traditional theories, such as Erikson's, held true under these conditions (Espín, 1985, 1987c; Espín, Stewart, & Gómez, 1990). The answer to my question was both yes and no. First, I confirmed that a strong ego, even at a young age, is able to withstand extreme stresses without necessarily becoming warped by pathology. But I also confirmed that the process becomes altered and is modified by unique circumstances. The uniqueness of this study was not in its results but in the process of the research itself. I was inspired to do this study after reading Allport's *Letters from Jenny* (1965). When I initially undertook the study, it was obvious to me that a qualitative approach was the most appropriate and relevant to the material. I used a method to analyze personal documents that had been developed by Stewart and her colleagues (Stewart, Franz, & Layton, 1988) and was impressed with the clarity of the results. But journal editors were not about to accept data not illustrated by numbers. After several unsuccessful attempts at publishing the qualitative study, the data were scored and analyzed statistically. The results were not different from those of the qualitative analysis I had initially undertaken, and this time, the article was accepted for publication. But in the new version, the words of the author of the letters were mostly lost and silenced, as only the numbers that now symbolized her experience were available to the reader.

This unintended and ironic "experiment" reaffirmed my conviction about the validity of qualitative approaches. On the other hand, the process of publishing this paper taught me a very important lesson about the rigidity with which psychology gate-keepers continue to value one paradigm over another. In spite of all the recent social constructionist and feminist critiques of Western epistemology's emphasis on decontextualized "objectivity" (e.g., Unger 1983, 1988; Hare-Mustin & Marecek, 1987; Gergen, 1985; Hubbard, 1988; Morawski, 1990), psychology continues to define as "scientific information" only those ideas presented quantitatively.

My dissatisfaction with the accepted research methodology in psychology had a deeper root than my personal preferences or competence. As Reinharz (1983) puts it, "personally experienced dissatisfaction with conventional methods is not an intrapsychic, private problem but derives from structural inconsistencies and skewed assumptions underpinning the methods themselves" (p.166). Hidden within the "scientific" bias of psychology is a narrow perspective determined by privilege. And privilege, indeed, has a thundering voice.

We call "scientific" those definitions of reality created by those who hold power and "unscientific" and/or "biased" those definitions of reality created by those who are oppressed or without power. Throughout history, the privilege to define what is "normal" or "scientific" is conferred by power (Kitzinger, 1991). From this perspective, those who are different in any way are seen as either "deficient" (and thus not worthy) or "naturally different" (and thus unable to change) (e.g., Fine & Gordon, 1989). In either case, privileges are justified as deserved, and the power structures that sustain those privileges are perceived as "realities" that could not or should not be altered.

The ethnocentric bias (which is also the androcentric bias, since both are intertwined in the Anglo-Saxon perspective in psychology) manifests itself in the emphasis on measuring individual "differences" and in a research methodology that fits the experience of white, heterosexual males in North America and Europe. Any focus on "differences" assumes that something or someone is the norm and those who are "different" are "deviant" from that norm. Because psychology focuses so much on the study of "differences," it does not know how to look at human variability and diversity. In reality, however, human variability is the norm and each group's experiences and perspectives are nothing but a part of the total human experience. To limit our definition of the human to the characteristics of one group is narrow thinking and a limitation on our knowledge.

Indeed, the issue of inclusion is not about "affirmative action" or about generous reaching out to those who are less privileged, out of a duty to help them. It is about *the nature of knowledge* in the discipline of psychology. The theories and the research we now have are, for the most part, simply pieces of faulty knowledge, no matter how elegant they may seem to us (Espín, 1991a). In addition, an analysis of human diversity based only on difference camouflages oppressive structures and "naturalizes" those differences (Fine & Gordon, 1989). And, more important, the fact that power differentials in society play a role in these differences is totally obscured.

Power and privilege in fact blind those who are privileged into believing that their truth and experience constitute what is (or should be) normal. As Simone Weil stated years ago, "Someone who does not see a pane of glass does not know that she does not see it" (cited in Young, 1990, p.39). In psychology as in other disciplines, those who do not partake of all the privileges are more aware of the existence of Simone Weil's pane of glass. They know that in spite of its apparent non-existence it is next to impossible to pass through this barrier—the more effective precisely because it is unseen. That is why Freire (1970) believes that oppressed people tend to have a clearer vision of reality than their oppressors. They hear the sound of others' experiences because they have heard the sound of their own in spite of its apparent silence. That is why it is incumbent on those people to reveal the existence of that pane of glass, to give voice to the silent components of human experience, to give witness to the validity of other realities. We all have partial understanding of reality and no one perspective can encompass all there is to know about human experience. That is why all perspectives and different approaches to them are needed (Howard, 1991) and that is why all perspectives are to some extent biased.

Psychology holds enormous power over our willingness to see diversity among human beings as acceptable and good or as a "problem" to be decried. In this society, psychology is in a unique position to influence perceptions and attitudes towards human variability, not only because in North America we psychologize everything but also because the business of psychology is precisely to figure out what human beings are really like. And indeed, some of the knowledge generated by psychology is (or should be) useful in our understanding of diversity. Regretfully, most of psychological theory is based on research done on white males who are sophomores in U.S. colleges (Sears, 1986). In spite of the limitation imposed by this narrow pool, those results are generalized and considered to be universal and valid information about all human beings regardless of their race, gender, sexual orientation, social class, language, ethnicity, and so forth. Doing research that focuses on gender, ethnicity, or sexual orientation is still seen as a specialized interest, not central to the profession. However, post-modern understandings of the multiplicity of realities that constitute the reality of the world leave no room for naive descriptions of people, the world, or human life that incorporate only one perspective on that reality. No matter how privileged that perspective may have been in the past, it is as partial as all others. If we believe that "Africans show Africa; Asians, Asia; and Euro-Americans, the world" (Trinh, 1989, p.373), we are limiting our possibility of knowing that world to the partial perspective of Euro-Americans.

One interesting example from outside psychology can illustrate the importance of a multiplicity of perspectives. In the field of primatology, it has become very clear that the female scientist-observer sees different activities among primates than male primatologists do. What the women observe is different because they observe female actors with different eyes. On the other hand, the female perspectives on primatology frequently give us a picture of the lonely white woman fighting the African poachers, which naively oversimplifies economic realities in those countries (Sperling, 1991).

Although it is true in all fields that the more a critical mass of professionals exists within the discipline who represent diversity in gender, ethnicity, class, sexual orientation, and so forth, the more chances that diversity would be incorporated at the core of the discipline. This is particularly important in psychology precisely because the subject of study in psychology is so close to the lives of the researchers and practitioners.

It must be clear from all I have said so far that I believe a social constructionist position holds the promise of fruitful possibilities in developing psychological theory (Gergen, 1985). A social constructionist paradigm that sees psychological characteristics as a result of social and historical processes, not as natural, essential qualities of one or another group of people, is a much more productive approach in the study of human diversity than some of the other traditional paradigms accepted in psychology (Espín & Gawelek, 1992). From a social constructionist perspective, the development of psychological theory itself is dependent on forms of negotiated understanding that are the product of historically situated interchanges determined by the categories we posses to define reality (Gergen, 1985).

It must also be clear by now that theories of the psychology of oppression and resistance to oppression have helped me understand the impact of the sociocultural context in the development of personality and in the psychotherapeutic context. I have already referred to Freire's (1970) and Martín-Baró's (1994) description of the impact of internalized oppression in determining behaviors and aspirations that seem individually determined. Other useful perspectives are provided by Bulhan (1985), who has studied the effect of internalized oppression on violent behavior and the expression of anger, and Lykes (1985), who has developed a theory of social individuality to describe the intricacies of a self developed within a social context rather than the usual interpretation of the self as individualized and totally autonomous. She has extended the implications of her theory to her studies of

Guatemalan Indian women (Lykes, 1989b) and to her analysis of caring and power-lessness (Lykes, 1989a). I would like to continue expanding the implications of these approaches to the psychological impact of oppression to my developing understanding of the psychology of women of color, particularly immigrant Latina women.

As I stated earlier, language is an important and much neglected variable in personality development and identity formation. It is very clear from the work of post-structuralists that the structure of reality is modified by the language used to describe it. From this perspective, language is an active creator of experience. For those people who speak more than one language, there is yet another component in the development of personality and the expression of psychopathology. From what I have gleaned in therapy with bilinguals, it is apparent that self-expression in areas such as sexuality is highly influenced by the use of one or the other language (Espín, 1984). The expression of pathological affect, strong emotional states, and the experience of the self are affected by the language used (Marcos, 1976; Marcos, Eisma, & Guimon, 1977). A recent article by Kallifatides (1992) describing the impact of the Swedish language on his Greek identity echoed my experiences with language as a bilingual person in the United States, Canada, and Belgium. Eva Hoffman's (1989) description of her sense of feeling split between her Polish-speaking and her English-speaking selves, illustrated within psychology by some of the research conducted by Marcos and his collaborators (Marcos et al., 1977), also echoed the experiences of many of my psychotherapy clients. Yet, the clinical literature remains mostly silent about these treatment considerations when working with bilingual clients. This is another silence I would like to continue to break.

My thinking and practice has been enriched also by learning about models of psychological development provided by other cultures (Espín & Gawelek, 1992). These models can enrich psychological theory and teach us about other possibilities for being human. For example, according to Watson-Franke (1988), in matrilineal societies there is a different valuing of mothers (and women) and different father and husband roles for men than those we are accustomed to. Although in patriarchal societies matrifocal families are seen as less valid than male-headed households, in matrilineal societies, matrifocus represents the legitimate philosophy. Western theoreticians, raised within a patriarchal context, find it difficult to conceptualize as "healthy" a family context in which women are central. The female-headed family of all races is seen as deviant in most of the Western world and described as "dysfunctional." However, what would happen if we examined these families from the perspective of a different developmental paradigm? Clearly, the necessity of a nuclear family structure for healthy personality development becomes questionable when we observe other societies where children develop to be healthy human beings through different family structures. What implications would this have, say, for object relations theories? The basic psychodynamic postulate of the existence of an unconscious with a life of its own assumes the separate existence of an internal individual world that is shaped by interactions with the mother during infancy. Psychodynamic thinking has consistently assumed as universal a heterosexual family structure where the mother is the primary caretaker. Although this might be the experience of many individuals raised in our society, it is certainly not a universal experience. Even in the United States, only 11% of families have a "traditional" structure. How are we to understand psychological development based on relations with an other (the object) if the role of this other and the relationship between the developing child and this other are significantly different in different cultures? Variations in child-rearing practices, such as the use of wet nurses, the involvement of the extended family, the raising of children by siblings or grandmothers, the presence or absence of father, impact the development of personality. However, healthy human beings develop all over the world, even when the conditions we consider essential may not be present. The cultural boundedness of our theories becomes more obvious.

That is one reason I also feel the need to continue looking at the rituals of therapy, which, in spite of transformations, to this day reproduces the format adopted by Freud within Victorian society. Are some of those rituals as essential now as they were then? Should that structure change with the increased number of women therapists or as ethnic minorities enter into the practice of psychology? What can or should be changed and what should remain unchanged? How does therapy, as we know it, or other forms of healing (Espín, 1988) apply across cultures, classes, and so forth?

In the preceding brief summary I have tried to address some areas of psychology in which silences still prevail, some experiences that require witnessing on the part of psychologists if psychology as a science and a profession is to be truly a means for human welfare. I hope to continue to pursue some of them in the future, and I encourage others to do so as well.

At this point in the history of our profession it is becoming obvious that psychology is undergoing a paradigm shift (Kuhn, 1970) as well as a membership shift. Even though there is still strong resistance to this shift from some sectors of the profession, a number of recent publications, research studies, theoretical developments, new divisions of the American Psychological Association (APA), policies, and other manifestations, too numerous to even attempt to cite, bear witness to the extent of this slow but consistent transformation of what psychology as a science, a profession, and a means for human welfare stands for. Even as the APA enters its second hundred years, many of its members would not recognize as theirs the exclusive stands of G. Stanley Hall and the other 25 white male charter members who constituted the APA in 1892.

Within organized psychology, in the academy, and among practitioners, there is an increased awareness that the ubiquitous white, Anglo-Saxon, heterosexual, college sophomore male cannot represent all human beings. This slow but sure shift has opened the door for new theorizing, new methodological approaches to inquiry, and a new focus on experiences previously conceptualized as different from the norm. In other words, the paradigm shift we are witnessing points towards a truer psychology, better able to describe human experiences. I am proud to know that I have done my small part to foster that transformation.

For whatever reason, my intuition told me that when experiences are reported repeatedly, they become legitimized, "normal"; when silence is given voice, it becomes real; when life is witnessed, it becomes presence. With more or less awareness of what I was doing, this is what my career has been about. I felt a need, wanted to understand silenced people and their experience, and therefore taught and wrote about an area of study without prestige in the field. I was really not that political or savvy about what an academic career in a research university entailed. Had I been, I might never have taken these risks and may have resigned myself to living and working in a professional world silent to the issues at the core of my deepest self. But, perhaps because my ancestors come from the land of Don Quijote, I could not avoid the pull of a different path. Through a web of psychotherapy practice, teaching, consulting, and research, I have tried to explore and give voice and witness to the experiences of women from different cultural backgrounds and life paths. I know that "one of the rules fundamental to the traditional construction of psychology is that it is an apolitical domain of technological expertise" (Kitzinger, 1990, p.124). Even though I have received an award for my contributions to the profession, I realize that a lot of my career has gone against psychology's cherished notions of detached objectivity. There are questions that are alive in psychology today as they were 20 years ago at the beginning of my career. However, I continue to believe that true science is not "head shrinking" but "mind expanding," and I believe that resisting limiting notions of what constitutes psychology (Kitzinger, 1990) is essential for the development of true science and responsible practice in our discipline. I imagine a new future for the second century of psychology, a future that is already being created, and I want to contribute to that future so that psychology can truly become a science and a practice of human experience.

Notes

Reprinted from Espín, O.M. (1993). Giving Voice to Silence: The Psychologist as Witness. *American Psychologist*, 48(4), 408–414. Presented at the 100th Annual Convention of the American Psychological Association, Washington, DC, August 1992. (Acceptance address, 1991 APA Award for Distinguished Professional Contribution to Public Service.)

References

Allport, G. (1965). *Letters from Jenny.* New York: Harcourt Brace Jovanovich.
Angyal, A. (1965). *Neurosis and treatment: A holistic theory.* New York: Viking.
Bandura, A. (1982). The psychology of chance encounters and life paths. *American Psychologist*, 37, 747–755.
Bulhan, H.A. (1985). *Franz Fanon and the psychology of oppression.* New York: Plenum.
Buxbaum, E. (1949). The role of a second language in the formation of ego and superego. *Psychoanalytic Quarterly*, 18, 279–289.
Cole, M. (1990). Cultural psychology: A once and future discipline? In J.J. Berman (Ed.), *Nebraska Symposium of Motivation 1989: Crosscultural perspectives* (pp.279—335). Lincoln: University of Nebraska Press.

Espín, O.M. (1980). Perceptions of sexual discrimination among college women in Latin America and the United States. *Hispanic Journal of Behavioral Sciences, 2*(1), 1–19.

Espín, O.M. (1984). Cultural and historical influences on sexuality in Hispanic/Latin women: Implications for psychotherapy. In C. Vance (Ed.), *Pleasure and danger: Exploring female sexuality* (pp.149–164). London: Routledge & Kegan Paul.

Espín, O.M. (1985, March). *Letters from V: Traumatic historical events and female adolescent development.* Paper presented at the meeting of the Association of Women in Psychology, New York.

Espín, O.M. (1987a). Issues of identity in the psychology of Latina lesbians. In Boston Lesbian Psychologies Collective (Eds.), *Lesbian psychologies: Explorations and challenges* (pp.35–55). Champaign: University of Illinois Press.

Espín, O.M. (1987b). Psychological impact of migration on Latinas: Implications for psychotherapeutic practice. *Psychology of Women Quarterly, 11*, 489–503.

Espín, O.M. (1987c, August-September). *Traumatic loss and female adolescent development: A case study.* Paper presented at the 95th Annual Convention of the American Psychological Association, New York.

Espín, O.M. (1988). Spiritual power and the mundane world: Hispanic female healers in urban U.S. communities. *Women's Studies Quarterly, 16*(3–4), 33–47.

Espín, O.M. (1991a, August). *Ethnicity, race, and class, and the future of feminist psychology.* Invited address presented at the 99th Annual Convention of the American Psychological Association, San Francisco.

Espín, O.M. (1991b). Roots uprooted: Autobiographical reflections on the psychological experience of migration. In F. Alegria & J. Ruffinelli (Eds.), *Paradise lost or gained: The literature of Hispanic exile* (pp.151–163). Houston: Arte Público.

Espín, O.M., & Gawelek, M.A. (1992). Women's diversity: Ethnicity, race, class and gender in theories of feminist psychology. In L.S. Brown & M. Ballou (Eds.), *Personality and psychopathology: Feminist reappraisals* (pp.88–107). New York: Guilford.

Espín, O.M., Stewart, A., & Gómez, C. (1990). Letters from V.: Adolescent personality development in sociohistorical context. *Journal of Personality, 58*, 347–364.

Fine, M., & Gordon, S.M. (1989). Feminist transformations of/despite psychology. In M. Crawford & M. Gentry (Eds.), *Gender and thought: Psychological perspectives* (pp.146–174). New York: Springer-Verlag.

Fonow, M.M., & Cook, J.A. (1991). *Beyond methodology: Feminist scholarship as lived research.* Bloomington: Indiana University Press.

Freire, P. (1970). *Pedagogy of the oppressed.* New York: Salisbury.

Fromm-Reichmann, F. (1950). *Principles of intensive psychotherapy.* Chicago: University of Chicago Press.

Gergen, K.J. (1985). The social constructionist movement in modern psychology. *American Psychologist, 40*, 266–275.

Grier, W., & Cobbs, P. (1968). *Black rage.* New York: Basic Books.

Hare-Mustin, R.T., & Marecek, J. (1987). The meaning of difference: Gender theory, postmodernism, and psychology. *American Psychologist, 43*, 455–464.

Hoffman, E. (1989). *Lost in translation.* New York: Dutton.

hooks, b. (1984). *Feminist theory: From margin to center.* Boston: South End.

Horney, K. (1937). *The neurotic personality of our time.* New York: Norton.

Howard, G.S. (1991). Culture tales: A narrative approach to thinking, cross-cultural psychology, and psychotherapy. *American Psychologist, 46*, 187–197.

Hubbard, R. (1988). Some thoughts about the masculinity of the natural sciences. In M.M. Gergen (Ed.), *Feminist thought and the structure of knowledge* (pp.1–15). New York: New York University Press.

Kallifatides, H. (1992, May). *Language and identity.* Paper presented at the annual meeting of the Society for the Advancement of Scandinavian Study, Minneapolis.

Kitzinger, C. (1990). Resisting the discipline. In E. Burman (Ed.), *Feminists and psychological practice* (pp.117–136). London: Sage.

Kitzinger, C. (1991). Feminism, psychology and the paradox of power. *Feminism and Psychology,* 1(1), 111–129.

Krapf, E.D. (1955). The choice of language in polyglot psychoanalysis. *Psychoanalytic Quarterly,* 24, 343–347.

Kuhn, T.S. (1970). *The structure of scientific revolutions.* Chicago: University of Chicago Press.

Lambert, W. (1992). Challenging established views on social issues: The power and limitations of research. *American Psychologist,* 47, 533–542.

Lykes, M.B. (1985). Gender and individualistic vs. collectivist bases for notions about the self. *Journal of Personality,* 53, 357–383.

Lykes, M.B. (1989a). The caring self: Social experiences of power and powerlessness. In M. Brabeck (Ed.), *Who cares? Theory, research and educational implications of the ethic of care* (pp.164–179). New York: Praeger.

Lykes, M.B. (1989b). Dialogue with Guatemalan Indian women: Critical perspectives on constructing collaborative research. In R. Unger (Ed.), *Representations: Social constructions of gender* (pp.167–185). Amityville, NY: Baywood.

Marcos, L. (1976). Bilinguals in psychotherapy: Language as an emotional barrier. *American Journal of Psychotherapy,* 30, 522–560.

Marcos, L.R., Eisma, J., & Guimon, J. (1977). Bilingualism and sense of self. *American Journal of Psychoanalysis,* 37, 285–290.

Martín-Baró, I. (1994). *Writings for a liberation psychology.* Cambridge, MA: Harvard University Press.

Morawski, J.G. (1990). Toward the unimagined: Feminism and epistemology in psychology. In R. Hare-Mustin & J. Marecek (Eds.), *Making a difference: Psychology and the construction of gender* (pp.150–183). New Haven, CT: Yale University Press.

Padilla, A.M., & Aranda, P. (1974). *Latino mental health: Bibliography and abstracts* (DHEW Publications Nos. 73-9144). Washington, DC: National Institute of Mental Health.

Reinharz, S. (1979). *On becoming a social scientist.* San Francisco: Jossey-Bass.

Reinharz, S. (1983). Experiential analysis: A contribution to feminist research. In G. Bowles & R.D. Klein (Eds.), *Theories of women's studies* (pp.162–191). London: Routledge & Kegan Paul.

Sears, D.O. (1986). College sophomores in the laboratory: Influences of a narrow database on social psychology's view of human nature. *Journal of Personality and Social Psychology,* 51, 515–530.

Sperling, S. (1991). Baboons with briefcases: Feminism, functionalism, and sociobiology in the evolution of primate gender. *Signs: Journal of Women in Culture and Society,* 17(11), 1–27.

Sue, D.W. (1973). Asian-Americans: The neglected minority [Special issue]. *Personnel and Guidance Journal,* 51(6), 385–414.

Sue, S. (1992). Ethnicity and mental health: Research and policy issues. *Journal of Social Issues,* 48, 187–205.

Stewart, A.J., Franz, C., & Layton, L. (1988). The changing self: Using personal documents to study lives. *Journal of Personality,* 56, 41–74.

Thomas, A., & Sillen, S. (1972). *Racism and psychiatry.* Secaucus, NY: Citadel.

Trinh, M. (1989). *Woman, native, other.* Bloomington: Indiana University Press.

Unger, R.K. (1983). Through the looking glass: No wonderland yet! (The reciprocal relationship between methodology and models of reality). *Psychology of Women Quarterly,* 8(1), 9–32.

Unger, R.K. (1988). Psychological, feminist, and personal epistemology: Transcending contradiction. In M.M. Gergen (Ed.), *Feminist thought and the structure of knowledge* (pp.124–141). New York: New York University Press.

Watson-Franke, M.B. (1988, July). *Siblings vs. spouses: Men and women in matrilineal societies (South America and North America).* Paper presented at the international Congress of Americanists, Amsterdam, The Netherlands.

Young, I.M. (1990). *Justice and the politics of difference.* Princeton, NJ: Princeton University Press.

2

Roots Uprooted: Autobiographical Reflections on the Psychological Experience of Migration

> *. . . each of us confronts our respective inability to comprehend the experiences of others even as we recognize the absolute necessity of continuing to do so.*

> —Linda Brodkey

Ethnic minority and women researchers frequently find themselves dissatisfied the traditional methods of research that are considered valid by other social scientists while struggling to establish their legitimacy in the academic world. The result, more often than not, is that we find ourselves involved in research projects that do not feel methodologically "right" to us in order to achieve this legitimacy. Or, alternatively, we devote ourselves to what "feels right" at the risk of losing tenure battles or other academic "blessings" from our colleagues.

Shulamit Reinharz, discussing a research method that she denominates "experiential analysis" (1979, 1983), states that "the first step in articulating a new method (of research) is to understand that one's personally experienced dissatisfaction with conventional methods is not an intrapsychic, private problem but derives from structural inconsistencies and skewed assumptions underpinning the methods themselves" (1983, p.166). In her formulation, the personal experience of the researcher is not only valid but essential in the development of studies that would be contextual and relevant. For Reinharz, a relevant research project should provide "an opportunity for catharsis or self-discovery" (1983, p.176) for both researcher and subjects and a "research product likely to provide resources or answers to pressing problems in living" (p.176). "The record of the researcher's feelings and ideas is also data" (p.175) because "all knowledge is contingent on the situation under which it is formed" (p.177) and for all researchers "one's own race, class, religion and gender predispose us to consider some settings more interesting and important than others" (p.179).

Denzin (1986, 1989) and Runyan (1982), using life narratives for sociological and psychological research, respectively, have demonstrated the value of studying life histories and biography for the social sciences in general and psychology in particular. Through their psychobiographical and interpretive interactionist studies they have demonstrated that the data provided by life narratives produces a richness that could not be obtained through the use of other methods. Plummer (1983), in a review of different approaches to life narrative study, summarizes their possibilities.

I am sure that, by now, we are all disabused of the notion that "value-free" research exists at all. But we are probably very well trained to doubt the validity of our personal experiences and life as sources of data. Interestingly enough, if we were not the researchers, probably some outsider to our cultures could get some grant money to study our lives and get a few good publications out of the analysis of data based on interviews about our experiences. Why not, then, take the role of that "outsider" while remaining ourselves; combine the perspectives of experiential analysis, interpretive interactionism, and psychobiography; and do some experiential studies of data provided by our lives and the lives of individuals with similar experiences?

As a social scientist, and on the basis of my own personal experiences, I believe that there is much to be learned from the individual narrative. For the past few years I have been engaged in the experiential analysis of my own migration story as a research project. I believe there is a void in the literature that could be filled through the use of life narratives to understand the psychological impact of the experience of uprootedness from a scientific (as opposed to just human interest) point of view. That is why I would like to share with the readers the results of my own experiential analysis of this process and the life narrative on which it is based. My intention is to demonstrate both the importance of studying this topic and the usefulness of this methodology for its study.

In 1984 I returned to Cuba for a two-week visit for the first time after an absence of 23 years. I left Cuba when I was 22 years old, so at the time of this visit I had lived, roughly, half of my life in Cuba and half of my life away from Cuba. This coincidence made the time and timing of the visit particularly significant. The visit provoked in me innumerable reflections on the experience of uprootedness in my life and on the significance of having lived half of my life away from my country of birth.

The purpose of this essay is to share some of those reflections and some of the experiences that led to them. The experiences I want to share refer to the uprootedness of the second half of my life as well as to the intense experiences involved in that two-week trip to Cuba. I believe that these reflections can shed light on the experiences of exile and uprootedness in the lives of others.

I do not intend to discuss Cuban politics, to take positions pro or against the Cuban revolution, or even argue the soundness of my decision to leave Cuba in 1961. Obviously, my life experiences, like anybody else's, are deeply connected to a specific time, place, and historical event. However, any discussion of the specifics of this historical event (i.e., the Cuban revolution), would distract from the subject of this essay, namely, some psychological consequences of uprootedness and historical dislocation and the description of a methodology to study them.

Even though my experience of uprootedness is in one sense absolutely mine, individual, and unique, it is in another sense generalizable to any person who has ever undergone the effects of historical dislocation. Because I am a psychologist and I see the meaning of my experiences mostly in psychological terms, I will describe the psychological impact on me of historical dislocation in the hope of generalizing my experiences to those of other people, particularly women, who have experienced similar events. Reinharz (1979, 1983) and Runyan (1982) have amply demonstrated that the experiential analysis and psychobiographical approaches used in this paper are valid forms of inquiry for the social sciences.

After this preamble, let me describe briefly the experiences of historical dislocation and uprootedness as I have felt them in my life and as they became intensely obvious to me as a consequence of my visit to Cuba in 1984.

I was barely 20 years old when Fidel Castro came to power in January 1959. By then, I had already experienced a number of events that had created in me the sense of instability that usually precedes actual uprootedness. For example, Batista's first takeover and his dismissal of my father from the Armed Forces, together with that of all others who were not his sympathizers just two years after my birth; Batista's defeat in the presidential elections of 1944; his second takeover in 1952, after the suicide of one of Cuba's most honest political leaders; the terror and tensions of the Batista years; and, finally, the entrance in Havana of Castro's Rebel Army in January 1959, a joyful event also characterized by suddenness and intense emotions The Bay of Pigs invasion in 1961 culminated for me a series of unexpected changes and surprising turning points. Through all those years, historical events had transformed the course of my life. Although I had previously been aware of the dangerousness of other historical events, such as the Second World War, Roosevelt's death, the atomic bombs in Hiroshima and Nagasaki, these events were happening far away and their impact on my life was not the same as that of the political events happening in Cuba.

I—like other Cubans of my generation; like thousands of young people in Europe before and during World War II; like thousands of young people yesterday and today in Central America, the Middle East, Southeast Asia, throughout the world—had learned to live immersed in a situation of constant danger without being consciously aware of that fact. I first recognized that I had been living in daily subliminal terror while watching a film in a theater in Madrid, Spain, when I left Cuba for a brief period in 1958. I was suddenly overcome by the realization that I could enjoy the movie without needing to keep a part of me on the alert, worrying about the possibility that a bomb might go off, that the police might raid the theater, or that something similarly dangerous might occur. Mind you, in my years in Cuba I was never hurt by a bomb, nor was I ever arrested. Yet bombs had killed and maimed many young people; some of my adolescent friends had been executed or imprisoned; and I *knew* it could happen to me too. The most amazing aspect of this experience was the realization that I had learned to always be alert *without even knowing* that I had learned it.

Elie Wiesel has written that once you have been in a situation of constant danger, you never feel fully safe again (Wiesel, 1984–1985). His description, although referring to the incomparable horror of the Holocaust, fits my experience. Rahe and Holmes (Holmes & Rahe, 1967; Rahe, 1972), who have done research on the effects of stressful events on illness and health, tell us that events such as getting a new job, moving to a new place, or losing a partner create stress that can lead to the development of physical illness. Needless to say, the stress created by living under the fear of bombs, government persecution, or other similar life-endangering situations is probably greater and capable of producing even more dramatic effects. Studies of learned helplessness demonstrate that when individuals find themselves trapped in situations they cannot control they tend to become seriously depressed (Seligman, 1975). Since I have never been seriously ill or particularly depressed about these issues, and neither have been most of the people I know who grew up under similar conditions, it seems that there are inner resources that sustain people in these extreme situations that we psychologists do not know much about. Studies involving children and adults who have been exposed to situations incredibly more dangerous than anything I have ever experienced shed some light on how psychological survival, development, and growth are achieved in spite of the negative effects produced by violent events created by disruptive political situations and historical dislocation (see, e.g., Coles, 1986; Dimsdale, 1980; Loomis, 1962; Reinharz, 1971; Williams & Westermeyer, 1986).

The most immediate feeling experienced after leaving such a situation of constant danger is relief, together with sadness and grief for those left behind. Confusion and frustration about all the new places and people and customs encountered soon add further burdens. But then, slowly, the unfamiliar starts becoming familiar, daily events start blurring the intense feelings of the first few weeks and years, and life settles into a new routine. Years go by and life goes on.

I lived in several countries after leaving Cuba, earned several higher education degrees, got married and divorced, developed important relationships and friendships along with a sense of better self-understanding, worked hard, and enjoyed life. Cuba was not constantly in my mind. For the most part, I remembered the events of my 22 years in Cuba as intrapsychic events and memories of *my* individual life. Here and there I was confronted with my uprootedness, but it was not a constant or acute pain.

Perhaps I was lucky; if I lived away from Cuba, at least I was living in other Latin American countries. The sense of being "different" was not as vivid there as it later became in the United States. But in spite of similarities in language, customs, and values, I always had a sense of not fully belonging. There was the sound of popular folk music that was familiar to everyone but me. And there was my memory of another popular folk music that only I knew. There was the unfamiliar taste of food that was a daily staple for the others. And there were tastes that I longed for which were unknown or inaccessible in that particular country. Even though we were all conversing in Spanish, there were words and expressions that seemed unusual and even offensive to me. And there were expressions I used which did not have any meaning for my closest friends.

So I learned to speak my Spanish with a Costa Rican accent while my Cuban one receded and I learned to enjoy Costa Rican food and to love Costa Rican music. My friends, co-workers, and classmates forgot to include me in their list of foreigners. And yet, once in a while, the subject of my nationality would come up when someone was angry with me or when I could not remember events in Costa Rican history. To this day, those years in Costa Rica are very close to my heart. My Costa Rican friends continue to be central in my life. But they know, as I know, that I am not really Costa Rican.

There were things I shared with them, however, that I cannot share now with my close friends in the United States. No matter how fluent I am in English, my innermost feelings *are* in Spanish, and my poetry is in Spanish. This deepest part of myself remains hidden from people who are extremely important to me, no matter how hard we all try. I can translate, but translated feelings like translated poetry are just not the same. If there was a difference between my friends and me in Costa Rica, there is an even greater difference between my friends and I in the United States. It is amazing how much hamburgers and Coke versus black beans and coffee remind an uprooted person of that difference!

Indeed, the loss experienced by an uprooted person encompasses not only the big and obvious losses of country, a way of life, and family. The pain of uprootedness is also activated in subtle forms by the everyday absence of familiar smells, familiar foods, familiar routines for doing the small tasks of daily life. It is the lack of what has been termed "the average expectable environment" (Hartmann, 1964) which can become a constant reminder of what is not there anymore. It is the loss of this "average expectable environment" that can be most disorienting and most disruptive of the person's previously established identity. In some cases, this disruption of the "average expectable environment" and its impact on the individual's identity (Garza-Guerrero, 1974; Levy-Warren, 1987) can be at the core of profound psychological disturbance. Although the lack of my "average expectable environment" was not destructive for me in this way, I have experienced its loss, more or less keenly, throughout the second part of my life. My return to Cuba in 1984 brought into focus what this loss had entailed for me.

After 23 years away from there, I realized that I needed to go to Cuba. As if I did not trust my own decision to go, I planned for my trip hastily. But the more I had to wait for my permit from the Cuban government, the more I knew I needed to go. I was not sure how it would feel to be there, but I knew that I had to do it and I knew that I had to do it alone. Without friends. Without people who had never been to Cuba before. Without people who had also been born in Cuba and thus had their own feelings about being there. This was my own emotional journey.

My journey back to Cuba did not start with the actual trip. For weeks before it I had sudden flashbacks of familiar scenes, places, events that I had forgotten or at least not remembered for the past 23 years. During the year after the trip I also had flashbacks of the events and places of my trip and of my previous life in Cuba. These flashbacks were so vivid and powerful that they absorbed me and distracted me from the activity of the moment. They made me think of the flashbacks, of almost hallu-cinatory quality, that are sometimes experienced by people suffering from Post-Trau-matic Stress Disorder or involved in mourning and bereavement (Parkes, 1972). In fact, it seems that I have been involved in a grieving process, no matter how unaware of it I may have been, and it is possible that I will continue to be involved in it for the rest of my life whenever these feelings are reactivated.

After a 45-minute flight from Miami, I arrived in Havana around 5:00 a.m. The transition was quick and dramatically abrupt. You have to understand that for me there had been not 90 miles between Cuba and the United States, but almost a quarter of a century and a dense wall of memory. The lights of Havana brought tears to my eyes. They had been so close and so out of my touch for so many years! By 7:00 a.m. I had checked in at the hotel, taken a shower, had breakfast, and cried, because for the first time in 23 years I had had Cuban sugar in my morning coffee. The moment I stepped out of the hotel I knew exactly where I was, what corners to turn, what buildings would be waiting for me on the next block, and which one of the buses going by would take me to which place in the city. In a few hours I had walked through my old neighborhoods, I had gone by my school, I had walked familiar streets and had come back to the hotel without ever having the slightest confusion about where I was or getting lost.

Cuba had been like a forbidden paradise for half of my life. Suddenly, this forbid-den paradise was all around me. For years Cuba had been a dark and painful mem-ory. Suddenly, it was present and clear, and the sky was blue, and everything was as it always was and as it was always supposed to be. And everyone spoke with a Cuban accent! This deep sense of familiarity, of everything being right, of all things being as they are supposed to be was something I had never experienced since 1961.

The experience of total familiarity was, of course, facilitated by the fact that there has been minimal construction in most Cuban cities during the past 30 years. But aside from the familiarity of the physical environment, there was something more to my experience than just the same buildings and the same bus routes, probably best illustrated by my intense reaction to Cuban sugar and the Cuban accent. Strangers almost always assumed that I was not a visitor; only on a few occasions did some of my clothes give me away. I was even told at one of the dollar stores in Santiago that they could not sell me the t-shirt I wanted to buy; didn't I know that these stores were only for foreign visitors?

But the joy in this sense of belonging was made painful by the realization that it will never again be part of my life on a continuous basis. I believe that, in the deepest sense, this is what uprootedness is all about: that you do not fully fit or feel comfortable in your new environment and that most of the time you do not even know that you don't. It takes an experience like my going back to Cuba to realize that what you have mistaken for comfort does not compare with what the feeling of belonging really means.

On my first morning in Havana I went to the school I attended from first grade to senior year in high school. The main door to the school was closed, but the door of what had been the chapel was open. The statues of the Virgin Mary, the Sacred Heart of Jesus, Saint Joseph, and the Crucifix were not there. Neither were the pews or the confessional boxes. The floor was covered with mattresses, the room was full of gymnastics equipment, and a small group of girls about five to eight years old were gracefully exercising to the rhythm set by music and a teacher's voice. I had visions of myself and other little girls receiving our First Communion in that same space, and I could not stop thinking about what my life would have looked like if I had done gymnastics rather than Communion in that place. And I wondered what the lives of these little girls would look like in the future.

As part of my emotional pilgrimage, I also wanted to visit the homes where I had lived. In spite of all the previous experiences, nothing had prepared me for what I would encounter in the apartment where we lived before leaving Cuba. I went there for the first time on the evening of my second day in Havana. As I walked to the door, a shadow on the side attracted my attention. It was too dark to see, but I knew what it was. I touched it and my fingers confirmed what I had realized in a fraction of a second: my father's nameplate was still affixed to the column at the entrance. Nobody was home that evening, so I returned the next day. And there, in the daylight, was my father's name on a bronze plate. It had not been removed after 23 years! This time a young man opened the door, and I told him the purpose of my visit and asked for his permission to come in. If the sight of my father's name on that bronze plate had sent chills through my spine, the insides of that apartment provided me with an even stranger experience. All of the furniture was the furniture that we had left, the same furniture that had been part of the first 22 years of my life. In fact, the man who opened the door had been taking a nap on my parents' bed, the bed on which I was conceived!

I am sure some of you own pieces of old family furniture. I am sure some of you have gone back to old family houses. But I do not know if you have ever experienced the impact of a physical space where nothing has been moved in a quarter of a century, since you were last there, yet where other people and their lives are now occupants.

A daughter of the poet Carl Sandburg had shared a cab with me from the Havana airport to the hotel. When I had told her that this was my first visit to Cuba in 23 years, she had told me that the house of her childhood, now a museum of her father's life, was both a familiar and strange place for her. At that moment, I had not fully understood her. Two days later, standing in the middle of the apartment that had been my home for several years, I knew what she had meant.

In addition to what I have described, my trip to Cuba made me realize that my memories had a geography—that what I remembered had actually happened in a definite physical space that continues to exist in reality and not only in my memory; that Cuba, in fact, exists beyond what I think or feel or remember about her. This realization, which may seem all too obvious, was the more powerful because before my return I never knew that I felt as if Cuba did not have a real existence beyond my memory.

My trip evoked other strong feelings as well. It may not come as a surprise to know that in spite of the intense and powerful sense of belonging that I experienced in Cuba, I was always alert and vigilant. Among everything that Cuba triggers in me, the need for being vigilant and alert is always included.

Beyond this powerfully intense experience of familiarity and strangeness, my trip put me in touch with childhood friends and made me reflect about the differences in our lives, about the choices to stay or leave that have dramatically influenced our life projects. None of us has any way of knowing what our lives would have looked like without the historical dislocations that have marked them. The only known fact is that powerful historical events have transformed the life course of those of us who left and those of us who stayed in Cuba. Those who stayed, if not uprooted, have also been under the effects of dramatic historical transformations. It is impossible to know if our decisions have resulted in a better life project for any of us, although we each hope and believe we have made the best decision. Bandura's (1982) discussion on the importance of chance encounters for the course of human development addresses the impact that chance may have as a determinant of life paths. For some people, chance encounters and other life events are additionally influenced by historical and political events far beyond their control. It is true that all human beings experience life transitions, but for people who have been subjected to historical dislocations life crossroads feel, intrapsychically, more drastic and dramatic.

It seems rather obvious that the impact of sociocultural and historical change on psychological development should be incorporated in any discussion of human development (Elder, 1981). As Bandura (1982) asserts "a comprehensive developmental theory must specify factors that set and alter particular life courses if it is to provide an adequate explanation of human behavior" (p.747). This is particularly important if we want to understand the experiences of individuals whose lives have been dramatically influenced by traumatic historical and political events because "the danger of any period of large-scale uprooting and transmigration is that exterior crises will, in too many individuals and generations, upset the hierarchy of developmental crises and their built-in correctives; and [make us] lose those roots that must be planted firmly in meaningful life cycles" (Erikson, 1964, p. 96). It seems that the use of a methodology that includes life history narratives and an experiential analysis of those experiences could provide social scientists with a tool to understand what the experience of historical dislocation and uprootedness entails for psychological development. Considering that these experiences are part of so many lives in the world in which we live, the importance of such an endeavor for the social sciences seems quite obvious.

In my case, what I learned once again from this trip is that who I am is inextricably intertwined with the experience of uprootedness. And what this uprootedness entails, particularly after this return trip, is an awareness that there is another place where I feel at home in profound ways that I did not even know or remember. That place, however, is not fully home anymore. And this reality is, precisely, the most powerful reminder of my uprootedness. My daily routine is not the daily routine of people in Cuba; their way of life is not my way of life; their perceptions of reality sometimes clash dramatically with mine. I have learned new things about myself—and what is important for me—that do not fit in Cuban life anymore. Even if I wanted to adapt in order to be there, I do not know if they have any use for someone like me. I would love to have the possibility of being back in Cuba for a long period of time, but I know that Cuba could never be my permanent home again. Believe it or not, I missed my daily life here while I was in Cuba.

Let me also say that I do not believe I have "a corner on uprootedness." In fact, I do not believe that my experience has been particularly difficult. During the past 30 years I have been lucky enough to secure reasonably good jobs, I have developed meaningful friendships that I deeply treasure, I have learned new things about myself and the world that I might not have learned had I stayed in Cuba, and I have evolved valuable adaptive skills as a result of coping with so many changes. It is precisely because my adaptation has been relatively successful and yet so painful at times that I am convinced of the profound psychological impact that uprootedness can have. If I, who have been able to survive and make sense of my experiences in a productive way, have felt and experienced what I have just described, it is reasonable to assume that the pain and confusion experienced by other women less fortunate than me will be more extreme and difficult to survive.

The obvious next step for me as a researcher is to collect life narratives from other people who have undergone similar experiences, particularly from individuals who may have returned to their countries of birth after many years of absence, and compare those experiences. I believe there is invaluable data to be gathered through this process and powerful generalizations to be made that would further our understanding of human development in general and of the impact of the experience of uprootedness in psychological development in particular (e.g., Ortiz, 1985).

I have found that sharing my own experiences produces a cathartic and self-exploratory effect in the audience as well as helping clinicians empathize with patients who have undergone similar experiences. I have also had several conversations with women who have returned to their countries of origin after long periods of time. Their experiences parallel mine to a remarkable degree. It seems evident to me that the details of my own narrative as well as other life narratives may provide invaluable information for understanding the experiences of other immigrants and possibly be useful in structuring programs of psychological assistance and mutual support.

I hope I have succeeded in demonstrating that there is value in the data provided by our own lives and that these data can be a point of departure for valuable analyses of other lives. By incorporating our own experiential perspectives in the research enterprise, ethnic minority researchers can thus innovate not only the focus of social science research but also the methodological approaches with which to study its content. This approach, both in content and process, constitutes a creative endeavor necessary to include new points of view in our disciplines rather than just adapting an established paradigm that, in both content and process, does not fully include the lives of our communities.

Notes

Reprinted from Espín, O.M. (1991). Roots Uprooted: Autobiographical Reflections on the Psychological Experience of Migration. In F. Alegría & J. Ruffinelli (Eds.), *Paradise Lost or Gained: The Literature of Hispanic Exile* (pp.151–163). Houston: Arte Público Press. Another version of this paper, entitled "Roots Uprooted: The Psychological Impact of Historical/Political Dislocation," appeared in E. Cole, O.M. Espín, & E.D. Rothblum (Eds.), (1992). *Refugee Women and Their Mental Health: Shattered Societies, Shattered Lives.* (pp.9–20) New York: Haworth.

References

Bandura, A. (1982). *The psychology of chance encounters and life paths. American Psychologist,* 37(7) 747–755.

Brodkey, L. (1987). Writing critical ethnographic narratives. *Anthropology and Education Quarterly,* 18, 67–76.

Coles, R. (1986). *The political life of children.* New York: Atlantic Monthly Press.

Denzin, N.K. (1986). Interpretive interactionism and the use of life histories. *Revista Internacional de Sociología,* 44, 321–337.

Denzin, N.K. (1989). *Interpretive interactionism.* Newbury Park, CA: Sage.

Dimsdale, J. (1980). *Survivors, victims and perpetrators.* Washington, DC: Hemisphere.

Elder, G.H. (1981). History and the life course. In D. Bertaux, (Ed.), *Biography and society: The life history approach in the social sciences* (pp.77–115). Beverly Hills, CA: Sage.

Erikson, E.H. (1964). *Insight and responsibility.* New York: Norton.

Garza-Guerrero, C.A. (1974). Culture shock: Its mourning and the vicissitudes of identity. *Journal of the American Psychoanalytic Association,* 22, 408–429.

Hartmann, H. (1964). *Essays on ego psychology.* New York: International Universities Press.

Holmes, T.H., & Rahe, R.H. (1967). The Social Readjustment Rating Scale. *Journal of Psychosomatic Research,* 11, 213–218.

Levy-Warren, M.H. (1987). Moving to a new culture: Cultural identity, loss, and mourning. In J. Bloom-Fesbach & S. Bloom-Fesbach (Eds.), *The psychology of separation and loss* (pp.300–315). San Francisco: Jossey-Bass.

Loomis, C. (1962). Toward systematic analysis of disaster, disruption, stress and recovery—Suggested areas of investigation. In G. Baker & L. Cottrell, Jr. (Eds.), *Behavioral science and child defense* (Publication #997). National Academy of Science–National Research Council.

Ortiz, K.R. (1985). Mental health consequences of the life history method: Implications from a refugee case. *Ethos*, 13, 99–120.

Parkes, C.M. (1972). Bereavement: Studies of grief in adult life. New York: International University Press.

Plummer, K. (1983). *Documents of life: An introduction to the problems and literature of a humanistic method.* London, UK: Allen & Unwin.

Rahe, R.H. (1972). Subjects recent changes and their near-future illness susceptibility. *Advances in Psychosomatic Medicine*, 8, 2–19.

Reinharz, S. (1971). *Coping with disaster.* Unpublished manuscript, Department of Psychology, University of Michigan.

Reinharz, S. (1979). *On becoming a social scientist.* San Francisco: Jossey-Bass.

Reinharz, S. (1983). Experiential analysis: A contribution to feminist research. In G. Bowles & R.D. Klein (Eds.), *Theories of women's studies* (pp.162–191). Routledge & Kegan Paul.

Runyan, W.M. (1982). *Life histories and psychobiography: Explorations in theory and method.* New York: Oxford University Press.

Seligman, M.E.P. (1975). *Helplessness: On depression, development and death.* San Francisco: W.H. Freeman.

Wiesel, E. (1984–1985). The refugee. *Cross-Currents*, 34,(4), 385–390.

Williams, C., & Westermeyer, J. (1986). *Refugee mental health in resettlement countries.* Washington, DC: Hemisphere.

Part Two

Feminist Psychology and Psychotherapy

In the chapters in this section, I expand on the insights presented in the first section. Chapters 3, 4, and 5 are focused on feminist theory in psychology and its applications to the practice of therapy.

Chapter 3 was written at the request of Mary Ballou and Laura Brown, coeditors of a book on feminist revisions of personality theory. It was initially intended to illuminate the silences on diversity in all theories of psychology; other chapters in that book addressed silences on gender. As the authors of the other chapters critiqued the theories, they discussed these theories in terms of gender as well as other diversity issues. I was challenged to turn my attention to a broader critique of psychology in general and to feminist theories within psychology in particular. Somewhat overwhelmed by this challenge, I asked my longtime friend and colleague Mary Ann Gawelek to coauthor this piece with me. Eventually, after many sessions of intellectually exciting conversations and note taking, we produced the essay. We mutually revised each other's thoughts and writing in each subsequent draft. When we submitted the piece for publication, we still had many more things to say and ideas to share. This was the last piece I wrote while still living in Boston. It was the first in a series that questioned the development of psychological theory and feminist psychology. I hope that our critique, together with those of others, stimulated thought among theoreticians. This piece, probably more than any other, stimulated for both of us productive discussions with other feminist psychologists. We received the Women of Color Psychologies Award from the Association for Women in Psychology for this essay.

Chapter 4, "Feminist Approaches to Therapy with Women of Color," crystallizes insights derived directly from practice on the relevance of the theory and practice of feminist psychology for the lives of women of color. Drawn from my years of practice as a therapist, this piece is focused on what the practice of therapy entails in the context of a multicultural society.

Chapter 5, "On Knowing You Are the Unknown," the final chapter in this section was initially presented in San Diego at a meeting organized by the local group Women for Change. Clearly, the piece profited from the discussions Mary Ann Gawelek and I shared over the previous piece. It also benefited from new insights I gained in my new intellectual home in women's studies at San Diego State University. In the original version, I sought to develop an understanding of the sources of "mirroring" and "idealizing" for women of color in the feminist movement. In other words, I used traditional psychological theory to understand the position of women in the movement. The text that appears here is a significantly revised version of that initial paper. The book in which the present version first appeared received a Distinguished Publication Award from the Association for Women in Psychology.

In Chapter 5 I assert much more strongly what I said only tentatively in "Roots Uprooted." These two pieces, together with the chapter written in collaboration with Gawelek, reiterate that those who are "different" from the mainstream, have something significant to say. In them, I contend that firsthand knowledge of two or more distinct realities hones one's vision and makes one see oneself and others in a new, more creative light. These chapters also assert my view that knowledge or political understanding are not the property of a particular group in society, regardless of that group's privilege or claim to knowledge and theoretical developments.

All these essays complement each other, arguing that all feminists must coproduce a more encompassing set of psychological theories. In the three pieces in this section, I argue for recognition of women of color in feminism and feminist theory. I also emphatically argue that women of color have been involved in the development of the feminist movement in significant ways. That their involvement and impact may not be always recognized by them or by others is yet another consequence of their social invisibility.

3

Women's Diversity: Ethnicity, Race, Class, and Gender in Theories of Feminist Psychology

with MARY ANN GAWELEK

Theories of psychological development and psychopathology have been notorious for their neglect of cultural variability as well as gender issues. Most psychological theory is literally Anglo-Saxon in its perspectives and conceptions of human nature. Psychology's preoccupation with scientific objectivity has divorced it from an understanding or description of human experience in its fullness and has circumscribed it to data that are mostly based on the experience of white Anglo-Saxon men. Data on white women or ethnic minority people of both sexes have mostly either been excluded as "nuisance variables" or included only as "difference," and frequently understood as deficiencies. Robert Levine says that psychology, as we know it, is nothing but the "folk beliefs of the West" (1981, personal communication). One might add that it is really "the folk beliefs of white, middle-class, North American males."

This chapter discusses weaknesses in feminist psychological theory that are derived from its inception in Western psychological theory. We seek to make explicit the connections between white middle-class culture in the United States and feminist psychological theory. We try to demonstrate that current feminist psychological theory is encumbered by a scientific paradigm of psychology, and try to present a case for a feminist theory in psychology that would truly encompass the diversity of female experience. We conclude by describing how a critique of theories of personality development will benefit from incorporating ethnicity, race, and class, as well as gender, at the core of its understanding of human development.

Although some of the comments we make are relevant and applicable to other behavioral sciences and mental health disciplines, we are confining our discussion to psychology in order to keep the comments focused—and, simply, because psychology is the discipline in which we were educated and in which we practice.

Psychology and Human Variability

Basically, psychology has understood human diversity from two diametrically opposed perspectives. Either diversity is a reflection of abnormalities or deficiencies, in which case efforts should be made to change the individuals and make them healthy, or these differences are dictated by nature rather than a result of the sociocultural context, so there is no need for any intervention.

As noted by feminist scholars (Fine, 1989; Hare-Mustin & Marecek, 1987), because psychology is the discipline that studies individual differences in human nature it does not know how to study human diversity except as "difference." And differences, even when created by societal power structures, are defined as inherently abnormal or innate.

An analysis of diversity based only on "difference," camouflages oppressive structures and "naturalizes" those differences without a recognition for the need to alter the social context (Fine, 1989). The fact that power differentials in society play a role in these differences is totally obscured.

The work of feminist theoreticians in psychology has also fallen prey to the tendency to "naturalize" psychological characteristics associated with gender differences. Most feminist psychological theory assumes that the psychological characteristics exhibited by white middle-class women (e.g., connectedness, empathy, nurturance, affiliative orientation, emphasis on the value of human interaction) are core to the psychology of all women (Jordan, 1984; Miller, 1986; Surrey, 1983). This essentialist assumption is made with little consideration that these characteristics, in fact, may be the consequence of defense mechanisms developed by women to deal with oppression. Only if the social conditions that have determined most women's behavior could be removed would we be able to assess if the characteristics ascribed to women are in fact part of "women's nature" (Espín, Gawelek, Christian, & Nickerson, 1989).

This criticism does not deny the value of a feminist psychology of women as it has evolved in the past two decades or so. Rather, we celebrate the impressive development of feminist theory in psychology while we give witness to and acknowledge the difficulty in actually examining the effects of the broad range of culturally determined variables on all women. In this chapter, the emphasis is on developing a feminist psychological theory which encompasses women of all cultures, races, and social classes.

Is Feminist Theory for All Women?

Elsewhere (Espín, 1977; Espín et al., 1979; Espín, Gawelek, & Rodríguez-Nogués, 1981), we have addressed the concern that what is currently published as psychology of women literature is actually reportage of research and practice on white, middle-class women and we have offered some alternatives to deal with this bias. Here we discuss how feminist psychology has addressed or failed to address the experiences of all women. It is obviously important to assess how a feminist perspective in psychology has been more or less successful in achieving the inclusion of all women. We must be prepared to undertake this assessment of how a feminist psychological theory includes other aspects of human variability besides gender, how it has or has not focused on feminist diversity.

Feminist scholars (e.g., Brown, 1990) have begun to express their distress with a data base and theoretical perspective that equate "women" with white, middle-class women because "lack of data and lack of awareness go hand in hand to create trained-in insensitivity . . . and ignorance" (p.5). An isolated chapter on black women in women's psychology books is not an adequate response to the ethnocentric perspective of most psychology of women.

This ethnocentric perspective is expressed through the focus on white women in the development of feminist theory in the United States as well as by a disregard and lack of knowledge of feminist perspectives being developed in other areas of the world. While French feminists (who are white and European) are recognized by name by North American feminists and have been translated into English, perspectives and theories on the psychology of women being developed in Latin America (e.g., Burín, 1987; Coria, 1988; Lombardi, 1988) or in other parts of the world (e.g., Katoppo, 1979) or even some perspectives on feminism developed by African-American feminists in the United States (e.g., hooks, 1981, 1984; Joseph & Lewis, 1981), remain either untranslated into English or largely unknown to most white, North American feminists.

White Privilege and Feminist Theory

There are several factors that contribute to the focus of psychology of women theories on the experience of white, middle-class women. As much as feminist theoreticians and therapists are conscious of the fact that the power structures of society are the cause of women's oppression, we tend to disregard our own participation in this structure of power when we are its beneficiaries. White, middle-class women, by virtue of their being members of the dominant race, have greater opportunities than women of color to be in positions of power, to engage in research, to publish the results of that research, and to otherwise be involved in professional and academic institutions where such knowledge is generated and distributed. Even when decrying the lack of feminist theory development by nonwhite women, white feminists (e.g., Jaggar, 1983) ignore the lack of access to sources of power by women of color, while minimizing the fact of their own connection to the sources of power in society.

Privilege leads white women to make the assumption that their experiences are universal, normative, and representative of others' experiences, although well-motivated, white, middle-class feminist scholars have fallen into the trap of presenting the experiences of "mainstream" women as the yardsticks of women's experiences. Therefore the impacts of racial, cultural, and class-based factors are ignored, not only for women of color but also for white women. Most white women are unaware of the fact that their racial privilege is an important cultural influence/factor in their lives (McIntosh, 1988).

This is not to say that feminist theoreticians are not well intentioned. It is only to note that they are constricted by the limitations of their own phenomenological context, that is, their existence as dominant cultural beings (McIntosh, 1988). Regrettably, much of feminist theory has done to the experience of women of color what men have done to the experience of women: ignore and/or silence it.

Personality theory about all women will not be developed until nonwhite, non-middle-class women are shaping the questions to be asked and interpreting the results, thus creating the theory. Because "the personal is political" in feminist thinking, it is the lived experiences of the women theorists that determines what is "political," in other words, what is considered essential and important for feminists to focus on. Thus it is not surprising that white feminists focus on their own experiences.

The main source of data for feminist theorizing is the lived experience of women. The political and social context in which a woman lives has importance as a force influencing her psychology. These are basic principles from which feminist psychology evolves. As such, we recognize that our own personal histories (as a white Cuban woman immigrant with English as second language and a Polish-American, working-class woman) have informed our awareness of the limitations of current feminist personality theories and our vision of what they should be like.

Feminist Psychology as a Reflection of Female Diversity

If feminist personality theory is to reflect the diversity of womankind, we must look for data that reflects all women's experiences. Naturalistic sources of data (Espín, Stewart, & Gómez, 1990; Fine, 1989) such as women's letters, journals, and stories must be encouraged as rich sources of data. Feminist therapists working with women of color need to be collecting and reporting data from their clinical experiences.

We must begin by recognizing that gender may not be a salient organizing variable in the lives of all women (Brown, 1990). *Salient* is the key word. For women of color, race or class rather than gender may be a more centrally determining factor in their identity. This should not be taken to assume that gender does not play a determining role in these women's lives. In fact, gender is always one of the most powerful organizers of behavior and self-understanding for all human beings. In all cultures, the experience and developmental contexts of women are different from those of their male peers. As such, all women, despite their racial/ethnic or social class background have their phenomenological experience dramatically molded by the variable of gender. But the culture or social class context from which each woman comes will influence how gender is experienced.

Because of this interplay among factors, the relative conscious salience of gender varies across societies and among individuals. Conscious awareness and saliency of a factor are not the same as its psychological impact. This is clearly illustrated by the fact that although white, middle-class women often fail to recognize the impact of white privilege on their lives, this does not mean that their lives are not powerfully determined by their white skin. The salience of gender is modified by the racial and class variables shaping a woman's life. If a woman is part of the dominant culture, the impact of her race and social class is usually not acknowledged either by the woman herself or by most psychologists. In this case, her gender appears as the most salient differentiating characteristic. In contrast, for a woman raised in a context where social class and/or ethnic background place her in a subordinate societal position, the salience of the gender variable may be less conscious and may seem less important. The need to identify with one's ethnicity or class is strong due to the common oppression experienced by all individuals in that group regardless of gender. Because she is a woman, a black, working-class woman does not necessarily have more in common with a white, upper-class woman than with a black, working-class male. However, she is most likely to have more in common with other women of color than with the black male.

Hurtado (1989) has developed an analysis of the experience of subordination for different groups of women based on the premise that "each oppressed group in the United States is positioned in a particular and distinct relationship to white men, and each form of subordination is shaped by this relational position" (p.833). According to Hurtado, white women's oppression by white men takes the form of seduction, while the oppression of women of color takes the form of rejection. This difference in the subordinate position of white women and women of color determines profound differences in the subjective experience of womanhood and thus accounts for differences in the phenomenological world of these two groups of women. Tensions between white feminists and feminists of color are "affected in both obvious and subtle ways by how each of these two groups of women relate to white men" (p.834). Although the experiences of both groups are conditioned by the fact that they are women, being a woman means different things.

To recapitulate, the importance of gender as a variable which affects the development of personality is unquestionable. However, the effect of gender is modulated by other variables such as social class, race, ethnicity, and culture, which always affect personality development in critical ways. Understanding how the experience of gender is shaped by one's social position of power will help us understand the wide range of female experience.

In addition, understanding gender as a static variable may be a fundamental misperception that leaves the researcher with a clearer research paradigm but a lack of understanding of the depth of this concept. Unger (1989) speaks to this issue when she says that "gender is constantly altered by social context, by culture, by cross-personal interactions, and by the consciousness of the individuals themselves. It is an inconsistent and sometimes contradictory category" (p.3).

Thus, the first challenge in broadening the psychology of women to apply to all women is to understand that gender is but one variable which shapes women's lives and, secondarily, that femaleness—the notion of what it is to be a woman—changes based on intrapsychic variables and the social context.

Ostrander (1984), Komarovsky (1987), and Rubin (1976) have demonstrated the pervasive differences in the lives of women due to social class. Stack (1974) and Sennett and Cobb (1972) have shown the important structural and emotional differences observed in individuals and families of diverse social and ethnic backgrounds. Watson-Franke (1988) addresses the differences in gender roles and values found in men and women raised in matrilineal societies. Earlier, Vygotsky (in Wertsch, 1985) and most recently Rogoff (1990) have built a powerful case for the social constructionist nature of cognitive skills. We can safely assume that those differences must impact the personality development of individuals raised in diverse social and cultural contexts.

Maria Root's (1992) chapter on the impact of trauma on personality opens up another perspective in looking at the experiences of different groups of women. She expands the conventional notion of trauma to include not only direct trauma but also indirect trauma and insidious trauma. She believes that women are more prone to suffer indirect trauma because of their tendency to empathize with others and others' suffering. Thus a woman of color is bound to feel empathy for the pain suffered by men of color due to discrimination in the world of work and other forms of racism. This type of reaction may be seen by white feminists as a proof that women of color continue to be male-identified, but the situation is rather that the white feminists fail to recognize the woman of color's empathy and identification with the trauma suffered by men as well as women whom she loves.

The third type of trauma discussed by Root is insidious trauma, which includes but is not limited to emotional abuse, racism, anti-Semitism, poverty, heterosexism, dislocation, and ageism. The effects of insidious trauma are cumulative and are often experienced over the course of a lifetime. Needless to say, women of color are subject to different degrees of insidious trauma throughout their lives. According to Root, exposure to insidious trauma activates survival behaviors that might be easily mistaken for pathological responses when their etiology is not understood. Misdiagnosis of pathology can be a consequence of lack of understanding of the impact of insidious trauma on women who have lived their lives under the impact of racism, hetero-sexism, or class discrimination.

An additional effect of insidious trauma caused by negative social stereotypes is their self-fulfilling influence. The destructive behavioral consequences of negative, self-fulfilling prophecy affect the personality development of the stigmatized person in dramatic ways (Allport, 1958; Snyder, Decker-Tanke, & Berscheid, 1977).

Social Construction Theory as a Basis for Feminist Psychology

The challenge of these notions leads one to a consideration of social construction theory as a viable alternative for interpreting the varieties of women's experiences. According to Gergen (1985), the assumptions of the social constructionist orientation include:

1. The view that what we know of the world is determined by the categories (linguistic and conceptual) that we possess to define it.
2. The terms by which the world is understood are social artifacts, products of historically situated interchanges among people.
3. The degree to which a particular form of understanding prevails across time is not fundamentally dependent on its empirical validity, but on the vagaries of social process.
4. Forms of negotiated understanding are of critical significance in social life.

Social constructionism clearly challenges established accepted beliefs in Western psychology as well as much of the work done within the psychology of women field. While this perspective has had increasing acceptance among feminist scholars, our re-search, theory, and practice are still conceived in the language and paradigm of main-stream psychology. Moreover, as we have stated earlier in this chapter, when we try to escape traditional psychology's descriptions of female psychology, we frequently fall into the trap of embracing an essentialist position (in which observed characteristics are assumed to represent the essential "nature of women," with its inherent biological deterministic ideology) or, worse, of confusing characteristics developed by women as strategies for survival in the midst of oppression as essential and intrinsic characteristics of being female (Espín et al., 1989; Lykes, 1989a, 1989b).

The social constructionist paradigm, which sees psychological characteristics as resulting from social and historical processes, not as natural, essential qualities of one or another group of people, is a much more productive approach for a psychology of women that aims to include the full diversity of the female experience.

The basic tenets of social constructionism—that one must challenge the objective basis of conventional knowledge; that knowledge is basically a social artifact; and that knowledge, no matter how substantiated by empirical validity it may appear to be, is socially and historically constructed—have important implications for theory building in feminist psychology.

The assumptions of social construction theory are not new to feminist thinkers. Feminist psychologists have consistently acknowledged the importance of the social, external structure of a woman's life in influencing the development of her sense of self. Feminist thinkers have recognized the importance of the individual experience of women and of the interplay of individual development and social context—an interaction which is so deeply entwined that it is fair to say there is no definition of an individual without a definition of her social context. One factor fails to exist without the other. A social constructionist perspective would mandate an examination of each theoretical orientation to determine if the sociocultural context of an individual is included as a central factor in how the theory describes the development of personality.

A feminist theory built on the social construction model would also necessitate an emphasis on pluralism. In recognizing differences and valuing their uniqueness, the complex entwining of race, ethnicity, class, religion, and sexual orientation can be understood. This understanding must include an assessment of the impact of prejudice, privilege/subordination, and how one's social roles are valued or devalued.

Theories of the psychology of oppression and resistance to oppression help us understand the impact of the sociocultural context in the development of personality and in the psychotherapeutic context. For example, Freire (1970) has described the impact of internalized oppression in determining behaviors and aspirations that seem completely individually determined. Bulhan (1985) has studied the effect of internalized oppression on violent behavior and the expression of anger. Lykes (1985) has developed a theory of social individuality to describe the intricacies of a self developed within a social context rather the usual interpretation of the self as individualized and totally autonomous. She has extended the implications of her theory to her studies of Guatemalan Indian women (Lykes, 1989a) and to her analysis of caring and powerlessness (Lykes, 1989b). Harré (1986) and others whose work is collected in that volume have studied how a variety of deep-seated individual emotions are in fact socially constructed and determined by culture, history, and other factors.

The lack of realization that sociocultural factors continually shape the development of individual personality creates distortions of the human experience in most psychological theories, including feminist theories. Understanding the influence of these distortions is critical in understanding why personality theories are lacking in their ability to incorporate and describe the whole of human experience. Conversely, the incorporation of the sociocultural context as an essential variable in theory opens possibilities heretofore unexplored in our understanding of human beings.

Social constructionism means that we must continually question ideology and methodology that may deny gender its broader cultural and systemic meaning. Some of the issues that extend cognitive mechanisms are: the many ways the different cultures negotiate issues of gender, the function of gender (as well as other race and class categories) as a social control mechanism, and the role of consciousness (in the sense of awareness of and reflection upon our own behavior) in mediating the effects of gender upon us all. (Unger, 1989, p.89)

Identity Development as Social Construction

In the light of these reflections about the value of a social construction orientation for the psychology of women, let us consider the very process of identity development.

Atkinson, Morten, and Sue (1979) have developed a model of ethnic minority identity development, and Cass (1979) has developed a similar one related to homosexual identity formation. Both models describe a progression that starts at a "conformist" or "confused" stage (in which images of the self are mostly negative because they are derived from society's negative attitudes towards those who are different). Several intermediate stages in both models describe a questioning of the negative images, more or less strong reactions of anger at the realization that one has been the victim of societal oppression that has become internalized. Finally, both models describe the achievement of a "synergetic articulation" (Atkinson et al., 1989) or "identity synthesis" (Cass, 1979) characterized by more stable patterns involving higher self-esteem and commitment to combating the causes of the original negative identity.

> Although these two models are not identical, they describe a similar process that must be undertaken by people who must embrace negative or stigmatized identities. This process moves gradually from a rejected and denied self-image to the embracing of an identity that is finally accepted as positive. . . . The final stage for both models implies the acceptance of one's own identity, a committed attitude against oppression and an ability to synthesize the best values of both perspectives. (Espín, 1987a, p.39).

For lesbians of all colors, as well as for all men and women of color, the development of identity is quite complex. The more a person deviates from those who represent the "ideal type" in society, namely heterosexual, white, middle-class males, the more their identity development will require an additional effort to incorporate these differences. This developmental process will most likely mandate periods of conflict and separation as those who are "different" struggle to incorporate their experience of subordination to and rejection of the standards of society.

Bernal and her associates (Bernal, Knight, Garja, Ocampo, & Cota, 1990) have done research on children's efforts to understand and incorporate awareness of their ethnicity. They have demonstrated that the development of cognitive abilities in children is intertwined with their capacity to incorporate self-awareness of their ethnicity. This effort to incorporate an understanding of ethnic difference and its implications for the self is an additional developmental task required of children of color that begins for them at an early age.

Language is also an important and much neglected variable in personality development and identity formation. It is very clear from the work of poststructuralists (e.g., Weedon, 1987) that the structure of reality is modified by the language used to describe it. Moreover, language is not simply "transparent and expressive, merely reflecting and describing (pre-existing) subjectivity and human experience of the world" (Gavey, 1989, p.463) but is, rather, an active creator of that experience. Extensive discussion of the affective and cognitive implications of bilingualism and language use for personality development is beyond the scope of this chapter. However, it is important to state that for those women who speak more than one language, there is yet another component in the development of personality and the expression of psychopathology. From what can be gleaned in therapy with bilinguals, it is apparent that self-expression in areas such as sexuality is highly influenced by the use of one or the other language (Espín, 1984). The expression of pathological affect, strong emotional states, and the experience of the self are affected by the language used (Marcos, 1976, 1977). An important aspect of language usage for women of color is its connection with self-esteem and identity development. Languages and speech do not occur in a vacuum. In the United States, black English and bilingualism are associated with an inferior social status. The differential valuing of languages and accents has a profound impact on the development of self concept and identity. Bilingual skills are devalued, and with them, those parts of the self that have been developed in the context of another language (Espín, 1987b).

Yet another example is provided by matrilineal societies. "The importance of the matrilineal message is that it puts sex and sexuality in a different perspective. . . . In this context the absence or low incidence of rape as well as the extremely negative views toward rape reported for some matrilineal systems are of interest" (Watson-Franke, 1988, pp.14–15).

The above examples illustrate how societal standards and expectations deeply affect the development of identity and other components of personality. They illustrate how a social construction perspective serves as a better tool in understanding how personality comes to be. Through the preceding discussion of factors affecting the development of identity for women of color, we hope to have demonstrated the significance of a social construction perspective for the understanding of the experiences of all women and thus for the psychology of women.

A Brief Look at Theories from a Feminist/Cross-Cultural Perspective

We now turn to an evaluation of traditional theories of personality development in a context which recognizes the reciprocal impact of individual development and social structure on development and meaning-making in the internal structure of personality.

The sexist bias in psychodynamic theories has been the object of discussion among feminists of diverse theoretical persuasions from Karen Horney (1924/1967) to the present (Chodorow, 1978; Lerman, 1986). Most psychodynamic theories place great emphasis on the interactions between infant and mother. This emphasis, as well as the basic psychodynamic postulate of the existence of an unconscious with a life of its own, assume the separate existence of an internal, individual world that is shaped by interactions with the mother during infancy.

Our most important criticism of psychodynamic theories is their inability to recognize the cultural relativity of child rearing. Deep-seated beliefs about the influence of mothers in object relations theory, for example, presuppose a certain form of family organization that is not only sexist but also culturally and class biased. How are we to understand psychological development based on relations with an other (the object) if the role of this other and the relationship between the developing child and this other are significantly different in different cultures? What psychodynamic thinking has consistently assumed as universal is a heterosexual family structure where the mother is the primary caretaker. Although this might be the experience of many individuals raised in our society, it is certainly not a universal experience. Recent developments of psychoanalytic theory such as object relations theory and self-psychology, although disagreeing with Freud and traditional psychoanalysis in many respects, still maintain this bias of considering the mother as the primary caretaker, with the mother/infant dyad as the source of the most serious psychological trauma or distress. Feminist discussions of object relations theories in terms of their emphasis on mother and their potential for mother-hating seldom question the sociocultural context in which the mother is immersed (Brown, 1990). Much less do they question aspects of that context that might be equally as influential as the mother in the psychological development of the child.

The importance of women's role in childbirth and caretaking is almost universal; however, different cultures assign different meanings to this role and may limit the role in significant ways. The variance of child-rearing practices, such as the use of wet nurses, the involvement of the extended family, the raising of children by siblings or grandmothers, the presence or absence of fathers, all dramatically affect the developments of personality. In addition, how the culture makes meaning of these practices also impacts the development of the individual.

For example, in poor, urban, black and Latino families in the United States, young mothers frequently turn over the care of their children to their mothers, who by then are in their late thirties and more able to take care of children than when they were young and had their own. Matrilineal societies provide us with another example of alternative relationships between mothers and children. According to Watson-Franke (1988), *matrilining* creates a different valuing of mothers (and women) and different father and husband roles for men than those we are accustomed to. "In congruence with the centrality of women, matriliny creates strong female role models, with the mother playing the essentially significant part" (Watson-Franke, 1988, p.4). While in patriarchal societies matrifocal families are seen as less valid than male-headed households, in matrilineal societies, matrifocus represents the legitimate philosophy. Western theoreticians, raised within a patriarchal context, find it difficult to conceptualize as "healthy" a family context in which women are central. "The centrality of women in female-headed families has no publicly acknowledged and supported structural force" (Watson-Franke, 1988, p.14). The female-headed family of all races is still seen as deviant in most of the Western world. Because the model of "healthy family" derived from patriarchal society resists and rejects a central position for women, it describes many black and Latino families, as well as all lesbian families, as "dysfunctional."

What implications does this have for object relations theories? Clearly, the necessity of a nuclear family structure as we know it in Western Society for healthy personality development becomes questionable. Moreover, the culture-boundedness of the theories developed within a patriarchal context become more obvious. It also makes explicit that psychodynamic theorists have not addressed the value-laden messages internalized by individuals concerning the societal assessment of being male or female, black or white. The basic understanding of the development of the unconscious appears to be questionable, since these societal messages have not been taken into account.

Within feminist theory, it has been pointed out that interpretations of psychoanalytic theories and their variations, such as Chodorow's (1978) work, have tended to disregard variability across racial and class lines (Spelman, 1988).

Early feminists heralded behavioral theories and therapy as helpful to women, since they recognized the importance of social variables on personality development. However, the recognition of how these variables affect the individual did not address how the social structure might be unhealthy or how the individual might internalize these messages. The most significant criticism of behavioral theories has been their lack of attention to the interplay between the internal and external factors in an individual's life. The advent of the "cognitive revolution" in psychology has modified this approach into the more accepted cognitive-behavioral perspective. Because cognitive-behavioral theories incorporate the tenets of social constructionism, their potential for addressing the experiences of all women seems to be greater. As such, cognitive-behavioral approaches to the psychology of women are already developing (Gergen, 1988; Unger, 1989; Crawford & Gentry, 1989). However, ethnic minority psychologists frequently take issue with the limitations created by research samples of exclusively white people as the source for the development of this theory (e.g., Casas, 1988). From a feminist perspective, Ballou (1990, 1992) questions the validity of a "scientific" claim that focuses on adaptation without questioning who is to decide what is "adaptive." Ballou also questions the emphasis on individual change without enough attention being given to needed changes in the environment.

Given their emphasis on the phenomenological world of the person, humanistic, person-centered theories have been well received by feminists. Hearing and respecting a woman's experience as a person are upheld by this theoretical school. However, there are two basic premises which are part of this person-centered philosophy that are quite problematic for feminist psychology theory. The first is that a person's "story" is reflected and accepted as told. While this may seem validating, it may also create the opposite effect. Since all women are victims of an oppressive society, simple acceptance and reflection may result in validation of the oppressive status quo or in defining as pathological that which is a defensive reaction to an oppressive situation (e.g., the high incidence of depression in women). The second assumption of person-centered theory is that the locus of control lies within the individual. This assumption is simply untrue for women who experience multiple discrimination: by definition, the external world is a major source of controlling factors in the lives of women, as we have already discussed extensively. Humanistic, person-centered techniques can be helpful to women when they are contextualized within an understanding of the women's social experiences.

The Future of Feminist Psychology Theory

The question remains: How does one develop a feminist theory that will adequately address womanhood, as shaped by all sociocultural variables and one's critiques of established theories? How does one, in fact, transform all psychological theory of personality development and psychotherapy to include the experiences of all human beings? As such, in analyzing any theoretical conceptualizations generated in regard to the psychology of women, one must emphasize the subjectivity of knowledge and understand the fact that phenomenological understandings of women will never be complete if only a certain group of individuals (white, middle-class women) have their experiences described.

A feminist paradigm must be the basis from which old theories are critiqued and new theories developed. Lerman (1986) and Ballou (1990) have articulated the basic tenets of this paradigm, with Lerman placing greater emphasis on a paradigm which integrates theory into practice and Ballou focusing more on basic theoretical points. Their assumptions are parallel to those of social construction theory. Following Lerman and Ballou, we believe that the primary factors to be considered in the development of a feminist personality theory are:

1. *All women's experiences must be heard, understood and valued.* This premise has serious implications when evaluating any theory—first, to assess whose experiences have been listened to as the basis for theoretical development; second, to assess whether the diverse experiences have been appreciated on their own merits or used only in comparison to existing cultural standards; and last, to assess the level of respect afforded to the populations discussed.

2. *Attention to the contextual influences is essential.* The internal experience of a woman is always and ever mediated by her social context, and the social context shifts as people change internally. "Social context," however, includes more than gender. Variables such as race, class, and ethnicity are not merely descriptors of a woman's characteristics, but powerful, active forces determining who she is. Theoretical postulates must always be assessed for their cultural relativity. Issues of social power, valuing, and opportunity for individual change must be variables considered.

3. *The psychology of women must be pluralistic.* We must recognize the vast differences among women based on sociocultural variables. Not only must these differences be identified but one must develop an attitude in which differences are equally

appreciated. "The demand of diversity is not merely gaining information about other races, cultures, classes, and ethnicities, to know them in 'our' terms. It is considering diversities through 'their' own realities and modes of knowing" (Ballou, 1990, p.33). Thus theories must be continually challenged to consider whether they are truths or social artifacts in order to expand the range of cultural forms and structures.

4. *Egalitarian relationships must be at the base of the development of the theory.* Where power is shared between partners (i.e., researcher/subject, theoretician/participant, therapist/client), the research participant or therapy client has to be perceived as the shaper of knowledge for the reality of subjective knowledge to be appreciated. Understanding how a theoretical frame allows for the sharing of information is critical in this respect. Otherwise, the "knowledge" included in the theory may be applicable to a limited group of women similar in characteristics to the researcher or theoretician.

Concluding Remarks

To analyze and reinterpret psychological theories of personality development and psychopathology, a feminist point of view that recognizes the centrality of variables of race, class, ethnicity, and culture, as well as the centrality of gender, is essential. This is not an impossible process but clearly a humbling one. The brief examples in this chapter serve to illustrate some of the tasks involved in theorizing about human psychological development with an inclusive perspective and with a social constructionist theoretical frame. It may be that our attempts to prove and justify psychology as a science within dominant academic structures has led us to miss the fact that all science is in fact constructed by human processes (Hubbard, 1988). Thus, in order for a feminist theory to be developed and articulated from this perspective, theorists must recognize their subjective stance. Most psychological theory is created and presented as if psychological reality were objectively definable and as if that reality were represented by that of white women. According to the principles of social construction theory, reality—particularly psychological reality—is constantly being constructed, rather than discovered, by scientists.

In developing a theoretical approach to the psychology of women, it is clear that the experiences of women of color must be incorporated. But to "add women of color and stir" will not produce an integrated theory. Moreover, the endless groups of women and their experiences that would need to be "stirred in" would condemn this approach to failure. But if we rely on social construction principles, the psychological make-up of all women will be seen as determined by social forces. This approach will provide us with a context from which to look not only at the experiences of women who are "different" but at the experiences of all women. The psychological impact of either social privilege or oppression because of factors other than gender, the impact of insidious trauma, the processes involved in the development of ethnic identity, the emotional implications of language use, the variety of cultural messages concerning sexuality, and other factors will be incorporated into the theory as constituting the experiences of all women.

In the articulation and construction of feminist psychological theory, and of all psychological theory that includes women, the presence of theorists from a wide variety of backgrounds is essential. Otherwise, feminist theory would continue to express more or less directly the structures of power in society that it attempts to change. The participation of theorists from a diversity of backgrounds will provide for the development of "feminist theory from margin to center" (hooks, 1984).

In summary, feminist theory should be a working theory that is evolving and regenerated by the inclusion of the experience of all women, and it should become a ferment in the development of all theory. "Feminist theory is [or should be] . . . vision guided by experience and experience corrected by vision" (Morawski, 1988, p.187). This vision will only be clear if it includes the experiences of all women.

Notes

Reprinted from Espín, O.M. & Gawelek, M.A. (1992). Women's Diversity: Ethnicity, Race, Class and Gender in Theories of Feminist Psychology. In L.S. Brown & M. Ballou (Eds.), *Personality and Psychopathology: Feminist Reappraisals* (pp.88–107). New York: Guilford.

References

Allport, G. (1958). *The nature of prejudice.* Garden City, NJ: Doubleday Anchor.

Atkinson, D., Morten, G., & Sue, D.W. (Eds.). (1979). *Counseling American minorities.* Dubuque, IA: William C. Brown.

Ballou, M.B. (1990). Approaching a feminist-principled paradigm in the construction of personality theory. In L.S. Brown & M.P.P. Root (Eds.), *Diversity and complexity in feminist theory* (pp.23–40). New York: Haworth.

Ballou, M.B. (1992). Introduction. In L.S. Brown & M.B. Ballou (Eds.), *Personality and psychopathology: Feminist reappraisals* (pp.3–7). New York: Guilford.

Bernal, M.E., Knight, G.P., Garja, C.E., Ocampo, K.A., & Cota, M.K. (1990). The development of ethnic identity in Mexican-American children. *Hispanic Journal of Behavioral Sciences,* 12(1), 3–24.

Brown, L.S. (1990). The meaning of multicultural perspective for theory building in feminist therapy. In L.S. Brown & M.P.P. Root (Eds.), *Diversity and complexity in feminist theory* (pp.1–21). New York: Haworth.

Bulhan, H.A. (1985). *Franz Fanon and the psychology of oppression* New York: Plenum.

Burín, M. (Ed.). (1987). *Estudios sobre la subjetividad femenina: Mujeres y salud mental.* Buenos Aires, Argentina: Grupo Editor Latinoamericano.

Casas, J.M. (1988). Cognitive-behavioral approaches: A minority perspective. *The Counseling Psychologist,* 16(1), 106–110.

Cass, V.C. (1979). Homosexual identity formation: A theoretical model. *Journal of Homosexuality,* 4, 219–235.

Chodorow, N. (1978). *The reproduction of mothering.* Berkeley: University of California Press.

Coria, C. (1988). *El sexo oculto del dinero: Formas de la dependencia femenina* (3rd ed.). Buenos Aires, Argentina: Grupo Editor Latinoamericano.

Crawford, M., & Gentry, M. (Eds.). (1989). *Gender and thought*. New York: Springer.

Espín, O.M. (1977, March). *Women cross-culturally: The counselor and the stereotype.* Paper presented at the annual convention of the American Personnel and Guidance Association, Dallas.

Espín, O.M. (1984). Cultural and historical influences on sexuality in Hispanic/Latin women: Implications for psychotherapy. In C. Vance (Ed.), *Pleasure and danger: Exploring female sexuality* (pp.149–171). London: Routledge & Kegan Paul. (2nd ed., London: Pandora, 1994)

Espín, O.M. (1987a). Issues of identity in the psychology of Latina lesbians. In Boston Lesbian Psychologies Collective (Eds.), *Lesbian psychologies: Explorations and challenges* (pp.35–55). Champaign: University of Illinois Press.

Espín, O.M. (1987b). Psychological impact of migration on Latinas. Implications for psychotherapeutic practice. *Psychology of Women Quarterly,* 11(4), 489–503.

Espín, O.M., Gawelek, M.A., Christian, L., & Nickerson, E.T. (1989, March). *Intimacy and autonomy: A stereoscopic view of the psychology of women.* Paper presented at the annual meeting of the Association for Women in Psychology, Newport, RI.

Espín, O.M., Gawelek, M.A., & Rodríguez-Nogués, L. (1981, June). *Feminism and ethnicity: How they intersect in women's lives.* Paper presented at the meeting of the National Women Studies Association, Storrs, CT.

Espín, O.M., Gawelek, M.A., Warner, B., Rodríguez-Nogués, L., Shapiro-Wayne, N., & Telles, P. (1979, March). *Feminism and ethnicity: Searching for "roots" and their implications.* Paper presented at the annual meeting of the Association for Women in Psychology, Pittsburgh.

Espín, O.M., Stewart, A., & Gómez, C. (1990). Letters from V.: Adolescent personality development in sociohistorical context. *Journal of Personality,* 58(2), 347–364.

Fine, M. (1989). Coping with rape: critical perspectives on consciousness. In R. Unger (Ed.), *Representations: Social constructions of gender* (pp.186–200). Amityville, NY: Baywood.

Fine, M., & Gordon, S.M. (1989). Feminist transformations of/despite psychology. In M. Crawford & M. Gentry (Eds.), *Gender and thought: Psychological perspectives* (pp.146–174). New York: Springer-Verlag.

Freire, P. (1970). *Pedagogy of the oppressed.* New York: Seabury.

Gavey, N. (1989). Feminist poststructuralism and discourse analysis: Contributions to feminist psychology. *Psychology of Women Quarterly,* 13, 459–475.

Gergen, K.J. (1985). The social constructionist movement in modern psychology. *American Psychologist,* 40, 266–275.

Gergen, M.M. (Ed.). (1988). *Feminist thought and the structure of knowledge.* New York: New York University Press.

Hare-Mustin, R.T., & Marecek, J. (1987). The meaning of difference: Gender theory, postmodernism and psychology. *American Psychologist,* 43, 455–464.

Harré, R. (Ed.). (1986). *The social construction of emotion.* Oxford, UK: Basil Blackwell.

hooks, b. (1981). *Ain't I a woman? Black women and feminism.* Boston: South End.

hooks, b. (1984). *Feminist theory: From margin to center.* Boston: South End Press.

Horney, K. (1967). *Feminine psychology.* New York: Norton. (Original work published in 1924)

Hubbard, R. (1988). Some thoughts about the masculinity of the natural sciences. In M.M. Gergen (Ed.), *Feminist thought and the structure of knowledge* (pp.1–15). New York: New York University Press.

Hurtado, A. (1989). Relating to privilege: Seduction and rejection in the subordination of white women and women of color. *Signs: Journal of Women in Culture and Society,* 14(4), 833–855.

Jaggar, A. (1983). *Feminist politics and human nature.* Totowa, NJ: Rowman & Allanheld.

Jordan, J. (1984). *Empathy and self boundaries* (Work in Progress, No. 16). Wellesley, MA: The Stone Center.

Joseph, G.I., & Lewis, J. (Eds.). (1981). *Common differences: Conflict in black and white feminist perspectives.* New York: Anchor.

Katoppo, M. (1979). *Compassionate and free.* New York: Orbis.

Komarovsky, M. (1987). *Blue-collar marriage.* New York: Random House.

Lerman, H. (1986). *A mote in Freud's eye: From psychoanalysis to the psychology of women.* New York: Springer.

Lombardi, A. (1988). *Entre madres e hijas: Acerca de la opresión psicológica.* Buenos Aires, Argentina: Paidós.

Lykes, M.B. (1985). Gender and individualistic vs. collectivist bases for notions about the self. *Journal of Personality,* 53, 357–383.

Lykes, M.B. (1989a). Dialogue with Guatemalan Indian women. Critical perspectives on constructing collaborative research. In R. Unger (Ed.), *Representations: Social constructions of gender* (pp.167–185). Amityville, NY: Baywood.

Lykes, M.B. (1989b). The caring self: Social experiences of power and powerlessness. In M. Brabeck (Ed.), *Who cares? Theory, research, and educational implications of the ethic of care* (pp.164–179). New York: Praeger.

Marcos, L. (1976). Bilinguals in psychotherapy: Language as an emotional barrier. *American Journal of Psychotherapy,* 30, 522–560.

Marcos, L. (1977). Bilingualism and sense of self. *American Journal of Psychoanalysis,* 37, 285–290.

McIntosh, P. (1988). *White privilege and male privilege: A personal account of coming to see correspondence through work in Women's Studies* (Working paper No. 189). Wellesley, MA: Center for Research on Women, Wellesley College.

Miller, J.B. (1986). *Toward a new psychology of women* (2nd ed.). Boston: Beacon.

Morawski, J.G. (1988). Impasse in feminist thought? In M. M. Gergen (Ed.), *Feminist thought and the structure of knowledge* (pp.182–194). New York: New York University Press.

Ostrander, S.A. (1984). *Women of the upper class.* Philadelphia: Temple University Press.

Rogoff, B. (1990). *Apprenticeship in thinking: Cognitive development in social context.* New York: Oxford University Press.

Root, M. (1992). Reconstructing the impact of trauma on personality. In L.S. Brown & M. Ballou (Eds.), *Personality and psychopathology feminist reappraisals* (pp.229–265). New York: Guilford.

Rubin, L.B. (1976). *Worlds of pain: Life in the working class family.* New York: Basic Books.

Sennett, R., & Cobb, J. (1972). *The hidden injuries of class.* New York: Vintage Books.

Snyder, M., Decker-Tanke, E., & Berscheid, E. (1977). Social perception and interpersonal behavior: On the self-fulfilling nature of social stereotypes. *Journal of Personality and Social Psychology,* 35, 656–666.

Spelman, E.V. (1988). *The inessential woman: Problems of exclusion in feminist thought.* Boston: Beacon.

Stack, C.B. (1974). *All our kin: Strategies for survival in a black community.* New York: Harper & Row.

Surrey, J.L. (1983). *Self-in-relation: A theory of women's development.* Wellesley, MA: The Stone Center.

Unger, R. (Ed.). (1989). *Representations: Social constructions of gender.* Amityville, NY: Baywood.

Watson-Franke, M.B. (1988, July). *Siblings vs. spouses: Men and women in matrilineal societies (South America and North America).* Paper presented at the International Congress of Americanists, Amsterdam, The Netherlands.

Weedon, C. (1987). *Feminist Practice and Poststructuralist theory.* Oxford, UK: Basil Blackwell.

Wertsch, J.V. (1985). *Vygotsky and the social formation of mind.* Cambridge, MA: Harvard University Press.

4

Feminist Approaches to Therapy with Women of Color

It is a rather pervasive belief among some white feminists and some people of color that feminism does not have anything to offer women of color and that consequently women of color would not benefit from a feminist approach to therapy. The assumptions made or the arguments advanced by these people are that most women of color in the United States come from poor or working-class backgrounds and are, more often than not, preoccupied by immediate issues of survival. Thus, goes this line of reasoning, issues related to women's rights are secondary to the pressing needs of everyday life. Feminism is perceived from this perspective to be the concern of white middle-class, educated women intent on reaching economic and political parity with men of their social class and race.

Regrettably, there is much that could be said about the insensitivity, racism, and classism of feminists in psychology (e.g., Brown, 1990; Espín & Gawelek, 1992) and of the women's movement in general (e.g., Anzaldúa, 1990; hooks, 1984). I would contend that the near-sightedness of white feminists as to the possibilities of the movement and the far reaching consequences of its ideas is very much to blame for the narrowness of some definitions of feminism and for the movement's goals being perceived as limited and exclusionary. As Gloria Anzaldúa (1990), bell hooks (1984), Audre Lorde (1984), and other feminists of color (e.g., Combahee River Collective,

1979) have stated, white middle-class women do not "own" feminism, nor is feminism irrelevant to the experiences of women of color. Rather the oppression of women of color in a white-dominated society takes on specific characteristics related to both gender and race (e.g., Anzaldúa, 1990; Hurtado, 1989; Joseph & Lewis, 1981; Lorde, 1984). These characteristics are molded by forces that multiply and reinforce each other as well as by the particular situation of men of color in this society.

white racism combines with sexism in unique ways to influence the oppression of women of color. The poverty and lack of education and resources that many women of color suffer from are a consequence of centuries of racist denial of the opportunities this country is supposed to provide for all of its citizens. Poor and working class women of color and their children, as we know, are at the bottom of the social and economic pyramid in this country. Racism influences the experiences of women of color directly. Sexism is also a powerful force in their lives.

When "being a man" is defined by white upper-middle-class opportunities and standards that are unattainable by most men of color, the expression of manhood becomes distorted. For poor and working-class men of color, asserting dominance over women and children may be nothing but a last desperate gesture to "prove their manhood" in a world that both expects all men to achieve a certain success and systematically destroys the chances of some men to achieve that position. Domineering, aggressive, and sometimes violent behavior towards women on the part of these men may be understood as this desperate gesture. However, this understanding does not in any way diminish or justify the suffering it causes to women and their children. The oppression to which all women are subjected in one form or another is intensified in the case of poor and working-class women of color by the oppression of these men.

The fewer outlets there are in the world at large for men of color to assert their domination and "masculinity" through economic, political, educational, or professional roles, the more they will turn to the territory of personal relationships and the family as the arena where they can, in fact, dominate and "prove" that they are indeed "real men" like the white men who deprive them of opportunities.

Women and children then become suitable recipients for the displaced anger of an oppressed man. Violence takes many forms: incest, rape, wife-beating. It is not unusual to hear supposedly "enlightened" persons defending the violent behavior of men of oppressed groups on the grounds that their only outlet is to beat their wives. Even if the displacement is understandable in individual cases, to accept and justify it is to condone injustice and another form of violence against women. (Espín, 1984).

As a reaction to the oppression experienced by these men, women of color may subordinate their needs even further. Root's (1992) analysis of the impact of trauma on personality helps us understand the experiences of different groups of women. She expands the conventional notion of trauma to include not only direct trauma, but also indirect trauma and insidious trauma. She believes that women are more prone to suffer indirect trauma because of their tendency to empathize with others and their suffering. Thus a woman of color is bound to feel empathy for the pain suffered by men of color due to discrimination and racism. This type of reaction may be seen by white feminists as a "proof" that women of color continue to be "male-identified," and thus the white feminists fail to recognize that it is a consequence of empathy and identification with the trauma suffered by others.

Not as unfortunate as his poor counterpart, the middle-class, professional man of color strives for what should "legitimately" be his, "as a man," frequently without any more understanding than white males about the fact that what men perceive as their "legitimate" right frequently impinges on the rights of the women closest to them. Thus it can be asserted that in a world where male dominance is expected, rewarded, and approved of, middle-class men of color are as likely as middle-class white men to act from a patriarchal position and to become abusive, domineering, and oppressive to women in their lives.

In fact, although negative reactions to the feminist movement as narrowly defined by the interests and experiences of white women are indeed justified (e.g., hooks, 1984), a lot of the opposition to feminist ideas on the part of men of color is nothing but a reaction by yet another group of men to women's efforts to change their subservient position. Because the feminist movement is indeed guilty of racism, the sexism that is as prevalent in communities of color as in the dominant white society hides insidiously behind a cloak of ethnic loyalty.

While affirmative action efforts to enable some men of color to become "more like white men" may reduce certain gaps between these groups of men, thus creating a trend towards equalization, these efforts may tend to have the opposite effect on real equality for women. For example, it is common knowledge that when non-white men begin to emulate white men, they often pressure non-white women to become more "like white women," which in this society is still interpreted as meaning "more like a middle-class, suburban, presumably idle, housewife," precisely the trap that white middle-class women have been trying to escape. There is nothing surprising about this trend among young middle-class men of color. The standards for the "good life" in this country have been defined in terms of the white middle and upper classes, so it is understandable that young people of color who are professional and/or middle class would aim to achieve that lifestyle for themselves. However, for young women of color, emulating those standards means that at some point in the future they are likely to find themselves in the same situation which many white middle-class women are still trying to leave. Assuming that at least superficial "equality" could be achieved on the basis of these standards and that the state of the economy and social climate would allow it, one could predict a situation in the future in which middle-class women of color could find themselves in positions which would again be belittled by society, because being a "middle-class, suburban, presumably idle, housewife" may not be appreciated by society at large by the time they achieve this status (Espín, 1979).

For the young ethnic minority woman who is in the process of obtaining a college degree, the lifestyle associated with the middle-class, suburban housewife may be a great temptation, with little consideration given to possible future disadvantages. However, most professional, middle-class women of color do not hold too many fantasies about the promises of a housewife role. Women of color who are professional and/or middle class encounter both racism and sexism in their daily lives. The sense of responsibility for their less fortunate sisters and brothers is an inherent component of the lived experience of these women. Their access to middle-class professions and lifestyles adds specific circumstances that need to be negotiated in their daily lives (e.g., Combs, 1986; Trotman, 1984).

For the woman of color of all socio-economic classes, an understanding of the oppression men of color experience in the world at large creates a double-bind. Wanting to support and understand those men, including their own brothers, fathers, and sons, they can feel trapped in situations of domination, abuse, and oppression at the hands of the men in their lives just as white middle-class women do, even though their experiences may appear to be so different. On the other hand, the experiences of women of color remain in the end vastly different from those of white women (e.g., Greene, 1986; Hurtado, 1989). Just the fact that white women partake of white privilege (McIntosh, 1988; Rave, 1990; Spelman, 1988) creates profound psychological and material differences between these groups of women.

Women of Color and Mental Health

Anyone who has a sense of the connections between life stress and mental health understands that "mental health" is not an exclusively intrapsychic and individual/existential concept. To be subjected to the constant stress of racism and sexism has a definite impact on a person's mental health. Attempts at restoring a person's well-being (or "mental health") that do not include a consideration of all stressors in a person's life are obviously doomed to failure.

Root's (1992) discussion of insidious trauma, which includes but is not limited to emotional abuse, racism, anti-Semitism, poverty, heterosexism, dislocation, ageism is relevant here. The effects of insidious trauma are cumulative and are often experienced over the course of a lifetime. Needless to say, women of color are subject to different degrees of insidious trauma throughout their lives. According to Root, the exposure to insidious trauma activates survival behaviors that might be easily mistaken for pathological responses when their etiology is not understood. Misdiagnosis of pathology can be a consequence of lack of understanding of the impact of insidious trauma on women who have lived their lives under the impact of racism, heterosexism, or class discrimination. An additional effect of insidious trauma caused by negative social stereotypes is their self-fulfilling influence.

For those women of color who are lesbians, the experience of being a woman of color is compounded by conflicting loyalties and additional tasks in the development of their identity as women of color and asl lesbians, which could be additional sources of insidious trauma (Espín, 1987a; Greene, 1986).

The above discussion illustrates some of the life situations women of color may bring to the therapeutic context that resemble "typical" situations presented by white women to white feminist therapists. It also points to some of the unique stressors characteristic of the experience of being a woman of color.

From its beginning, feminist therapy has been concerned with the psychological effects of social forces. Although its focus has mostly been the impact of everyday sexism on the lives and mental health of women rather than the combined effect of racism and sexism, the fact that it emphasizes the social construction of women's psychology and the necessity of attending to the social world in order to understand and restore the integrity of the psychic world give it a unique perspective. To acknowledge the impact of social forces on mental health makes feminist therapy uniquely suited to the needs of women of color rather than foreign or irrelevant to those needs. As Comas-Díaz (1987) states, "defined as a set of political, economic and social values which support balanced power relations between the sexes, feminism is potentially relevant to all women. However, in order to be effective with Hispanic women (and other women of color), this perspective needs to be culturally embedded" (p. 40).

An examination of the principles of feminist therapy and their possibilities for becoming more directly "culturally embedded" and sensitive to differences among women is in order at this point.

Defining Feminist Therapy

Feminist criticism of psychotherapy prompted a re-evaluation of the field in the early 1970s. The result of this re-evaluation was the development of feminist therapy. Feminist therapy challenges the authoritarian, patriarchal approaches of traditional psychotherapy that tend to reinforce women's sense of dependency and inadequacy, to treat women's unhappiness as pathology and illness, and to make adjustment to traditional roles the goal of treatment for women. Feminist therapists attempt to reconceptualize the goals of therapy and the role of the therapist in order to make the therapy process compatible with the new theories of women's psychology and the goals of the women's movement. Feminist therapy is distinguishable not only from the traditional, more or less sexist forms of therapy but also from a nonsexist approach to therapy. The distinctive feature of feminist therapy is the analysis of the social, political, and economic oppression that affects women individually and as a group. This analysis informs the therapist's understanding of women's psychological development and the therapeutic process (Donovan & Littenberg, 1981).

A crucial aspect of the work of the feminist therapist is in helping her clients distinguish the situations in their lives for which they are personally responsible from circumstances and intrapsychic attitudes that reflect broader social problems. In feminist therapy it is as important to help clients to set goals and develop skills to make appropriate individual changes as it is to validate the client's experiences of frustration or powerlessness and to encourage the client to meet with others who suffer from similar problems (Donovan & Littenberg, 1981; Espín, 1985; Greene, 1986).

The explicit commitment to feminist values as a basis for conceptualizing therapy is what distinguished feminist therapy from other forms of therapy. Simply to be non-sexist and to attempt modification of existing approaches is inadequate. What is necessary is a critical recognition of sociocultural agents and factors as generating emotional distress in women, and the development of special expertise in working with women's issues and concerns. (Faunce, 1985, p.1)

"Important is the philosophy that determines the attitudes with which techniques are used and theories supported" (Faunce, 1985, p.1.) And probably the most basic principle of feminist philosophy is that *the personal is political.* In simple terms, this means that the individual experience expresses the collective situation while, at the same time, "a feminist perspective . . . regards the individual's behavior as best understood by examining the social structure" (Comas-Díaz, 1987, p.52). The feminist philosophical postulate that "the personal is political" has profound implications for the work of the feminist therapist because it presupposes that changes in the lives of women necessitate changes in the basic structure of society. Feminist therapists believe that therapy is not value-free and that the therapist has to understand and acknowledge her values. This means that the therapist has to be aware of and struggle against her own sexism, racism, classism, and heterosexism. The feminist therapist is aware of the fact that there are no individual solutions for social, moral, and political problems that are at the root of her clients' distress. Thus she recognizes the need to join others to work for social change and the importance that such activity has for her clients' validation and empowerment (Donovan & Littenberg, 1981). As a consequence, from a feminist point of view, "in both therapy and politics, transformation means finding a way to give voice to the unheard, to embody the invisible" (Hill, 1990, p.57). Because women of color are the most invisible and unknown among women (Espín, 1991), it is relevant to examine what a feminist approach to therapy can offer them.

Guidelines for Feminist Therapy

Although total agreement on the theory and practice of feminist therapy has not been achieved yet, Butler (1985) offers a set of guidelines that distinguish a feminist therapy approach from other approaches to therapy:

1. *Recognition of women's oppression based on gender, race, and class.* The basis for feminist therapy is a recognition of the harmful effects of the sexist society in which we live. Real oppression of women based on gender as well as class and race is the basis for the conflicts, low self-esteem, and powerlessness reported by many women who seek therapy. (p.33)
2. *Relevance of the socio-cultural context.* Feminist therapy explores with clients the inherent contradictions in the prescribed social roles for women. Re-

jected is the medical model of psychiatry, which locates the source of human conflict within the individual, that is, in a vacuum, with no relationship to the socioeconomic system within which we live. Emphasized is a sociocultural and systems approach to psychological growth and change. (pp.33–34)

3. *Focus on women's empowerment.* Feminist therapists support women in an exploration of their inner resources and capacity for nurturance and self-healing. They encourage the process of individual goal-setting and support those client goals that transcend traditional sex-role stereotyping. They encourage the exploration of various lifestyles and sexual orientations and support the acquisition of skills for self-directed and interdependent living. (p.34)

4. *Diverse therapeutic modalities.* Feminist therapy distinguishes itself from traditional therapies by its nonsexist frame of reference. Feminist therapists utilize appropriate existing therapeutic modalities and develop new techniques compatible with the underlying philosophy of feminist therapy. (p.35)

5. *Demystification of power in the therapeutic relationship.* Feminist therapists work on demystifying the power relationship inherent in any therapeutic situation. Doing so requires a feminist therapist to be open about her own values and attitudes. (p.35)

6. *The therapist and other women as role models.* Feminist therapy affirms that matching women clients with women therapists is often the most therapeutic choice for women. Feminist therapists use both individual and group approaches to therapy. Affirmed, in particular, is the value of an all-women's group therapy model. The group model enables women to (1) validate each other's strengths, (2) develop mutual support systems, (3) break down their isolation from each other, and (4) help each other perceive various possibilities for growth. (p.36)

7. *The therapist's on-going self-examination and reflection on her values.* Feminist therapy requires that a therapist (1) conduct an ongoing evaluation of her practice; (2) make provision in her practice for low-income clients; (3) examine her lifestyle and values as they relate to her therapeutic approach; (4) identify with the goals and philosophy of feminism; and (5) examine her own race, class, and sexual orientation as they may lead to therapeutic blind spots with clients. (p.37)

8. *Encouragement of growing experiences in addition to therapy.* Feminist therapists acknowledge that therapy per se is not a cure-all, and they encourage women to consider other avenues for growth and support instead of or in addition to therapeutic experience. (p.37)

I believe that these guidelines coincide with what women of color would need from the therapeutic relationship. In particular, it is relevant that they emphasize the importance of empowerment, choice, and active social action as healing factors that would foster mental health for all women.

Positive Contributions of Feminist Therapy to the Mental Health of Women of Color

Feminist therapy's central tenet of the importance of socio-cultural factors in the psychology of all women is its most obvious positive contribution to the effective delivery of mental health services for women of color.

Of particular relevance for women of color seeking psychotherapy is that a central focus of feminist therapy is to *empower women.* "Empowerment is usually understood as the process of helping a powerless individual or group to gain the necessary skills, knowledge or influence to acquire control over their own lives" (Smith & Siegel, 1985). It is clear that women of color need to be empowered individually and as a group, and it is also clear that such empowerment will be psychologically healing and validating. Several authors who have discussed the empowering effects of feminist approaches to therapy with women of color (Comas-Díaz, 1987; Mays & Comas-Díaz, 1988; Solomon, 1982) state that feminist approaches help women of color to acknowledge the deleterious effects of sexism, racism, and elitism; deal with negative feelings imposed by their status as ethnic minorities; perceive themselves as causal agents in achieving solutions to their problems; understand the interplay between the external environment and their inner reality; and perceive opportunities to change the responses from the wider society.

Although consideration of life choices for women is not limited to reproductive issues, these issues constitute an extremely important component of women's life choices. Thus, another positive contribution of a feminist approach to therapy with women of color derives from the feminist conceptualization of reproductive choice. Both in terms of access to birth control and abortion as well as in the right to be protected from forced sterilization, feminist positions reaffirm women's right to control their own bodies. For all women of color, the access to safe abortion and birth control and the governmental funding of such programs is of primary importance. But perhaps even more so is the issue of forced sterilization for poor ethnic minority women. Regrettably, this is an issue that has not attracted as much attention from white feminists, although it has been of primary importance for women of color (Davis, 1981).

The issue of forced sterilization has galvanized the energy of women of color, but so have other issues that have prompted them to become involved in social action. Housing and the homeless, neighborhood safety, pregnant teenagers, educational opportunities, drugs, the AIDS crisis, and violence in the family are examples of some of the issues that have served as catalysts for the involvement of women of color in social change projects. Because the psychological effects of oppression have their roots in the social world as feminists maintain and the psychological healing of women does not occur only through a focus on the intrapsychic, changing the conditions of oppression under which women live is both a promoter and a consequence of psychological healing. For women of color, involvement in social action represents a form of empowerment, a productive expression of anger, and a way of testing their inner strength and resources. Involvement in social action becomes a powerful antidote to the helplessness engendered by oppressive social conditions. Thus, feminist therapy's encouragement of participation in activities outside therapy provides a support that is uniquely relevant for women of color.

Women of color by virtue of their constant exposure to instances of racism and sexism are frequently in touch with their anger. Since the acknowledgement and expression of angry feelings is seen as contradicting the cultural image of the "good" woman, women of color find their femininity questioned when they express their justified anger.

One of the contributions of feminist therapy to the treatment of women is the validation of women's anger and the facilitation and management of that anger as a source of strength in oppressive social contexts. In feminist therapy, women of color can find their anger validated, examine their experience of anger, learn to manage it, and circumvent depression through freedom to express anger in productive action both in their personal life and in their social world. For women to be able to express anger in articulate and appropriate verbalizations and confrontations is one of the goals of feminist therapy (Burtle, 1985). However, this presupposes a therapist who is able to deal with her own anger and with expressions of anger directed at her. This issue is particularly poignant when the therapist is a white woman because the anger of the woman of color can become threatening to the therapist or it could evoke feelings of guilt in her that would not be productive for the client.

Contradictions in Feminist Therapy with Women of Color

It is rather ironic that a theory that evolved from the awareness that socio-cultural factors are essential determinants in the psychology of women has been so slow to extend its own major insight to socio-cultural factors other than gender, thus excluding the experiences of the vast majority of women who are not white, and in that process excluding the impact of socio-cultural factors other than gender, such as race, class, and ethnicity, on the lives of all women, including white women (Espín & Gawelek, 1992; Spelman, 1988). Recent theoretical efforts at correcting this distortion within feminist psychology (e.g., Ballou, 1990; Brown, 1990; Espín & Gawelek, 1992) are still not widespread. Most therapists, regardless of their race, ethnicity, or class, continue to be trained in theories that are presented as universally valid (Greene, 1986) even though these theories are based on the specificity of life conditions of a population of mostly middle-class, white, Western, heterosexual males. Bradshaw (1990) provides an example of this bias in her discussion of Masterson's Theory and accurately describes the "racism cloaked in psychological jargon" (p. 75) present in so many theories. Thomas and Sillen (1972) provide innumerable examples of racist biases in both theory and practice.

Theories of psychological development and psychopathology have been notorious for their neglect of cultural variability as well as gender issues. Most psychological theory is literally Anglo-Saxon in its perspectives and conceptions of human nature. Psychology's preoccupation with scientific objectivity has divorced it from an understanding or description of human experience in its fullness and has limited it to data that are mostly based on the experience of white Anglo-Saxon men. Data on white women or ethnic minority people of both sexes have mostly been either excluded as "nuisance variables" or included only as "difference" and more often than not understood as deficiencies. Basically psychology has understood human diversity from two diametrically opposed perspectives. Either differences among people are a reflection of abnormalities or deficiencies, in which case efforts should be made to change the individuals and make them healthy, or these differences are seen as dictated by nature rather than a result of the socio-cultural context, so there is no need for any intervention (Espín & Gawelek, 1992; Fine & Gordon, 1989). Current feminist psychological theory has not fully escaped this bias and unfortunately is also encumbered by the scientific paradigm of psychology.

> Most feminist therapists and theoreticians, although trained in traditional systems and theories of personality and psychotherapy, have been quick to identify the masculinist biases inherent in other theories and practices that are associated with them. Many have also been able to cull out the heterosexist and homophobic biases. But the subtle aspects of racist and classist assumptions have been less visible and less salient to many white feminist therapists who have benefitted from privilege of race and class. (Brown, 1990, p.4)

Thus, the tendency to overgeneralize from data and information gathered from the experience of white women continues for the most part unchallenged, rendering women of color invisible yet one more time and limiting the development of a theory that should and could render them more visible (Brown, 1990; Espín, 1991; Greene, 1986).

In spite of this limitation, I still believe that feminist therapy has a lot to offer to women of color and their mental health, particularly if white therapists take seriously their own white privilege and actively engage in anti-racist self-education in this area (Katz, 1978; McIntosh, 1988; Rave, 1990).

Feminist Therapy with Women of Color

By definition the therapist in a feminist approach to therapy is a woman who is a feminist. But nothing much is said in feminist therapy's theory about the socio-cultural background of the therapist, such as her race, ethnicity, class, etc.

I would like to propose that the best form of therapy for women of color is a feminist ethno-specific approach. By a feminist ethno-specific approach I mean a therapeutic context in which the therapist is a woman from the same ethnic/racial background as the client. I am fully aware of the small numbers of feminist therapists who are women of color and thus of the difficulties involved in implementing this approach. Nevertheless, I would like to explain my rationale for stating that feminist ethno-specific therapy is the best approach to psychotherapy with women of color.

As feminist therapists maintain, the similarities in life experience between therapist and client provide a unique, perhaps the only, context in which women can feel both nurtured and empowered in therapy (e.g., Eichenbaum & Orbach, 1984; Gilbert, 1980; Kaschak, 1981). Arguments about the absolute importance of a woman therapist for women also provide the justification for the importance of cultural specificity in therapy. In spite of some contradictory information (Brody, 1984), it seems that the advantages of same gender as well as same culture/ethnicity/race between therapist and client are evident. I believe that these advantages are that (1) the therapist can understand the culture/ethnicity/race and the language (Espín, 1987b) of the client from firsthand experience; (2) the therapist can serve as a more adequate and effective role model for the client because a therapist from the same ethnic/racial group can, just through her presence, raise the client's consciousness as to what a woman of that background can accomplish; (3) the therapeutic relationship can be more equalized because therapist and client share the same culture/ethnicity/race, and thus the balance of power in the therapeutic context, rather than reproducing the inequalities of the world at large better approximates the feminist philosophy of therapy; and (4) the therapist is more likely to be invested in the client's success in therapy and life.

Obviously there are also some pitfalls in this approach, such as the danger of over-identification of therapist with client that could lead to excessive expectations or impatience about the client's progress and the danger of other countertransferential reactions evoked in the therapist that may interfere with the therapy and that could be triggered precisely by the similarity between the two parties involved. These dangers, however, are present in all feminist therapy by the very fact that both parties in the dyad are women. As Rave (1990) aptly puts it, white racism and privilege are still present in therapy when both parties involved are white women, because these forces are an inescapable component of all of our lives, not just the lives of those who are "different."

In spite of my belief that a feminist ethno-specific approach would be best suited to therapy with women of color, the reality is that the number of feminist therapists of color is so small that most women of color who seek out a feminist therapist will find themselves in therapy with a white woman. Good therapy provided in the woman of color client/white therapist dyad could be a tool for further understanding about differences and bridging gaps between races, classes, etc. for both therapist and client. On the other hand, this dyadic context could place the client in the position of "teaching" about culture, ethnicity, class, or race to the therapist, once again depriving the client from fully receiving what she needs. This dyad obviously involves the dangers of transferential/countertransferential reactions inherent in all therapy. But in addition it reproduces power differentials inherent in this society and thus a specific set of conflicts that exist prior to and outside the therapy. Once again the client finds herself in a context in which the white woman (this time as her therapist) has more power than her, thus defeating the possibility of empowerment that feminist therapy is supposed to offer all women (Gilbert, 1980; Kaschak, 1981). In this dyadic context it is essential that the therapist "acknowledges the deleterious effects of sexism and racism" (Comas-Díaz, 1987, p.41) on the life of her client and that these be addressed within the context of the therapy as well as acknowledged in the world at large, or else the therapy will be doomed to failure or fall short of what it should offer the client.

In those rare instances when the therapist is a woman of color and the client a white woman, another set of possibilities and pitfalls can become part of the transference and countertransference. A case example presented later will illustrate this point.

Comas-Díaz (1989) offers a rather encompassing and clear framework for understanding the different shapes that transferential and countertransferential reactions can take in cross-cultural contexts. Her framework is applicable to the varying compositions of the therapeutic dyad that may be found in feminist therapy.

Clinical Illustrations

It is sometimes naively assumed by people not involved in feminist therapy that such therapists spend their time "preaching feminism," rather than doing therapy per se. It is also assumed that feminist therapists attribute all psychological conflicts to the social context and pay little attention to intrapsychic individual conflicts. Rather than disputing these naive assumptions, I will refer the reader to authors who have described feminist therapy and its applications in detail (e.g., Comas-Díaz, 1987; Espín, 1985; Gilbert, 1980; Greene, 1986; Kaschak, 1981) and will devote the rest of this paper to clinical illustrations of feminist therapy with women of color. One vignette addresses the therapeutic dyad where the therapist is a woman of color and the client is white. This example was chosen because it illustrates poignantly some of the issues encountered when feminist therapy is done in a cross-cultural context. Details of the cases that are irrelevant to the illustration of a feminist approach to therapy have been omitted. All names as well as other identifying information have been modified.

Case 1: Amalia

Amalia was a 37-year-old Latin American woman who was an illegal immigrant. She was in a co-habiting relationship with a working-class white Anglo man who owned a small business. Amalia had two sons from a previous union who were 10 and 11 years of age, and a son and a daughter, ages 3 and 8 months respectively, from her present union. She had been taking some ESL classes at a community center, and one of her teachers there referred her to me for therapy because she was apparently depressed. We agreed on a fee that was affordable for her and acceptable to me and began to work steadily on her feelings of depression, although she frequently missed sessions.

Soon after we started working together, Amalia told me that Jim did not know she was in therapy and that he was abusive towards her and the children, particularly her two older sons. He could become violent when his wishes and commands were not followed. Because of her immigration status and her lack of education and English, it was clear that she could not afford to leave him. But more important, the thought that he did not have the right to be violent and domineering had not ever crossed her mind. When I shared with her that I did not like to see her trapped in this situation and that I would never tolerate that treatment from any man, she was extremely surprised, and her facial expression showed vividly how startled she was at my comment.

Amalia's father had been violent with her mother and the children, and Amalia's previous mate had also been violent. Her only sister was in an abusive marriage, and she believed all her brothers and other men she knew beat their wives as a matter of course. I explained to her that although I believed she probably was describing a reality, I thought this was a sad reality and one that should be changed. She commented at this point that she had heard some white American women say that but had never heard another Latina woman say that it was not right for a man to beat his wife. She expressed her excitement at the possibility of rebelling against Jim's violent treatment without having "to become too Americanized." I, in turn, was surprised at her response, because I do not believe that wife abuse is specific to Latino culture and because up to that point I had interpreted her submission to his violence to be a result of her violent family history and her economic and legal situation. It had not occurred to me to interpret it as an expression of her fear of becoming too acculturated into American values.

During the next few sessions Amalia became very inquisitive about my opinions on violence against women. She obtained a phone number from me and went as far as contacting a shelter for battered women that served mostly a Black and Latino population. Then, she got pregnant by Jim for a third time! I continued to work with her through her pregnancy and during that time explored with her her unconscious motivation to become pregnant at a time when she was beginning to question her relationship with Jim. During her pregnancy Amalia continued taking ESL classes and also started training as a beautician, which she had almost finished by the time her baby was born. Her therapy sessions became more regular during her pregnancy, and the violence at home subsided considerably to almost no violence directed against her and much less towards the children. She took advantage of this more calm environment to convince Jim that she ought to settle her immigration status legally, particularly considering that she now had three American children. Jim, who had more or less opposed this move by telling her that it was not necessary, agreed to it now, probably because she was more firm in expressing her wishes about this and other matters at home. When the baby was born, Amalia decided to terminate therapy because the beautician courses, the baby, and her other obligations already demanded 100% of her time.

Case 2: Camila

Camila came to the United States from Latin America with her family when she was 15. The family had decided to migrate because of political changes in her country. When she started therapy 3 years later Camila was studying at a university and had recently become sexually involved with an Irish-American woman in her dorm. Her grandmother, who was still living in her country of origin, had been more important to her as a maternal figure than her own mother. However, her grandmother was very opposed to Camila's lesbian relationships, which had started right before she immigrated to the United States.

She came to therapy wanting to speak in Spanish because, according to her, "her problems were in Spanish," and she also wanted a feminist therapist who would not reject her lesbianism. She actually was not sure that such a therapist really existed because she thought all feminist therapists were white and she had been in therapy for a short period of time with a Latino man, at the insistence of her family. This therapist had been intent on convincing her that her attraction to women was transitory and that she should try to get sexually involved with men. Camila, who is rather smart and to the point, told him that perhaps he should encourage his heterosexual female clients to get involved with women as a transitory stage too and left the therapy.

She was very pleased to see that rather than trying to encourage her to change her sexual orientation, I was interested in ways of helping her be happier in her relationships by choosing more appropriate partners (the woman she was involved with was an active alcoholic). We worked intensely on self-esteem issues and also on her relationship with her grandmother, her parents, and her partners. She worked in therapy on and off for about 7 years, coming to see me when she needed immediate help and taking extended breaks from the therapy when things were going well. When Camila finally terminated her therapy, she went back to her country for an extended visit with her grandmother. Her partner for the past 2 years, a Jewish woman she had met through their common interest in music, was coming to stay at the grandmother's home, at the grandmother's invitation, for part of the visit.

Case 3: Eileen

Eileen sought out a feminist therapist in order to deal with some relationship difficulties that she thought needed a feminist approach. She was 27, white, upper middle class, the third in a family of three daughters. Her father was an executive for a powerful international company he had worked for all his life. He was very successful, and the family lived in comfort. Her mother was a homemaker. Her two older sisters were married to very successful white men. Eileen had been involved in several relationships with Latino and black men, much to the disgust and opposition of her parents. All the relationships had ended with the men leaving after a lot of verbal fights in which they all said in one form or another that she was too needy. Although it was very clear that her parents had been cold and emotionally abusive throughout her childhood and continued to be as verbally abusive to her as she and her lovers were to each other, she insisted that they were good parents and she alone was to blame for her incapacity to sustain good relationships.

In her view, her choice of men of color as sexual partners was not an issue that needed to be discussed. She "just fell in love with the individuals" and was surprised that I could be "prejudiced like her parents in assuming that she should be with white men only." While agreeing that race should not be a factor against choosing a partner, I continued to question her pattern of always being involved with men of color and choosing me as a therapist, considering that there are so many more white women who are feminist therapists. Her response was always that she did not have "any of those prejudices" and "did not pay attention to a person's race or ethnicity" in choosing friends, lovers, or a therapist.

After some time in which she did not make much progress in therapy, she started referring to her father's questioning of my competence on a regular basis. Eventually, she directly asked about my credentials, but immediately made a comment about not wanting to know that I had "too many degrees" because then I "might be too good for her." When I confronted her with the implied racism in this statement and the implied self-deprecatory meaning of it, she denied that any of those interpretations were true.

Later in the therapy, when she finally started acknowledging the cold and verbally abusive atmosphere in which she had grown up, she mentioned in passing a novel about Black families she had read in adolescence. In this novel, all family members were loving and supportive of each other in spite of the fact that they were very poor. She added that when she had read the novel she had wished her father was not successful in his business; perhaps if they were poor, the family would be more loving.

This revelation brought on the unraveling of an elaborate fantasy that her relationships with men of color would be warmer and better than her sisters' marriages. Eventually, she was able to confront the role her fantasy about the warmth and loving characteristics of people of color had had in her choice of a Latina woman as her therapist. From that she went to a full acknowledgement of her emotional deprivation during childhood and her feeling that she would never be good enough because "no white person could really be loving enough." All she could hope for was that her therapist or her lovers, as people of color and thus able to love, could provide all the warmth and love she craved and was incapable of giving. At the same time that she held this over-idealized image of people of color, she also held strong racist views. Like her parents, she assumed that neither her therapist nor her lovers "were fit to lick her boots" (her father's words) and was intent on defeating her therapy and her relationships to prove this point. This was yet another effort to "prove" to herself and others that her parents were right and thus "good."

Needless to say, there were other issues in Eileen's therapy that have been left out of this account. The point I want to make by presenting this case vignette is that cross-cultural feminist therapy contexts present unique challenges. Because Eileen's issues expressed themselves in a rather strong fashion, they were more clearly observable. The powerful unconscious forces involved in cross-cultural therapy are made more obvious in Eileen's story precisely because these issues express themselves dramatically in this case and also because the usual cross-cultural pattern in feminist therapy of white Therapist/Woman of Color Client is reversed. But I believe that some variation of these issues is always present in cross-cultural therapy contexts. I believe that it is impossible to live in a racist society such as ours and not have those forces be present in the therapy room even when client and therapist share the experience of being female.

The strong tenet of feminist therapy that sexism always creeps into the therapy context when the therapist is male and the client is female is paralleled by the differences in race/ethnicity/class between client and therapist in feminist cross-cultural therapy. It would be naive to believe that the racism of white feminist therapists will never creep into their therapy with women of color clients. The cross-cultural context lends itself to the expression of these feelings and patterns in as powerful a way as the cross-gender therapy context. This is the reason why I believe that a feminist ethno-specific approach provides the best alternative for women of color, in spite of the fact that I am well aware of the limitation that the small numbers of feminist therapists of color imposes on this possibility.

Since most women of color seeking feminist therapy will probably be in therapy with white women therapists, it is incumbent on the white feminist therapist to be aware, educated, and actively involved in dealing with the influence of racism in her life in order to counter the existence of these forces in herself and in her therapy with women of color.

The Tapestry of Therapy with Women of Color

The case vignettes presented above provide an illustration of how feminist concerns are present in therapy with women of color, even when the focus seems to be on ethno-cultural issues, and how ethno-cultural issues are present even when the focus appears to be more on feminist concerns. In other words, all the threads of the social context are interwoven in the tapestry of therapy, and it is essential for good therapy that attention be paid to all of them.

For example, in Amalia's case, the effect of acculturative stress was expressed through her concern about becoming "too Americanized." This concern was an important factor in how she perceived and tolerated the expression of anger in herself and violent behavior on the part of others. While preventing the abuse of women is usually defined as a feminist concern, Ho (1990) warns us not to interpret and/or justify violent behavior towards women in ethnic minority communities under the guise of cultural traditions. "Violence hurts victims physically regardless of cultural heritage and customs" (Ho, 1990, p.147), and thus abusers "should not be allowed to use their cultural background as an excuse for their abusive behavior" (Ho, 1990, p.146).

Amalia's family background, her fear of the effects of acculturation, and her tenuous legal status combined to create a situation of helplessness that although to some extent specifically female was also amplified by stressors shared by both females and males in her legal, social, and acculturative situation.

In disclosing my unwillingness to tolerate violence in my life, I apparently modeled for her the possibility of refusing to tolerate violence and still remain faithful to Latina culture. Feminist therapy's emphasis on the relevance of appropriate therapist disclosure provided a vehicle for an apparently successful intervention. At the same time, the ethno-specific context of the therapy was essential for Amalia's acceptance of the relevance of the therapist's position for her own life as a Latina. It was the combination of both perspectives that produced an enhancement of Amalia's life situation and mental health.

With Camila, the open exploration of sexuality, in Spanish, also provided a form for the resolution of her ambivalence. In her previous experience, every Latino person (e.g., grandmother and psychiatrist) was rejecting of her lesbianism, and her sexuality could only be expressed in an English-speaking context where other aspects of her self-esteem were endangered (Espín, 1987a). The encouragement of individual goal-setting and transcendence of traditional sex-role stereotypes that are characteristic of a feminist perspective were, in her case, strengthened by the support of a Latina therapist who could accept Camila's sexuality and discuss it positively in Spanish from within the same cultural context in which she felt nurtured and supported in all other aspects of her life. The presence of this role model provided her with options she would not have been aware of otherwise.

In Eileen's case, the intermingling of the ethno-cultural and feminist themes presented itself in a more subtle, and even confusing, form. However, the same themes of racism, classism, and need for acknowledging the diversity of women's experiences that are usually identified as issues for women of color were clearly present in the therapy of this white upper-middle-class woman. The equalization of power in the context of her therapy operated under some peculiar conditions. Had I been more aware of the existence of issues of race and class as a significant factor in her life, rather than assuming that they were not as relevant for a white upper-middle-class woman, Eileen's therapy would probably have progressed more rapidly. Moreover, had I not taken at face value her apparent lack of racism and prejudice, we would have been able to uncover the elaborate fantasies that precluded her involvement in realistic relationships and disguised her intense self-denigration and self-hatred at a much earlier stage in her therapy.

Conclusion

Let me conclude by saying that I do not see a feminist approach to therapy as something that could be used or not, depending on circumstances. The preceding discussion of the case vignettes serves to illustrate this perspective. I believe that when a therapist has a feminist analysis of the social world and thus a feminist understanding of women's life experiences, there is an inherent feminist approach to her therapy as well as to her own life. Consequently, she will approach the therapy of all her clients from this vantage point. By the same token, when a therapist has an analysis and understanding of the impact of racism, social class, privilege, and sexual orientation as factors in the construction of personality, it is impossible and ineffective to approach any client without this perspective.

I will go as far as to assert that a therapist who does not have an analysis of the social world could not be a good therapist. That analysis includes an understanding of the impact of oppression due to gender, race, ethnicity, class, sexual orientation, disability, and age (and, conversely, of the impact of privilege on the lives of those who do not belong to oppressed groups in these categories). I believe that this analysis and awareness are as essential for good therapy as knowledge of psychological theory or practical therapeutic skills. Indeed, to espouse a theory or use a skill without understanding its embeddedness in the social context in which it was developed can, in fact, be dangerous and unethical (Katz, 1985).

Thus a therapist who has a feminist philosophy of treatment and who actively seeks to assist her women of color clients in their healing and empowerment will always, in one form or another, be doing feminist therapy, regardless of what the specific focus of the therapeutic work is at any given time.

Notes

Reprinted from Espín, O.M. (1994). Feminist Approaches [to Therapy with Women of Color]. In L. Comas-Díaz & B. Greene (Eds.), *Women of Color and Mental Health: Integrating Ethnic Identities in Psychotherapy* (pp.265–286). New York: Guilford.

References

Anzaldúa, G. (Ed.). (1990). *Making face, making soul/ Haciendo caras*. San Francisco: Aunt Lute Foundation Books.

Ballou, M.B. (1990). Approaching a feminist principled paradigm in the construction of personality theory. In L.S. Brown & M.P.P. Root (Eds.), *Diversity and complexity in feminist theory* (pp.23–40). New York: Harrington Park Press.

Bradshaw, C.K. (1990). A Japanese view of dependency: What can Amae psychology contribute to feminist psychology and therapy? In L.S. Brown & M.P.P. Root (Eds.), *Diversity & complexity in feminist theory* (pp.67–86). New York: Harrington Park Press.

Brody, C.M. (1984). Feminist therapy with minority clients. In C.M. Brody (Ed.), *Women therapists working with women: New theory and process of feminist therapy* (pp.109–115). New York: Springer.

Brown, L.S. (1990). The meaning of a multicultural perspective for theory building in feminist therapy. In L.S. Brown & M.P.P Root (Eds.), *Diversity and complexity in feminist therapy* (pp.1–21). New York: Harrington Park Press.

Burtle, V. (1985). Therapeutic anger in women. In L.B. Rosewater & L. Walker (Eds.), *Handbook of feminist therapy* (pp.71–79). New York: Springer.

Butler, M. (1985). Guidelines for feminist therapy. In L.B. Rosewater & L. Walker (Eds.), *Handbook of feminist therapy* (pp.32–38). New York: Springer.

Comas-Díaz, L. (1987). Feminist therapy with Hispanic/Latina women: Myth or reality? *Women and Therapy,* 6(4), 39–61.

Comas-Díaz, L. (1989, October). *Cross-cultural psychotherapy: The therapist/patient dyad.* Paper presented at Conference on Psychotherapy of Diversity: Cross-cultural Treatment Issues. Boston.

Combahee River Collective. (1979). A Black feminist statement. In Z. Eisenstein (Ed.), *Capitalist patriarchy and the case for socialist feminism* (pp.135–139). New York: Monthly Review Press.

Combs, H.G. (1986). The application of an individual/collective model to the psychology of Black women. In D. Howard (Ed.), *The dynamics of feminist therapy* (pp.67–80). New York: Haworth.

Davis, A. (1981). *Women, race and class.* New York: Vintage.

Donovan, V.K., & Littenberg, R. (1981). Psychology of women: Feminist therapy. In B. Harber (Ed.), *The women's annual: 1981* (pp.211–235). Boston: G.K. Hall.

Eichenbaum, L., & Orbach, S. (1984). Feminist psychoanalysis: Theory and practice. In C.M. Brody (Ed.), *Women therapists working with women: New theory and process in feminist therapy* (pp.46–55). New York: Springer.

Espín, O.M. (1979). The needs of Third World/minority women in historically white universities. *Debate and Understanding #5* (pp.27–31). Boston University, Martin Luther King Jr. Center for Academic Services and Minority Affairs.

Espín, O.M. (1984). Cultural and historical influences on sexuality in Hispanic/Latin women: Implications for psychotherapy. In C. Vance (Ed.), *Pleasure and danger: Exploring Female Sexuality* (pp.149–163). London: Routledge & Kegan Paul.

Espín, O.M. (1985). Psychotherapy with Hispanic women: Some considerations. In P. Pedersen (Ed.), *Handbook of cross-cultural counseling and psychotherapy* (pp.165–171). Westport, CT: Greenwood.

Espín, O.M. (1987a). Issues of identity in the psychology of Latina lesbians. In Boston Lesbian Psychologies Collective (Eds.), *Lesbian psychologies: Explorations and challenges* (pp.35–55). Champaign: University of Illinois Press.

Espín, O.M. (1987b). Psychological impact of migration on Latinas: Implications for psychotherapeutic practice. *Psychology of Women Quarterly,* 11(4), 489–503.

Espín, O.M. (1991, February). *On knowing you are the unknown: The psychology of women of color.* Presented at Knowing Women: A Gathering of Women Who Know—The New Psychologies of Women, San Diego, CA.

Espín, O.M., & Gawelek, M.A. (1992). Women's diversity: Ethnicity, race, class and gender in theories of feminist psychology. In M. Ballou & L.S. Brown (Eds.), *Theories of personality and psychopathology: Feminist reappraisals.* (pp.88–107). New York: Guilford.

Faunce, P.S. (1985). A feminist philosophy of treatment. In L.B. Rosewater & L. Walker (Eds.), *Handbook of feminist therapy* (pp.1–4). New York: Springer.

Fine, M., & Gordon, S.M. (1989). Feminist transformations of/despite psychology. In M. Crawford & M. Gentry (Eds.), *Gender and Thought: Psychological Perspectives.* (pp.146–174). New York: Springer Verlag.

Gilbert, L.A. (1980). Feminist therapy. In A.M. Brodsky & R. Hare-Mustin (Eds.), *Women and psychotherapy* (pp.245–265). New York: Guilford.

Greene, B.A. (1986). When the therapist is white and the patient is black: Considerations for psychotherapy in the feminist heterosexual and lesbian communities. In D. Howard (Ed.), *The dynamics of feminist therapy* (pp.41–65). New York: Haworth.

Hill, M. (1990). On creating a theory of feminist therapy. In L.S. Brown & M.P.P. Root (Eds.), *Diversity and complexity in feminist therapy* (pp.53–65). New York: Harrington Park Press.

Ho, C.K. (1990). An analysis of domestic violence in Asian American communities: A multicultural approach to counseling. In L.S. Brown & M.P.P. Root (Eds.), *Diversity and complexity in feminist therapy.* (pp.129–150). New York: Harrington Park Press.

hooks, b. (1984). *Feminist theory: From margin to center.* Boston: South End.

Hurtado, A. (1989). Relating to privilege: Seduction and rejection in the subordination of white women and women of color. *Signs: Journal of Women in Culture and Society,* 14(4), 833–855.

Joseph, G.I., & Lewis, J. (Eds.). (1981). *Common differences: Conflict in Black and white feminist perspectives.* New York: Anchor.

Kaschak, E. (1981). Feminist psychotherapy: The first decade. In S. Cox (Ed.), *Female psychology: The emergent self* (pp.387–401). New York: St. Martin's.

Katz, J. (1978). *white awareness: Handbook for anti-racism training.* Norman: University of Oklahoma Press.

Katz, J. (1985). The socio-political nature of counseling. *The Counseling Psychologist,* 13(4), 615–624.

Lorde, A. (1984). *Sister outsider.* Freedom, CA: Crossing.

Mays, V., & Comas-Díaz, L. (1988). Feminist therapies with ethnic minority populations: A closer look at blacks and Hispanics. In M.A. Dutton-Douglas & L.E. Walker (Eds.), *Feminist psychotherapies: Integration of therapeutic and feminist systems.* (pp.228–251). Norwood, NJ: Ablex.

McIntosh, P. (1988). *white privilege and male privilege: A personal account of coming to see correspondence through work in Women's Studies* (Working Paper No. 189). Center for Research on Women, Wellesley College, Wellesley, MA.

Rave, E.J. (1990). white feminist therapists and antiracism. In L.S. Brown & M.P.P. Root (Eds.), *Diversity and complexity in feminist therapy* (pp.313–326). New York: Harrington Park Press.

Root, M.P.P. (1992). Reconstructing the impact of trauma on personality. In M. Ballou & L.S. Brown (Eds.), *Theories of personality and psychopathology: Feminist reappraisals.* (pp.229–265). New York: Guilford.

Smith, A.J., & Siegel, R.F. (1985). Feminist therapy: Redefining power for the powerless. In L.B. Rosewater & L. Walker (Eds.), *Handbook of feminist therapy* (pp.13–21). New York: Springer.

Solomon, B.B. (1982). The delivery of mental health services to Afro-American individuals and families: Translating theory into practice. In B.A. Bass, G.J. Wyatt, & G.J. Powell (Eds.), *The Afro-American family: Assessment, treatment and research issues* (pp.201–237). New York: Grune & Stratton.

Spelman, E.V. (1988). *The inessential woman: Problems of exclusion in feminist thought.* Boston: Beacon.

Thomas, A., & Sillen, S. (1972). *Racism and psychiatry.* New York: Brunner/Mazel.

Trotman, F.K. (1984). Psychotherapy of black women and the dual effects of racism and sexism. In C.M. Brody (Ed.), *Women therapists working with women: New theory and process of feminist therapy* (pp.96–108). New York: Springer.

5

On Knowing You Are the Unknown: Women of Color Constructing Psychology

I recently found a quote from Paulo Freire in one of bell hooks's latest books that I think applies to what all liberation movements, including feminism, are about: "We cannot enter the struggle as objects in order to later become subjects" (1990, p.15). I find this thought particularly relevant when we are reflecting on the impact of racism on theories of the psychology of women.

I believe the feminist movement has functioned to provide opportunities for many women to develop and maintain a sense of self-worth. In its present historical reality, however, the women for whom the movement most fully provides such validation are white and middle class. Women of color, feminist or not, are seldom idealized, respected, valued, or presented as role models in whose footsteps other women would want to follow.

It is certainly true that women of color validate and respect each other. It is also true, however, that in a context of cultural imperialism those women of color who are developing feminist theoretical perspectives frequently do not feel fully validated by either white feminists or people of both genders in their own ethnic group. For the most part they are simply unknown to most white feminists and considered irrelevant by people in their own ethnic group. Most definitions of the concepts of "feminist" or "woman" assume either that all women are included in one version of feminism or that women of color "do not fully understand" what sexism really is and what feminism is supposed to mean. Women of color do not fully "belong" unless they are willing to learn from white women what feminism "really is." The term "feminist" is frequently attributed only to white women by women of color and white women alike.

When statements are made about the "need to include" women of color in theories or organizations, in the very statement of the need for their inclusion the assumption is being made that some other group (meaning, of course, *white* women) "owns" and defines the movement in which the women of color are to be included. Including women of color is seen as either a duty performed out of guilt or a generous act towards those less fortunate than the "owners" of the movement. However, guilt is for the most part useless and generosity tends to be humiliating for those who are the object of it. The thought that a true feminist movement, and feminist psychology in particular, are really non-existent as long as only some women are being mirrored and idealized by the movement does not occur to those who, consciously or unconsciously, see themselves as the guilty and generous "owners" of the feminist movement.

I would like to say very strongly that there will never be a true feminist movement, and more important for us as psychologists, there will not be valid theories of the psychology of women as long as this movement and these theories are based on a very limited sector of the population (Espín, 1991). Ironically, this is the same criticism that we as feminists have of a male-oriented psychology.

Indeed, this whole issue of inclusion is not about "affirmative action" but rather about *the nature of knowledge,* both in the psychology of women and in the discipline of psychology as a whole. The theories and the research we now have are, for the most part, incomplete and faulty pieces of knowledge, no matter how elegant they may seem. As I have written elsewhere,

> Post-modern understandings of the multiplicity of realities that constitute the reality of the world, leave no room for naive descriptions of women, the world, or human life that incorporate only one perspective on that reality. No matter how privileged that reality may have been in the past, it is as partial as all others. (Espín, 1991, p.5)

White feminists, for all their good intentions, are no more immune to blindness created by privilege than their male counterparts are (McIntosh, 1988). As Simone Weil put it many years ago (cited in Young, 1990, p.39), "someone who does not see a pane of glass, does not know that she does not see it." This is precisely the curse of the privileged: that they do not see anything that does not have to do with themselves, and on top of that, believe that what they see is universal truth. Thus there is an inhibition of the real capacity to know.

Those who do not partake of that privilege, however, know very well the existence of that pane of glass; they know it is impossible for them to go through this barrier—the more effective precisely because it is unseen. In fact, the non-privileged can be better "knowers" and more knowledgeable. Their vision tends to be clearer; they see themselves, they see the glass pane, and they know who is on the other side of that glass. That is why women and other oppressed people have a clearer vision of reality than white males and other oppressors.

bell hooks's (1990) comments about the Freire citation I opened with expand on this point:

> This statement compels reflection on how the dominated, the oppressed, the exploited make ourselves subject. How do we create [a] world view, a consciousness, an identity, a standpoint that . . . opposes dehumanization but [a] movement which enables creative, expansive self-actualization? Opposition in not enough. . . . [The] process [of becoming subjects] emerges as one comes to understand how structures of domination work in one's own life, as one develops critical thinking and critical consciousness, as one invents new, alternative habits of being, and resists from that marginal space of difference inwardly defined. (p.15)

What I interpret from the standpoint of a theory of feminist psychology as I read this statement is that women of color need to take a central position in the creation of feminist theory as *creators* of the theory, not as people who are generously or guiltily included by others. I also read in this statement that from the new consciousness and critical thinking born of our own experiences and our own "difference[s] inwardly defined" a new "creative, expansive self-actualization" will develop. But I don't think this is something women of color can, will, or should do in our own little corners or in small spaces on programs. I believe it is a contribution women of color will have to make as feminist psychologists for the benefit of *all* psychology, or in whatever profession or way of life we might be.

The success of this task presupposes both willingness and effort on the part of women of color to develop our own "critical consciousness" and "critical thinking" in order "to understand how structures of domination" have affected our psychology and in order to invent "new, alternative habits of being." Clearly, this is not a minor task, either personally or theoretically, considering that it is to be undertaken in a context of oppression and cultural imperialism where one is, indeed, the "unknown."

Up to now, the feminist movement and feminist psychology theory, as part of that movement, have suffered from the limitations created by the cultural imperialism prevalent in all of psychology. Iris Young (1990) writes:

> Cultural imperialism involves the paradox of experiencing oneself as invisible at the same time that one is marked out as different. The invisibility comes about when dominant groups fail to recognize the perspective embodied in their cultural experience as a perspective. These dominant cultural expressions often simply have little place for the experience of other groups, at most mentioning or referring to them in stereotyped and marginalized ways. This, then, is the injustice of cultural imperialism: that the oppressed group's own experience and interpretation of social life finds little expression that touches the dominant culture, while that same culture imposes on the oppressed group its experiences and interpretation of social life. (p.60)

This is, indeed, the experience of "knowing you are the unknown." It is the experience of knowing that the dominant cultural paradigm, including the relatively new paradigm of feminist psychology, sees you only as the different one, as the one who has only a partial view of reality, while it gives to itself the right to see its perspectives as universal rather than culturally determined and therefore also different from the perspectives of others in its own way.

To assume that race and class should only come into feminist psychology theory when we are referring to women of color misses the most important insight of feminism, i.e., that the psychology of each individual woman is influenced by her social context: that the personal is political and the political impinges upon the personal. In so doing, it limits the development of true feminist psychology in very serious ways because when the psychology of white women is assumed to be influenced only by their gender and not their race, a very important understanding is missing. Just as we can understand the sexism a woman of color experiences only when we understand its connection to the racism she does experience, to understand fully how the particular forms of sexism she experiences influence a white woman, we must understand its connection to the racism she does not experience. In fact, "attempts to isolate gender from race and class, typically operate to obscure the race and class identity of white middle class women" (Spelman, 1988, p.209) and thus limit the understanding of both white women's psychology and the psychology of women of color.

Some efforts by feminist therapy theorists, for example those of the Feminist Therapy Institute (Brown & Root, 1990) and the recent Women of Color Institute of the Association for Women in Psychology raise my hopes about a new understanding and opening among white feminists. Other contexts, however, continue to leave me very discouraged. Even though it has become somewhat common practice to add a few women of color to the lists of feminist foremothers or theoreticians, they, or their names, may be included in a token fashion, without real knowledge of their points of view or deep consideration of the meaning of those points of view for white feminists. Few white feminists would recognize names of feminist theorists of color such as Patricia Hill Collins, Audre Lorde, bell hooks, Gloria Anzaldúa, María Lugones, Aida Hurtado, Maria Root, or Trinh Minh-ha compared to the numbers who easily recognize white women theorists such as Gilligan, Miller, or Chodorow. For the most part, women of color continue to be mentioned in small asides, footnotes, or digressions from the main topic and almost always as the *object* of theorizing, rather than as the *subject* who theorizes and whose theories are part of the common knowledge. As bell hooks (1984) says, "In more recent years, racism has become an accepted topic in feminist discussion not as a result of [women of color calling attention to it] but as a result of white female input validating such discussions, a process which indicates how racism works" (p.51).

A feminist theory that is derived from the experiences of those theorizing requires the presence of women of color as generators of theory as *subjects* rather than *objects*. The focus on "difference" in psychology has walked into feminist theory unanalyzed; therefore, difference can be seen as natural and unchangeable and/or as signifying deficiency. Difference will continue to imply the existence of a norm and thus ab-normality on the part of those who are different from that norm, rather than vari-ability in human experience.

A few examples of how a focus on human variability—a perspective that makes the experience of women of color as central to psychology as that of any other hu-man group—could enrich both the psychology of women and psychology in general might help to illustrate my point. Since I cannot possibly cover in a few pages every aspect of what a feminist exploration of psychology could and should entail, I focus on a few illustrations based on my own interests within psychology.

Most feminist psychology theory (e.g., Chodorow, 1978; Gilligan, 1982; Miller, 1986) takes the psychological characteristics prevalent among contemporary middle-class women in Western societies to be the essential component of the psychology of women, without stopping to consider that most of these characteristics are rather de-fense mechanisms developed by women to deal with conditions of oppression. If women are so proficient at human relations, it is probably because that ability has been their survival tool in a male-dominated world, not because ability for human interaction is intrinsically connected with female chromosomes. Only if the oppres-sive social conditions that have determined most women's behavior can be removed will we be able to assess whether some of the values that society has abandoned to women are indeed part of "women's nature" (Espín & Gawelek, 1992).

I believe that a social constructionist paradigm that sees psychological characteris-tics as a result of social and historical processes, not as natural, essential characteris-tics of one or another group of people, is the more productive approach in the study of human diversity than some of the other traditional paradigms accepted in psy-chology. Theories of the psychology of oppression and resistance to oppression help us understand the impact of the socio-cultural context in the development of per-sonality and in the psychotherapeutic context. For example, Freire (1970) has de-scribed the impact of internalized oppression in determining behaviors and aspira-tions that otherwise seem completely individually determined.

Language is also an important and neglected variable in studies of personality de-velopment and identity formation. I agree with the post-structuralist concept that the structure of reality is modified by the language used to describe it. Language is not transparent and does not merely reflect and describe human experience. Rather, it is an active creator of that experience.

For women who speak more than one language, there is yet another component in the development of personality and the expression of psychopathology. What I have learned from doing therapy with bilingual individuals is that self-expression in areas such as sexuality is highly influenced by the use of one or the other language (Espín, 1987). Expressions of pathological affect, or of strong emotional states, and the experience of the self are affected by the language used to describe them. An im-portant aspect of language usage for women of color is its connection with self-es-teem and identity development. Language and speech do not occur in a vacuum. In the United States, the dominant society ascribes inferior social status to Black English and to bilingualism. The differential valuing of languages and accents has a profound impact on the development of self-concept and identity. When bilingual skills are devalued, also devalued are those parts of the self that have developed in the context of another language (Espín, 1987).

We need to look seriously at other societies and cultures, searching for models of development that, precisely because the Western/Anglo-Saxon model is different from them, may teach us about other possibilities for being human. Psychodynamic theories place great emphasis on the existence of an internal individual world that is shaped by interactions with the mother during infancy. Deep-seated beliefs about the influence of mothers, especially in object relations theory, presuppose a certain form of family organization that is not only sexist but also culturally and class biased. How are we to understand psychological development based on relations with an other (the object) if the role of this other and the relationship between the developing child and this other are significantly different in different cultures? (Espín & Gawelek, 1992).

According to Watson-Franke (1988), matrilineal societies provide us with an alternative perspective. In her view, *matrilining* creates a different valuing of mothers (and women) and different father and husband roles for men than those to which we in patrilineal cultures are accustomed. "In congruence with the centrality of women, matriliny creates strong female role models, with the mother playing the essentially significant part" (p.4). While in patriarchal societies matrifocal families are seen as less valid than male-headed households, in matrilineal societies, matrifocus represents the legitimate philosophy. Western theoreticians, raised within a patriarchal context, find it difficult to conceptualize as healthy a family context in which women are central. "The centrality of women in female-headed families has no publicly acknowledged and supported structural force" (p. 14).

The female-headed family of all races is still seen as deviant in most of the Western world. Because the model of healthy family derives from a patriarchal society that resists and rejects a central position for women, it describes many Black and Latino families as well as all lesbian families as "dysfunctional." But what would happen if we looked at them from a different paradigm? What implications would this have for object relations theories? Belief that an idealized nuclear family structure is essential to healthy personality development can be questioned when one observes or studies other societies where children develop and become healthy adults in different family structures.

Even feminist critiques of object relations theories in terms of their emphasis on mother and their potential for mother-hating seldom question the socio-cultural context in which the mother is immersed. Much less do they question aspects of that context that might be as influential as the mother in the psychological development of the child (Espín & Gawelek, 1992).

It is extremely important to take a critical look today at the ritual of therapy, a ritual that has changed perhaps too little since Freud's time. Feminist therapy has challenged many of the traditional models, but how do models of feminist therapy apply across cultures, classes, etc. (Espín, 1994)?

Women of color lead lives immersed in unique experiences which uniquely qualify them to transform the personal in their lives into the political or theoretical perspectives necessary to create a true psychology of all women. Women of color are therefore essential partners in the development of feminist psychology and feminist therapy.

Paraphrasing Gloria Anzaldúa (1987) and María Lugones (1990), women of color who are feminist live on "the borderlands." We know more than one world and "travel" between different "worlds." In doing so, we develop new experiences, new territories and new languages not known by those who inhabit only one world or speak in only one language. We know possibilities unknown by others. We can develop those possibilities to the enrichment of everyone, but only if we are *subjects,* known and respected as equals in the task of building a new world for all women. If we continue to be treated as *objects,* when acknowledged at all, we will never be known by others and perhaps not even fully by ourselves. The richness and knowledge we could offer the feminist movement in general and feminist psychology in particular will forever be lost. I believe that all of us in this book, as well as its readers, can play a role in steering the feminist movement in this most enriching direction. We are all, together, the *subjects* and the *owners* of this movement.

Notes

Reprinted from Espín, O.M. (1995). On Knowing You Are the Unknown: Women of Color Constructing Psychology. In J. Adelman & G. Enguidanos (Eds.), *Racism in the Lives of Women* (pp.127–136). New York: Haworth.

References

Anzaldúa, G. (1987). *Borderlands/La frontera.* San Francisco: Spinsters/Aunt Lute.

Brown, L.S., & Root, M.P.P. (Eds.). (1990). *Diversity and complexity in feminist therapy.* New York: Harrington Park Press.

Chodorow, N. (1978). *The reproduction of mothering.* Berkeley: University of California Press.

Espín, O.M. (1987). Psychological impact of migration on Latinas: Implications for psychotherapeutic practice. *Psychology of Women Quarterly,* 11(4), 489–503.

Espín, O.M. (1991, August). *Ethnicity, race and class, and the future of feminist psychology.* Invited address presented at the 99th Convention of the American Psychological Association, San Francisco.

Espín, O.M. (1994). Feminist approaches [to therapy with women of color]. In L. Comas-Díaz & B. Greene (Eds.), *Women of Color and mental health* (pp.265–286). New York: Guilford.

Espín, O.M., & Gawelek, M.A. (1992). Women's diversity: Ethnicity, race, class and gender in theories of feminist psychology. In L.S. Brown & M. Ballou(Eds.), *Personality and psychopathology: Feminist reappraisals* (pp.88–107). New York: Guilford

Freire, P. (1970). *Pedagogy of the oppressed.* New York: Seabury.

Gilligan, C. (1982). *In a different voice.* Cambridge, MA: Harvard University Press.

hooks, b. (1984). *Feminist theory: From margin to center.* Boston: South End.

hooks, b. (1990). *Yearning: Essays on race, gender and cultural politics.* Boston: South End.

Lugones, M. (1990). Playfulness, "world"-traveling, and loving perception. In G. Anzaldúa (Ed.), *Making face, making soul/Haciendo caras*. San Francisco: Spinsters/Aunt Lute.

McIntosh, P. (1988). *Understanding correspondence between white privilege and male privilege through women's studies work* (Working Paper #189). Center for Research on Women, Wellesley College, Wellesley, MA.

Miller, J.B. (1986). *Toward a new psychology of women* (2nd ed.). Boston: Beacon.

Spelman, E. (1988). *The inessential women: Problems of exclusion in feminist thought.* Boston: Beacon.

Watson-Franke, M.B. (1988, July). *Siblings vs. spouses: Men and women in matrilineal societies (South America and North America).* Paper presented at the International Congress of Americanists, Amsterdam, The Netherlands.

Young, I.M. (1990). *Justice and the politics of difference.* Princeton, NJ: Princeton University Press.

Part Three

Sexuality

Of all the pieces in this anthology, the two essays included in this section were written and published the earliest. Chapter 6, "Cultural and Historical Influences on Sexuality in Hispanic/Latin Women," was originally presented in the early 1980s as an invited paper at a Barnard College conference on women's sexuality. The conference generated much controversy among feminists because of some presenters' refusal to condemn sexual practices disapproved by others. This piece first appeared in print in the anthology *Pleasure and Danger: Exploring Female Sexuality* that collected the papers of that conference. That anthology and this paper have been cited widely in the past decade. Chapter 7, on the development of identity in Latina lesbians, was first presented in Boston at a nationwide conference on lesbian psychology. It was subsequently published in the anthology of papers presented at that conference. Both of these anthologies received Distinguished Publication Awards from the Association for Women in Psychology. *Pleasure and Danger* is now in its second edition in English and it has been translated into several other languages.

These two chapters, together with "Psychological Impact of Migration on Latinas" (included in Part 4), are also the most widely cited pieces I have authored. This may be due to their earlier publication dates and hence longer presence in the psychological literature on Latinas. These pieces appeared when virtually no one else wrote about Latinas' sexual issues. Both have been reproduced in several anthologies, cited in textbooks on the psychology of women, and used by well-known feminist writers in their articles and books. The wide diffusion of these pieces reflects their pioneer status. It also speaks to the scarcity of information on this topic. I am flattered by their inclusion in the cited references of some prominent feminist writers, but dismayed that some of my statements, particularly, concepts from "Cultural and Historical Influences on Sexuality in Hispanic/Latin Women," have been taken out of context and used to further stereotype Latina women's lives and sexuality. This has occurred when authors trying to demonstrate their inclusion of all ethnically diverse women had very little understanding of extant cultural complexities. In at least one case, this same piece was abridged and included without my permission in an anthology of readings on race and class. I want to believe that these uses are a statement of interest in my ideas, although misuse of this sort frustrates any scholar.

The greatest value of these two pieces, without doubt, is their significance for Latinas themselves and for those providing services to them. At many conferences, professional and college student Latinas as well as other professional women have told me these articles gave them a new sense of themselves or their therapy clients. Apparently, these essays have provided Latina women, their intimates, and their therapists with a new way of seeing themselves or a confirmation of their intuitions. As a result, these two articles have provided me with great personal and professional satisfaction.

Many pages have been written on the issue of women's sexuality since these two articles were published. Other articles and books on Latinas' sexuality appeared in the years since their publication. Deeper and more sophisticated understandings about the sexuality of Latinas and the processes of identity development for lesbians have been produced. As scholarship on women's sexuality, particularly that of Latinas, has increased since the late 1980s, other writers have confirmed and elaborated on the main point of these articles: that sexuality is profoundly affected by historical, political, and cultural contexts. Newer scholarship has reiterated the importance of the interplay of complex factors that affect the sexuality of women both individually and collectively. Ignoring social influences or, conversely, the reality of individual agency when confronting women's sexuality leaves us with a partial picture. Minimizing either factor diminishes the possibilities and richness of women's sexuality— another way of saying that sexuality is always multilayered and that individual desire is never purely individual.

The conceptualizations derived from social construction theoretical understandings were mostly unknown to psychology when these two chapters were written. But even though I did not have the vocabulary of social construction theory available to me at the time, a social construction perspective is present in these two chapters. Both make reference to the social construction of desire and the multilayered nature of sexuality and identity by emphasizing in different ways that "sexualities and sexual experience are produced, changed, and modified within an ever-changing sexual discourse" (Tiefer, 1995, p.19).

When I originally penned these articles, I did not ask who benefits from these culturally constructed beliefs assigned to women's sexuality. I hope my recent scholarship (presented in Part 5 of this book) begins to answer this question. Had I had access to some of the new insights at the time of my writing, I might have presented—and expanded on—the issues presented in these two essays from different theoretical perspectives. In particular, I would use newer theories of psychological identity to frame the study of Latina lesbian identity development, including interrogating the concept of identity from postmodern perspectives. I would reconceptualize identity formation less from an Eriksonian or developmental stage process and more as a process of understanding one's social location within a changing social context. The perspectives I would include now were not available to me then. Yet, I believe many of the points in the chapters still resonate as valid. In the 1980s, these essays helped open the way for discussion of these issues.

References

Tiefer, L. (1995). *Sex is not a natural act.* Boulder, CO: Westview Press.

6

Cultural and Historical Influences on Sexuality in Hispanic/Latin Women: Implications for Psychotherapy

The purpose of this paper is to present some ideas on the development of sexuality in Hispanic women and their implications for a psychotherapeutic relationship. This paper will examine four major factors which affect the development of sexuality in Latin women in the United States: historical influences, immigration, language, and the psychological effects of oppression.

Despite shared features of history and culture, attitudes towards sex-roles are extremely diverse among Hispanic women. For instance, some Latin women are willing to endorse "modern" and "liberated" sex-roles concerning education and employment, while maintaining very "traditional," "conservative" positions concerning sexual behaviors or personal relationships. Others are traditional in all respects and still others reject all traditional beliefs concerning the roles of women. Consequently, it is very difficult to discuss the sexuality or sexual behavior of Latin women without the danger of making some sweeping generalizations. The experiential and emotional distance between an immigrant worker of peasant extraction who barely knows how to write her name in Spanish and a "Latin princess" who comes to the United States to study at a private educational institution with all expenses paid by her parents is enormous. If these two women met each other, they probably would not acknowledge any commonalities between them. And yet, as their therapist, I can recognize a common thread and a historical background to their lives, a thread shared with daughters of immigrants born and raised in the streets of New York and in the rural areas of the Southwest.

What are the commonalities among Hispanic women in the United States that manifest themselves in spite of the enormous differences among them? Historical influences have left their mark in cultural processes and in class and race differentiation. Other commonalities have to do with the experience of separation implied in immigration, with the cognitive and affective effects of sharing a common language, and with the experience of oppression.

The enormous differences between the Spanish and British conquest of Latin America and North America set these two cultures apart (see: Beard & Beard, 1968; Prescott, n.d.). On the one hand, the British came with their families, escaping persecution; North America became a dumping ground for religious dissidents. The Puritans and many of those who followed turned away from England with no desire to return to the homeland, seeking a place where they could remain separated and independent from all those who were different or held different beliefs. The Spaniards, on the other hand, came to America as a male army for the specific purpose of conquering new land for their king. They landed anticipating territory full of gold and silver and abundance where land was fertile all year long. These resources, plus the centralization of power already achieved by the native Indian empires, provided an environment profoundly different from that encountered by the Pilgrims.

Most *conquistadores* were men without fortune, nobility, or other resources. The majority of them did not come with their wives or with any female relatives; marrying women of Spanish descent was practically impossible. They initially intended to return to Spain full of honors and riches in order to marry Spanish women of a higher class. Difficult communications and the hardships of an enterprise that did not produce gold at first sight as they had expected delayed their return to Spain indefinitely. Many of them never returned and, instead, stayed in the Americas for the rest of their lives.

Thus, the conquerors' temporary sexual use of Indian women developed into more enduring relationships. They set up homes with the native women who were originally taken only as concubines. These relationships—some temporary, some stable— created the Mestizo population of Latin America. Although the Spanish conquerors are known for their cruelty, many were willing to legally marry Indian or black women and to recognize, support, and pass their inheritance on to their children by those marriages. A similar behavior would have been unthinkable not only to the Puritans but to most white gentlemen in the United States to this day. It is well known that even Thomas Jefferson had children by a black woman. However, those children were never called Jefferson and that slave woman was never freed by him.

While Calvinist theology, with its emphasis on predestination, encouraged the separation of the races in North America, the Spanish Catholic clergy battled in Europe and America for the human rights of the Amerindians, following Catholic theological tenets which give the right to salvation to anyone who is baptized and fulfills appropriate duties as a Christian. Once the Indians were declared to be human by the Pope, they had the right to be Catholic and thus children of God (Kurtz, 1982).

The Catholic church's proclamation of the importance of virginity for all women, regardless of their race or social status, became a challenge to a social system that otherwise could have been even more oppressive to non-white women. By emphasizing that all women, regardless of race and social class, hold the duty and the right to remain virgins until marriage, and that all men were responsible to women whose honor they had "stained," the church discouraged consensual union and illegitimacy (Martinez-Alier, 1974). However, by upholding the standard of virginity as the proof of a woman's honorability, the church, and later the culture in general, further lowered the status of women who cannot or will not maintain virginity. This also fostered the perspective that once an unmarried woman is not a virgin, she is automatically promiscuous. These standards fell in a disproportionately harsh way on native and Mestizo women, who were less likely to be virgins because of the social and economic conditions in which they lived.

Historical circumstances combined to shape gender and race relations in Latin America in a very distinctive way. This is not to say that racial inequality or prejudice do not exist in Latin America, but that they differ from the forms found in North America. There is a fluidity in racial relationships among Latins that is difficult to understand in the United States. In Latin America, social status is affected more profoundly by factors other than race. Social class and income prevail over color (Martinez-Alier, 1974). Different shades of color among members of the same family are not denied. The number of political figures and upper-class Latin Americans who are "non-white" by North American standards attests to the difference in perspective. On the other hand, European ancestry and "whiteness" are highly respected. "Color" makes doors harder to open. People of color are overrepresented in the lower socio-economic classes, and many a descendant of an interracial marriage would carefully avoid such a marriage now. The non-white woman may still be seen as not deserving the same respect as the white woman. And if a white man fathers her children, she may not find the same protection as her white counterpart. Moreover, precisely because many of the conqueror's wives were not white, the lower status of all women was further compounded by racial factors.

Trends created centuries ago in the relationships between men and women of different races, cultures, and political status persist today in Hispanic cultures. Historical influences have been modified, amplified to give a certain character and tone to the lives of Hispanic women. In addition to their shared cultural, historical, and religious heritage described above, Hispanic women living in the United States today share many characteristics as a function of immigration, language, and the shared experience of oppression.

Although most Hispanic women in the United States are not immigrants, many of them come from immigrant families. A discussion of the psychological implications of *immigration* is relevant even if not applicable to all Hispanic women. Immigration or any other form of separation from cultural roots involves a process of grieving. Women seem to be affected by this process in a manner that is different from that of men. Successful adaptation after immigration involves resolution of feelings of loss; the development of decision-making skills; ego strength; and the ability to tolerate ambiguities, including sex-role ambiguities. Factors pertaining to the psychological make-up of the individual woman as well as specifics of the home culture and class interplay in unique ways with the characteristics of the host culture. Newly encountered patterns of sex-roles combine with greater access to paid employment for women and may create an imbalance in the traditional power structure of the family.

One of the most prevalent myths encountered by immigrant Hispanic women is that all American women are very free with sex. For the parents and the young women alike, "becoming Americanized" is equated with becoming sexually promiscuous. Thus, in some cases, sexuality may become the focus of the parents' fears and the girl's desires during the acculturation process.

Language is another important factor in the experience of Hispanic women. To discuss the affective and cognitive implications of bilingualism and languages will take us beyond the scope of this paper. However, it is important to keep in mind that even for those Hispanic women who are fluent in English, Spanish may remain as the language of emotions because it was usually the first language heard and learned and thus it is full of deep affective meaning (Espín, 1982).

The preference of the one language over another or the shift from one language to another might be an indication of more subtle processes than even the choice of words (Marcos & Urcuyo, 1979). For example, in a recent study of Cuban women in Miami (Espín & Warner, 1982), fluency in English appears as the single most important determinant of attitudes towards the role of women in society. Shifts between languages and the preference for one language or the other may be a means to achieve either distancing or intimacy. When the topic at hand is sexuality, the second language might be an effective tool to express what one does not dare to verbalize in the first language. Conversely, certain emotions and experiences will never be addressed appropriately unless they are discussed in the first language (Espín, 1982). "The emotional significance of a specific word for a particular individual generally depends on the individual's personal values and his [or her] developmental history" (González-Reigosa, 1976, p.325).

The emotional arousal evoked by saying taboo words decreases when they are pronounced in a foreign language (González-Reigosa, 1976). Presumably, erotic language is experienced differently when uttered or heard in either English or Spanish.

The condition of *oppression* under which most Hispanics live in the United States creates certain psychological effects for both men and women, although Latin women, oppressed both as women and Hispanics, suffer from physical and psychological consequences of oppression in a profound way. The conditions of oppression originating in the economic, political, and social structures of the world become psychological as the effects of these external circumstances become internalized (Freire, 1970). The external oppression of Hispanic women is expressed in political, educational, economic, and social discrimination. Psychologically, the oppression of Hispanic women develops through internalized attitudes that designate women as inferior to men, including Hispanic men, while designating all Hispanics as inferior to the white mainstream of North American society. Oppressive beliefs that affect all women and all Hispanics influence the lives and the sexuality of Hispanic women.

There are specific forms in which the psychology of oppression affects women from all ethnic minority groups. One involves the importance placed on physical beauty for women and, particularly, on standards of beauty inappropriate for non-white women. Women, regardless of ethnic group, are taught to derive their primary validation from their looks and physical attractiveness. The inability of most non-white women to achieve prescribed standards of beauty may be devastating for self-esteem.

Another psychological effect of oppression for Hispanic women is to further increase their subordination to men. As a reaction towards the oppression suffered by minority men in the larger society, minority women may subordinate their needs even further to those of men. Women and children may be suitable recipients for the displaced anger of an oppressed man. Violence takes many forms: incest, rape, wife-beating. Violence against women is produced and sustained by societal messages about women. The prevalent virgin/whore dichotomy in images of women fosters and condones the violence. It is not unusual to hear supposedly "enlightened" persons defending the violent behavior of men in oppressed groups on the grounds that their only outlet is to get drunk and beat their wives. Even if the displacement can be understood in the case of each individual, to accept and justify it is to condone injustice and another form of violence against women under the guise of understanding.

In addition, women from oppressed groups may be seen as an "easy prey" for white men or as "sexier" than their white counterparts. Their sexual behavior is supposed to be freer and less restrained when, in fact, the opposite might be true. On the other hand, a young woman's sexuality might be the only asset she has in her efforts to break away from oppressive conditions.

Contemporary Sexuality and the Hispanic Woman

If the role of women is currently beset with contradictions in the mainstream of American society (Miller, 1986), this is probably still more true for women in Hispanic groups. The honor of Latin families is strongly tied to the sexual purity of women. And the concept of honor and dignity is one of the essential distinctive marks of Hispanic culture. For example, classical Hispanic literature gives us a clue to the importance attributed to honor and to female sexual purity in the culture. La Celestina, the protagonist of an early Spanish medieval novel, illustrates the value attached to virginity and its preservation. Celestina was an old woman who earned her living in two ways: by putting young men in touch with young maidens so they could have the sexual contact that parents would never allow and by "sewing up" ex-virgins so that they would be considered virgins at marriage. Celestina thus made her living out of making and unmaking virgins. The fact that she ends by being punished with death further emphasizes the gravity of what she does. In the words of a famous Spanish playwright of the seventeenth century, *"al Rey la hacienda y la vida se han de dar, mas no el honor; porque el honor es patrimonio del alma y el alma solo es de Dios"* (Calderón de la Barca, n.d.). This quotation translates literally, "To the king you give money and life, but not your honor, because honor is part of the soul, and your soul belongs only to God."

Different penalties and sanctions for the violation of cultural norms related to female sexuality are very much associated with social class. The upper classes or those seeking improved social status tend to be more rigid about sexuality. This of course is related to the transmission of property. In the upper classes, a man needs to know that his children are in fact his before they inherit his property. The only guarantee of his paternity is that his wife does not have sexual contact with any other man. Virginity is tremendously important in that context. However, even when property is not an issue, the only thing left to a family may be the honor of its women and as such it may be guarded jealously by both males and females. Although Hispanics in the twentieth century may not hold the same strict values—and many of them certainly cannot afford the luxury to do so—women's sexual behavior is still the expression of the family's honor. The tradition of maintaining virginity until marriage that had been emphasized among women continues to be a cultural imperative. The Virgin Mary—who was a virgin and a mother, but never a sexual being—is presented as an important role model for all Hispanic women, although Hispanic unwed mothers, who have clearly overstepped the boundaries of culturally prescribed virginity for women, usually are accepted by their families. Married women or those living in common-law marriages are supposed to accept a double standard for sexual behavior, by which their husbands may have affairs with other women, while they themselves are expected to remain faithful to one man all of their lives. However, it is not uncommon for a Hispanic woman to have the power to decide whether or not a man is going to live with her, and she may also choose to put him out if he drinks too much or is not a good provider (e.g., Brown, 1975).

In fact, Latin women experience a unique combination of power and powerlessness which is characteristic of the culture. The idea that personal problems are best discussed with women is very much part of the Hispanic culture. Women in Hispanic neighborhoods and families tend to rely on other women for their important personal and practical needs. There is a widespread belief among Latin women of all social classes that most men are undependable and are not to be trusted. At the same time, many of these women will put up with a man's abuses because having a man around is an important source of a woman's sense of self-worth. Middle-aged and elderly Hispanic women retain important roles in their families even after their sons and daughters are married. Grandmothers are ever present and highly vocal in family affairs. Older women have much more status and power than their white American counterparts, who at this age may be suffering from depression due to what has been called the "empty-nest syndrome." Many Hispanic women are providers of mental health services (which sometimes include advice about sexual problems) in an unofficial way as *curanderas, espiritistas,* or *santeras* for those people who believe in these alternative approaches to health care (Espín, 1996). Some of these women play a powerful role in their communities, thanks to their reputation for being able to heal mind and body.

However, at the same time that Latin women have the opportunity to exercise their power in the areas mentioned above they also receive constant cultural messages that they should be submissive and subservient to males in order to be seen as "good women." To suffer and be a martyr is also a characteristic of a "good woman." This emphasis on self-renunciation, combined with the importance given to sexual purity for women, has a direct bearing on the development of sexuality in Latin women. To enjoy sexual pleasure, even in marriage, may indicate lack of virtue. To shun sexual pleasure and to regard sexual behavior exclusively as an unwelcome obligation towards her husband and a necessary evil in order to have children may be seen as a manifestation of virtue. In fact, some women even express pride at their lack of sexual pleasure or desire. Their negative attitudes toward sex are frequently reinforced by the inconsiderate behavior and demands of men.

Body image and related issues are deeply connected with sexuality for all women. Even when body-related problems may not have direct implications for sexuality, the body remains for women the main vehicle for expressing their needs. The high incidence of somatic complaints presented by low-income Hispanic women in psychotherapy might be a consequence of the emphasis on "martyrdom" and self-sacrifice, or it might be a somatic expression of needs and anxieties. More directly related to sexuality are issues of birth control, pregnancy, abortion, menopause, hysterectomy, and other gynecological problems. Many of these have traditionally been discussed among women only. To be brought to the attention of a male doctor may be enormously embarrassing and distressing for some of these women. Younger Hispanic women may find themselves challenging traditional sexual mores while struggling with their own conflicts about beauty and their own embarrassment about visiting male doctors.

One of the most common and pervasive stereotypes held about Hispanics is the image of the "macho" man—an image which generally conjures up rough, tough, swaggering men who are abusive and oppressive towards women, who in turn are seen as exclusively submissive and long-suffering (Abad, Ramos, & Boyce, 1974).

Some authors (Le Vine & Padilla, 1980) recognize that "machismo"—which is nothing but the Hispanic version of the myth of male superiority supported by most cultures—is still in existence in the Latin culture, especially among those individuals who subscribe more strongly to traditional Hispanic values. Following this tradition, Latin females are expected to be subordinated to males and to the family. Males are expected to show their manhood by behaving in a strong fashion, by demonstrating sexual prowess, and by asserting their authority over women. In many cases, these traditional values may not be enacted behaviorally but are still supported as valued assumptions concerning male and female "good" behavior. According to Aramoni (1982), himself a Mexican psychologist, "machismo" may be a reaction of Latin males to a series of social conditions, including the effort to exercise control over their ever-present, powerfully demanding, and suffering mothers and to identify with their absent fathers. Adult males continue to respect and revere their mothers, even when they may not show much respect for their wives to other women. As adolescents they may have protected their mothers from their fathers' abuse or indifference. As adults they accord their mothers a respect that no other women deserves, thus following their fathers' steps. The mother herself teaches her sons to be dominant and independent in relations with other women. Other psychological and social factors may be influential in the development of "machismo." It is important to remember that not all Latin males exhibit the negative behaviors implied in the "macho" stereotype, and that even when certain individuals do, these behaviors might be a reaction to oppressive social conditions by which Hispanic men too are victimized.

Sexually, "machismo" is expressed through an emphasis on multiple, uncommitted sexual contacts which start in adolescence. In a study of adolescent rituals in Latin America, Espín (1975) found that many males celebrated their adolescence by visiting prostitutes. The money to pay for this sexual initiation was usually provided by fathers, uncles, or older brothers. Adolescent females, on the other hand, were offered coming-out parties, the rituals of which emphasize their virginal qualities. Somehow, a man is more "macho" if he manages to have sexual relations with a virgin; thus, fathers and brothers watch over young women for fear that other men may make them their sexual prey. These same men, however, will not hesitate to take advantage of the young women in other families. Women, in turn, are seen as capable of surrendering to men's advances, without much awareness of their own decisions on the matter. "Good women" should always say no to a sexual advance. Those who say yes are automatically assumed to be less virtuous by everyone, including the same man with whom they consent to have sex.

Needless to say, sexual understanding and communication between the sexes is practically rendered impossible by these attitudes generated by "machismo." However, not all Hispanics subscribe to this perspective and some reject it outright. In a review of the literature on studies of decision-making patterns in Mexican and Chicano families, the authors concluded that "Hispanic males may behave differently from non-Hispanic men in their family and marital lives, but not in the inappropriate fashion suggested by the myth with its strong connotations of social deviance" (Cromwell & Ruiz, 1979, p.37). This article reviews only research on the decision-making process in married couples and, thus, other aspects of male-female relationships in the Hispanic culture are not discussed.

In the context of culturally appropriate sex-roles, mothers train their daughters to remain virgins at all cost, to cater to men's sexual needs, and to play "little wives" to their fathers and brothers from a very early age. If a mother is sick or working outside the home and there are no adult females around, the oldest daughter, no matter how young, will be in charge of caring not only for the younger siblings but also for the father, who would continue to expect his meals to be cooked and his clothes to be washed.

Training for appropriate heterosexuality, however, is not always assimilated by all Latin women. A seldom-mentioned fact is that, as in all cultures, there are lesbians among Hispanic women. Although emotional and physical closeness among women is encouraged by the culture, overt acknowledgement of lesbianism is even more restricted than in mainstream American society. In a study about lesbians in the Puerto Rican community, Hidalgo and Hidalgo-Christensen (1979) found that "rejection of homosexuals appears to be the dominant attitude in the Puerto Rican community" (p.118). Although this attitude may not seem different from that of the dominant U.S. culture, there are some important differences experienced by Latin lesbian women which are directly related to Hispanic cultural patterns. Frequent contact and a strong interdependence among family members, even in adulthood, are essential features of Hispanic family life. Leading a double life becomes more of a strain in this context. "Coming out" may jeopardize not only these strong family ties but also the possibility of serving the Hispanic community in which the talents of all members are such an important asset. Because most lesbian women are single and self-supporting and not encumbered by the demands of husbands and children, it can be assumed that professional experience and educational level of Hispanic lesbians will tend to be relatively high. If this is true, professional experience and education will frequently place Hispanic lesbian women in positions of leadership or advocacy in their community. Their status and prestige and, thus, the ability to serve their community are threatened by the possibility of being "found out."

Most "politically aware" Latinos show a remarkable lack of understanding of gay-related issues. In a recent meeting of Hispanic women in a major U.S. city, one participant expressed the opinion that "lesbianism is a sickness we get from American women and American culture." This is, obviously, another version of the myth about free sexuality of American women so prevalent among Hispanics. But it is also an expression of the common belief that homosexuality is chosen behavior, acquired through the bad influence of others, like drug addiction. Socialist attitudes in this respect are extremely traditional, as the attitudes of the Cuban revolution towards homosexuality clearly manifest. Thus, Hispanics who consider themselves radical and committed to civil rights remain extremely traditional when it comes to gay rights. These attitudes clearly add further stress to the lives of Latin women who have a homosexual orientation and who are invested in enhancing the lives of members of their communities.

They experience oppression in three ways: as women, as Hispanics, and as lesbians. This last form of oppression is in fact experienced most powerfully from inside their own culture. Most Latin women who are lesbians have to remain "clos-eted" among their families, their colleagues, and society at large. To be "out of the closet" only in an Anglo context deprives them of essential supports from their com-munities and families and, in turn, increases their invisibility in the Hispanic cul-ture, where only the openly "butch" types are recognized as lesbians.

Issues of Sexuality in Psychotherapy with Hispanic Women

What does therapy have to offer Hispanic women, especially in relation to sexuality? Unfortunately, psychotherapy could be, and in fact has been in many instances, an-other instrument for the oppression of all women. By helping people tolerate and adapt to established sex-roles and other structures of oppression, psychotherapy can perpetuate the status quo. On the other hand, by increasing the individual's self-awareness and allowing a better perspective on the forces that impinge on the self, psychotherapy can become an instrument of liberation. If psychotherapy is to be-come an effective mode of growth for the individual rather than just another instru-ment of society, it can do so only by taking some risks.

Good psychotherapy for Hispanic women should free the client's energy from the entanglement of emotional conflicts in order to enable her to make better and freer choices. Since the personal is political, these choices may entail engaging in activities which in the long run will benefit the status of women—and men—in the Hispanic community. An awareness of the reality of women's lives and the consequent under-standing that their conflicts are not exclusively intrapsychic is essential. In fact, an exclusive intrapsychic emphasis indicates a lack of understanding of the client's real-ity and a lack in the therapist's training. For good therapy to occur it is essential to help women distinguish between conflicts and suffering which have their source in socialization and oppression and conflicts arising from intrapsychic, individual sources. This distinction is not always neat and simple. But, contrary to partisans of an exclusively social perspective, each woman who comes to therapy carries her own particular internalized combination of externally determined and intrapsychic con-flicts. Good therapy thus necessitates attending to both categories of factors affecting her mental health and well-being.

This form of therapy implies a political commitment to the goal of making actual changes in the life situation of Hispanic women who are in therapy, rather than sim-ply attending to the alleviation of individual psychological symptoms. The political commitment implied in this mode of therapy, however, does not in any way detract from the therapist's professional seriousness and psychotherapeutic expertise (Rawl-ins & Carter, 1977). The therapist remains, as always, a professional with a given ex-pertise. The desired outcome of this approach to therapy is the self-empowerment of Hispanic women. But, precisely because of this perspective, therapy may be perceived as threatening by immediate members of the woman's family, who may not be ready to cope with changes she may make as the result of the therapy. When the therapy touches specifically on the issues of sexuality, an understanding of the delicate balance among all the forces described above as manifested in the life history of each individual Latin woman becomes more important than ever. Sexuality is that point where the full self-realization of a human being intersects vividly with her vulnerability. As discussed beautifully by Carole Vance (1984) in her introduction to *Pleasure and Danger,* where this chapter first appeared, sexuality is about pleasure and about danger. Because there is both pleasure and danger in sexuality, there are problems and possibilities in every aspect of sexuality. Sexual behavior may become both liberating and enslaving. Sexual choices, although deeply personal, may also be of far-reaching political consequences.

For women undergoing a process of acculturation, as many Hispanic women are, choices about sexual behavior may become important expressions of a multitude of different experiences and values. Sexuality and sex-roles within a culture tend to remain the last bastion of tradition. Rebellion against the culture of origin or loyalty to it can, in many instances, be expressed through sexual behavior. The relative degrees of guilt or joy that may be associated with choices about sexual behavior are frequently entangled with considerations which are not fully or exclusively personal but, rather, determined by external factors and considerations.

Sexual issues tend to be at the core of much family conflict concerning women and adolescent girls in immigrant families. The adoption of new ways of life or sexual behaviors, although satisfactory in many respects, may be associated with intense guilt and feelings of betrayal. In addition, because of the myths associating free sexuality with "Americanization," there is actual danger that young women may become promiscuous or self-destructive through sex. They may attribute their discomfort with their own behavior to parental influence or lack of adequate acculturation when, in fact, they may be adopting behaviors considered extreme by most American women.

Each culture allows women a different range of accepted sexual behavior. This range goes from what is fully approved and expected—the ideals and values of the culture—to what is accepted or tolerated, even if it is not in conformity with the ideal. Some cultures allow a very narrow range of sexual expression to women, while others tolerate greater degrees of variation. There is a different cost in each culture for women who overstep the boundaries of allowed or tolerable sexual behavior. Knowledge about values concerning female sexuality in a given culture is not sufficient in itself to understand individual women. Each woman, in fact, positions herself at some point along the range of behaviors allowed by the culture. Each woman's choice expresses something about who she is as an individual as well as what her cultural values are. Superficial knowledge of a culture may lead the therapist to accept as a cultural norm what might only be the client's expression of her individuality. Conversely, a behavior that conforms to strict cultural norms or violates them at a high personal cost can be interpreted by an unknowing therapist as a strictly individual choice with no cultural implications. For example, cultural norms can be invoked by the client or assumed, inaccurately, by the therapist to explain a woman's restricted sexual behavior, thus preventing the exploration of other causes which may be in the individual's life history. Or culturally appropriate reactions to the violation of sexual norms can be interpreted as inappropriate dependency or manifestations of personal neuroticism, thus increasing the client's guilt and confusion. To accept as "cultural" some behaviors or attitudes that might be self-defeating can be as damaging as being totally insensitive to cultural differences. There is a danger of being male-centered in the name of cultural values. Precisely because sex-roles and female sexuality tend to be the last bastion of traditional cultural values while other norms may be changing under acculturative pressures, it is possible to support these values without consider-ing their negative effects on women. This danger is present in therapy with Latin women for non-Hispanic and Hispanic therapists alike. Paradoxically, there might be a danger of compromising essential feminist values—namely, a woman's right to her own choices—because of an insistence on a "politically correct" feminist point of view that may run contrary to the client's perspective at the time. In other words, in trying to make a "liberated" woman out of each Hispanic female client the choices of each woman may not be appropriately respected. Being totally out of pace with the culture of origin and with the rest of the family may be extremely alienating and painful for a Hispanic woman, no matter how "liberated."

In therapy, sexuality and choices about sexual behavior have to be discussed and understand on the basis of each woman's needs and wants. Male-centered cultural values as well as mainstream or feminist beliefs about women have to be addressed and explored for what they are. Validation for each woman's sexuality and experience is provided through the expansion of feeling states and encouragement to under-stand their meaning. The clarification of relationships and autonomy struggles pro-vides a recognition of her legitimate rights beyond prescribed roles and expectations. An exploration of options with their ramifications and realities expands the range of possibilities and increases her sense of empowerment.

Although some aspects of the relationship between language and sexuality in bilingual individuals has already been briefly discussed, psychotherapy relies too heavily on language to ignore the psychological implications of language in the ther-apeutic process, especially for persons who constantly change between two languages or who are participating in therapy in a second language (e.g., Krapf, 1955; Marcos & Alpert, 1976).

Obviously, selecting reliable sources concerning every aspect of therapy with Latin women is imperative. Finding a competent supervisor, knowledgeable about the cul-ture and experienced in working with this population, is ideal. Although Hispanic therapists, especially women therapists, may not need these admonitions, the reality is that most therapists working with Hispanic women are not Latin themselves. For those who are Latin, their own loyalties to and/or conflicts with their background are, inevitably, part of what they bring to the psychotherapeutic relationship with Hispanic women. As always, it is important to keep in mind that, for each woman, validation and empowerment are always achieved against the backdrop of specific cultural circumstances as well as her life history. Good psychotherapy can be an instrument for positive growth and a vehicle for integrating a responsible and creative sexuality into their lives.

Notes

Reprinted from Espín, O.M. (1984). Cultural and Historical Influences on Sexuality in Hispanic/Latin Women: Implications for Psychotherapy. In C. Vance (Ed.), *Pleasure and Danger: Exploring Female Sexuality* (pp.149–164). London, UK: Routledge & Kegan Paul (2nd ed., London: Pandora, 1994).

References

Abad, O.M., Ramos, J., & Boyce, E., (1974). A model for delivery of mental health services to Spanish-speaking minorities. *American Journal of Orthopsychiatry*, 44(4), 584–595.

Aramoni, A. (1982). Machismo. *Psychology Today*, 5(8), 69–72.

Beard, C.A., & Beard, M.R. (1968). *The Beard's new basic history of the United States*. New York: Doubleday.

Brown, S., (1975). Love unites them and hunger separates them: Poor women in the Dominican Republic. In R.R. (Ed.), *Toward an anthropology of women* (pp.322–332). New York: Monthly Review Press.

Calderón de la Barca, P. *El alcalde de Zalamea*. (Multiple editions.)

Cromwell, R.E., & Ruiz, R.A. (1979). The myth of "macho" dominance in decision making with Mexican and Chicano families. *Hispanic Journal of Behavioral Sciences*, 1(4), 371–337.

Espín, O.M. (1975, November). *The "quinceañeras": A Latin American expression of women's roles*. Paper presented at the National Meeting of the Latin American Studies Association, Atlanta.

Espín, O.M. (1982, October). *Issues of psychotherapy with fluently bilingual clients*. Paper presented at the Stone Center, Wellesley College, Wellesley, MA.

Espín, O.M., (1996). *Latina healers: Lives of power and tradition*. Encino, CA: Floricanto.

Espín, O.M., & Warner, B. (1982). Attitudes towards the role of women in Cuban women attending a community college. *International Journal of Social Psychiatry*, 28(3), 233–239.

Freire, P., (1970). *Pedagogy of the oppressed*. New York: Salisbury.

González-Reigosa, F. (1976). The anxiety-arousing effect of taboo words in bilinguals. In C.D. Speilberger & A.R. Díaz-Guerrero (Eds.), *Cross-cultural anxiety* (pp.312–329). Washington, DC: Hemisphere.

Hidalgo, H., & Hidalgo-Christensen, E.(1979). The Puerto Rican cultural response to female homosexuality. In E. Acosta-Belén (Ed.), *The Puerto Rican woman*. New York: Praeger.

Krapf, E.E. (1955). The choice of language in polyglot psychoanalysis. *Psychoanalytic Quarterly*, 24, 343–357.

Kurtz, D.V. (1982). The Virgin of Guadalupe and the politics of becoming human. *Journal of Anthropological Research*, 38(2), 194–210.

Le Vine, E.S., & Padilla, A.M. (1980). *Crossing cultures in therapy: Pluralistic counseling for the Hispanic*. Monterey, CA: Brooks/Cole.

Marcos, L.R., & Alpert, M. (1976). Strategies and risks in psychotherapy with bilingual patients: The phenomenon of language independence. *American Journal of Psychiatry*, 33(11), 1275–1278.

Marcos, L.R., & Urcuyo, L. (1979). Dynamic psychotherapy with the bilingual patient. *American Journal of Psychotherapy*, 33(3), 331–338.

Martinez-Alier, V. (1974). *Marriage, class and colour in nineteenth century Cuba.* London: Cambridge University Press.

Miller, J.B. (1986). *Toward a new psychology of women.* Boston: Beacon.

Prescott, W.H. (n.d.). *History of the conquest of Mexico and history of the conquest of Peru.* New York: Modern Library. (Original work published in 1843 and 1847)

Rawlins, E.I., & Carter, D.K.(1977). *Psychotherapy for women: Treatment toward equality.* Springfield, IL: Charles C. Thomas.

Vance, C.S. (1984). Introduction. *Pleasure and danger: Exploring female sexuality* (pp.1–27). London: Routledge & Kegan Paul.

7

Issues of Identity in the Psychology of Latina Lesbians

Identity development for persons of ethnic or racial minority groups involves not only the acceptance of an external reality that can rarely be changed (e.g., being black, Puerto Rican, Jewish, or Vietnamese), but also an intrapsychic "embracing" of that reality as a positive component of one's self. By definition, in the context of a heterosexist, racist, and sexist society, the process of identity development for Latina lesbian women entails the embracing of "stigmatized" or "negative" identities. Coming out to self and others in the context of a sexist and heterosexist American society is compounded by coming out in the context of a heterosexist and sexist Latin culture immersed in racist society. Because as a Latina she is an ethnic minority person, she must be bicultural in American society. Because she is a lesbian, she has to be polycultural among her own people.

The dilemma for Latina lesbians is how to integrate who they are culturally, racially, and religiously with their identity as lesbians and women. The identity of each Latina lesbian develops through conscious and unconscious choices that allot relative importance to the different components of the self and thus of her identity as woman, as lesbian, as Latina.

Identity Development

The term *identity* is understood here as that which each woman tells herself about who she is when she is alone with herself. The term is also understood as that which

97

each context to which she is field sensitive calls forth in a given moment. In other words, identity is also associated with social image.

According to Erik Erikson, the crises conducive to the development of an integrated identity consist of "a state of being and becoming that can have a highly conscious (and, indeed, self-conscious) quality and yet remain, in its motivational aspects, quite conscious and beset with the dynamics of conflict." Because a "part of identity must be accounted for in that communality within which an individual finds himself [or herself]" there might be "fragments that the individual had to submerge in himself [or herself] as undesirable or irreconcilable or which his [or her] group has taught him [or her] to perceive as the mark of fatal 'difference' in sex role or race in class or religion" (Erikson, 1975, pp.19–20). For both lesbians and ethnic minority persons of both sexes and, indeed, for ethnic minority lesbians, the process of identity development is full of vicissitudes, and it frequently demands the submerging of different fragments of the self.

However, as Erikson has written, "certain historical periods present a singular chance for a collective renewal which opens up unlimited identities for those who, by a combination of unruliness, giftedness, and competence, represent a new leadership, a new elite, and new types . . . in a new people" (Erikson, 1975, p.21). We seem to be living in such a period, and ethnic minority lesbians seem to be at a crucial point of this psychohistorical process.

Obviously, different individuals are at different stages of identity development, that is to say, different stages of clarity about who they are, or are finding different ways of embracing the labels—imposed or chosen—by which people classify each other and themselves, including embracing those aspects of identity considered to be negative by the group or groups to which the individual belongs. The process is not necessarily linear for any given individual. In fact, identities are fluid as is the process of developing them. Donald Atkinson, George Morten, and Derald Wing Sue (1979; Sue, 1981) have evolved a model of identity development for ethnic minorities that captures the fluidity of the process and describes its phases in a clear and concise way. Vivienne Cass (1979) has developed a similar theoretical model in reference to homosexual identity formation. Both models incorporate the different possible reactions to a negative identity that ethnic minority persons and homosexuals can have at different points in life.

In the Atkinson, Morten, and Sue model, stage one, *Conformity*, is characterized by a preference for dominant cultural values over one's own culture. The reference group is likely to be the dominant cultural group, and feelings of self-hatred, negative beliefs of one's own culture, and positive feelings toward the dominant culture are likely to be strong. The second stage, or *Dissonance*, is characterized by cultural confusion and conflict. Information and experiences begin to challenge accepted values and beliefs. Active questioning of the dominant-held values operates strongly. In stage three, *Resistance and Immersion*, an active rejection of the dominant society and culture and a complete endorsement of minority-held views become evident. Desires to combat oppression become the primary motivation of the person. There is an attempt to get in touch with one's history, culture, and traditions. Distrust and hatred of dominant society is strong. The reference group is one's own culture. Stage four, *Introspection*, is characterized by conflict at the too-narrow and rigid constraints of the previous stage. Notions of loyalty and responsibility to one's own group and notions of personal autonomy come in conflict. In stage five, *Synergetic Articulation and Awareness*, individuals experience a sense of self-fulfillment with regard to cultural identity. Conflicts and discomfort experienced in the *Introspection* stage have been resolved, allowing greater individual control and flexibility. Cultural values are examined and accepted or rejected on the basis of prior experience gained in earlier stages of identity development. Desire to eliminate all forms of oppression becomes an important motivation of the individual's behavior.

Vivienne Cass's model (1979) proposes six stages of development that individuals move through in order to acquire a fully integrated identity as a homosexual person. In stage one, *Identity Confusion*, the individual realizes that feelings, thoughts, or behavior can be defined as homosexual, and this realization presents an incongruent element into a previously stable situation in which both the individual and the environment assumed the person to be heterosexual. As a result of this incongruence the individual arrives at a self-identity potentially that of a homosexual. "Where the task of stage one was to resolve the immediate personal identity crisis of 'Who am I?' the task of stage two, *Identity Comparison*, is to handle the social alienation that now arises" (pp.222–223). In stage three, *Identity Tolerance*, there is an increased level of commitment to the homosexual self-image. "At this stage, contacting homosexuals is viewed as something that has to be done in order to counter the felt isolation and alienation from others. The individual tolerates rather than accepts a homosexual identity" (p.225). Stage four, *Identity Acceptance*, is "characterized by continued and increasing contacts with other homosexuals. These contacts allow [the person] to feel the impact of those features of the subculture that validate and 'normalize' homosexuality as an identity and a way of life. [The individual] now accepts rather than tolerates a homosexual self-image" (p.229). Entrance into stage five, *Identity Pride*, is characterized by the incongruences that exist between a concept of self as totally acceptable as a homosexual and society's rejection of this concept. In order to manage this incongruence, heterosexuals and heterosexuality are devalued. A combination of anger and pride is developed, and confrontation with the environment may occur. More and more strategies previously used to conceal a homosexual identity are deliberately abandoned. Disclosure becomes a strategy for coping. Stage six, *Identity Synthesis*, starts "with an awareness that the 'them and us' philosophy espoused previously, in which all heterosexuals were viewed negatively and all homosexuals positively, no longer holds true. . . . Personal and public sexual identities become synthesized into one image of self receiving considerable support from [the] environment. . . . Homosexual identity . . . instead of being seen as the identity, is now given the status of being merely one aspect of the self. This awareness completes the homosexual identity formation process" (pp.234–235).

Although these two models are not identical, they describe a process that must be undertaken by people who must embrace negative or stigmatized identities. This process moves gradually from a rejected and denied self-image to the embracing of an identity that is finally accepted as positive. Both models describe one or several stages of intense confusion and at least one stage of complete separatism from and rejection of all representatives of the dominant society. The final stage for both models implies the acceptance of one's own identity, a committed attitude against oppression, and an ability to synthesize the best values of both perspectives and to communicate with members of the dominant group.

Latina Lesbians

It can be reasonably asserted that the development of identity in Latina lesbians must follow patterns similar to those described by these two models. However, I do not know of any studies on this topic. Indeed, the literature on Latina lesbians is scarce.

A professional presentation by Hortensia Amaro (1978) discussed the issue of coming out for Hispanic lesbians, and some literary discussions that address the experiences of Latina lesbians have been published by Cherrie Moraga (1983). Although there might be studies in progress on this population, very few have been published. Hilda Hidalgo and Elia Hidalgo-Christensen (1976–1977, 1979) have published two versions of a study of Puerto Rican attitudes toward lesbianism. Yvonne Escaserga and her collaborators (Escaserga, Mondaca, & Torres, 1975) studied the attitudes of Chicana lesbians toward psychotherapy. To my knowledge, no other research studies focus particularly on Latina lesbians or on the specific aspect of their identity development.

Although emotional and physical closeness among women is encouraged by Latin culture, overt acknowledgment of lesbianism is even more restricted than in mainstream American society. Hidalgo and Hidalgo-Christensen (1976–1977, 1979), for example, discuss the importance of *amigas íntimas* (intimate female friends) for Puerto Rican women and contrast it with the results of their research that show that most members of the Puerto Rican community strongly reject lesbianism. They found that "rejection of homosexuals appears to be the dominant attitude in the Puerto Rican community" (1976–1977, p.120). At a meeting of Hispanic women in a major U.S. city in the early 1980s, one participant expressed the opinion that "lesbianism is a sickness we get from American women and American culture." This is, obviously, an expression of the common belief that homosexuality is chosen behavior acquired through the bad influence of others. Socialist attitudes with respect to homosexuality are extremely traditional, as the attitudes of the Cuban and other revolutions clearly manifest. Thus, Latinos who consider themselves radical and committed to civil rights may remain extremely traditional when it comes to gay rights. I have previously discussed the impact of the prevalent Latino attitudes on Hispanic women who have a lesbian orientation (Espín, 1984). These attitudes clearly add further stress to the lives of Latina lesbians who are invested in participating in the life of their communities. Although these attitudes may not seem different from those of the dominant culture, some important differences experienced by Latina lesbians are directly related to Hispanic cultural patterns. Latin families tend to treat their lesbian daughters or sisters with silent tolerance: Their lesbianism will not be openly acknowledged and accepted, but they are not denied a place in the family either. Very seldom is there overt rejection of their lesbian members on the part of Hispanic families. The family may explain away the daughter's lesbianism by saying that "she is too intelligent to marry any man" or "too dedicated to her work to bother with dating, marriage, or motherhood." Nevertheless, because frequent contact and a strong interdependence among family members, even in adult life, are essential features of Hispanic family life, leading a double life may become more of a strain. Because of the importance placed on family and community by most Hispanics, the threat of possible rejection and stigmatization by the Latin community becomes more of a psychological burden for the Hispanic lesbian. Rejection from mainstream society does not carry the same weight. As Cherrie Moraga (1983) puts it, "that is not to say that Anglo culture does not stigmatize its women for 'gender transgression'—only that its stigmatization did not hold the personal power over me which Chicano culture did" (p.99).

To avoid stigmatization by the Latino community, Hispanic lesbians frequently seek other groups or networks in which their lesbian orientation will be more accepted than it is in their family and its community. However, as Hortensia Amaro (1978) states, "reliance on alternative support groups outside the Hispanic community would not occur without a cost. Loss of contact with the ethnic community and culture will mean lack of support for their identity as a Hispanic. On the other hand, staying within the Hispanic community and not 'coming out' will represent a denial of the identity associated with sexuality and intimate love relationships" (p.7). To be out of the closet only in an Anglo context deprives them of essential supports from their communities and families and, in turn, increases their invisibility in the Hispanic culture, where only the openly "butch" types are recognized as lesbian. To complicate matters even further, Latina lesbians sometimes experience discrimination or more subtle forms of racism, not only from the mainstream of American society but also within the context of the Anglo lesbian communities in which they continue to be in numerical minority.

Many Latina women who are lesbians choose to remain closeted among their families, their colleagues, and society at large. Coming out may jeopardize not only the strong family ties but also the possibility of serving the Hispanic community. This is particularly difficult because the talents of all members are such an important asset for any minority community. Because most lesbian women are single and self-supporting and not encumbered by the demands of husbands and children, it can be assumed that the professional experience and educational level of Hispanic lesbians will tend to be relatively higher than that of other Hispanic women. Because there are no statistics on Hispanic lesbians, this assertion cannot be easily proved. But if it is true, professional experience and education will frequently place Latina lesbians in positions of leadership or advocacy in their community. Their status and prestige, and thus the ability to serve their community, will be easily threatened by the possibility of being found out by the same people they are trying to serve.

Cuban Lesbians

Having provided some background on the development of identity in minority persons and on the experience of Latina lesbians, I will present what a group of Cuban lesbians have to say about the different components of their identity. I was prompted by a recognition of the problems encountered by Latina lesbians to study the relative importance of these identity components in a group of such women. I wanted to assess the relative degree of cultural and lesbian identity for this group. How did these women integrate the different components of the self in the process of identity formation? I decided to limit my study to Cuban women in order to reduce the number of intervening factors that may differentiate among Hispanic subgroups. Although the study focuses on Cuban women, the results serve to illustrate general principles relevant to the identity development of other Latinas and minority lesbians.

The Study

I distributed a questionnaire through friendship pyramiding among Cuban lesbians in several cities in the United States and analyzed the responses primarily through the use of qualitative methods. Qualitative methodology provides a legitimate and flexible format for an exploratory study based on a sample of convenience obtained through friendship pyramiding such as this one (see Bogdan & Taylor, 1975; Filstead, 1970; Glaser & Strauss, 1967).

I kept both the Atkinson, Morten, and Sue model (1979; Sue, 1981) of ethnic minority identity development and the Cass model (1979) of homosexual identity development as background for understanding the process of identity formation of the respondents. However, I made no effort at coding questions on the basis of the stages described in these two models. Because there is no other study published on this specific population of lesbians, I saw value in examining how they themselves described their experience without superimposing any previously determined model of analysis.

I mailed thirty-five questionnaires: fifteen to specific individuals and twenty in small packets of five to people who had offered to contact others. Sixteen completed questionnaires were returned. Although the sample is obviously small, it is important to remember that obtaining respondents in a population surrounded by secrecy while searching for a specific ethnicity as in this case is not a minor task. A response rate of almost half of questionnaires sent is not considered a low response rate in itself. In addition, ten subjects or even smaller numbers are considered to be sufficient in qualitative studies when the sample is saturated (see Bogdan & Taylor, 1975; Filstead, 1970; Glaser & Strauss, 1967).

The respondents expressed great enthusiasm for the study, and almost all of them asked to be sent results and to be kept informed about any future studies on this matter. It is important to acknowledge the possibility that respondents are only among those women who have embraced the multiple components of their identity enough to be willing to answer and return the questionnaire. In fact, I heard through the grapevine that some of the prospective respondents felt that their lesbianism was a "trial sent by God," which they had to suffer and endure, and thus they found the questionnaire too difficult and decided not to answer it. In addition, because the questionnaire was written in English, it presupposes literacy in English on the part of prospective respondents, at least to be able to read it. Respondents were encouraged to answer in Spanish if they preferred. However, although some Spanish was used, questionnaires were primarily answered in English. A further consideration is that respondents were highly educated and perhaps not representative of the population of Cuban lesbians in the United States.

The questionnaire was brief. It consisted of three pages preceded by a demographic fact sheet in which questions such as occupation, place of residence, and age were asked. Because I wanted to make the questionnaire easy and to the point, some richness of data may have been lost. If the study is to be expanded in the future, in-depth interviewing should be used to follow up. The questionnaire was completely anonymous. Respondents who were interested in the results of the study were asked to submit a request under separate letter or postcard.

Before presenting the data I must reiterate that both sexuality and ethnicity, regardless of how "in-born," "born into," or "given at birth," are, in fact, fluid, life-long processes. What I think of myself today in terms of either ethnicity or sexuality may not be what I thought yesterday or what I will think tomorrow. Because "what each woman thinks of herself" is what I define as identity for my purposes here, I have included those women who consider themselves appropriate participants of this study by responding to the questionnaire. That is why one of the respondents, a twenty-three-year-old woman born in Hialeah, Florida, a short while after her family immigrated into the United States, is included in the study. She defines herself as Cuban, so she can be considered as such for the purposes of this study.

Characteristics of the Group

The ages of the sixteen respondents range from twenty-three to forty-five with a mean of thirty-two years. Fifteen of the respondents were born in Cuba, and one was born in Florida. Eleven of the sixteen are either the oldest child or the oldest daughter in the family. Their places of residence are fairly evenly distributed across the United States. Responses came from Florida, California, the Midwest, and the Northeast.

On the basis of parents' occupation and education in Cuba and in the United States, it can be estimated that three come from an upper-middle-class socioeconomic background, seven from a middle-class background, and six from a low-middle or working-class background. The occupations of the respondents varied, but they were all highly educated. Three of the respondents held doctorates, one was a physician, one was a lawyer, and two were law students. Five had master's degrees and five bachelor's degrees, and one was a professional writer. This high level of education may be an effect of the friendship pyramiding process of recruiting participants for the study. On the other hand, it may be that the high level of education found in this group is a confirmation of what was hypothesized earlier in this chapter concerning the level of education of Latina lesbians compared to a general population of Latinas in the United States. Fourteen of the sixteen women were raised Catholic, one was Methodist, and one Episcopalian. Only three of them practiced their religion at the time of the study. These three women were members of Dignity, a national organization of gay and lesbian Catholics.

Of the sixteen women, fifteen were involved in a committed relationship. Nine of them were in relationships with Cuban or other Hispanic women, five in relationships with Jewish women, one with an Afro-American woman, and one with a white Anglo woman.

The fifteen women who were born in Cuba had arrived in the United States between 1956 and 1972. Thus their length of residence in this country ranged from seven to twenty-eight years, with a mean of eighteen years. Their age at leaving Cuba ranged from three to twenty-two. Twelve participants left Cuba between three and thirteen years of age, one left at seventeen, two at twenty, and one at twenty-two. Most of them left Cuba during their childhood years, and only three left in early adulthood.

Coming out as a lesbian occurred from twenty-one years earlier (1962) to as recently as a few months before the questionnaire was filled out. Age at coming out ranged from sixteen to thirty-three years old. As is usual with a lesbian population, chronological age does not correlate with the number of years of being out, except that those who had been out upwards of twenty years obviously were among the oldest respondents. Five of the women were out to all members of their family, including parents. Six were out to siblings or other relatives, and five were not out to anyone in their families. Most of them were out to friends, and most of them preferred to socialize with people who know they are lesbians.

Responses to the "Core" Questions

Several questions were considered to be the core questions of the study. Questions 5 and 6 asked the participants if they identified as Cuban and as lesbian, respectively. Questions 7 and 8 asked for a brief description of their process of identifying as Cuban and as lesbian. Questions 9 and 10 asked about the influence that living in the United States may have had on them as lesbians and as Cubans. Question 11 asked the relative importance that being Cuban or being lesbian had in their lives. Question 12 asked about their decision making in choosing friends among Latin people who were not gay or among Anglo lesbians. This last question was intended to elicit reflections on the process of emotional costs involved in this decision.

Fourteen of the women, including the young woman born in Florida, identify as Cuban. The two respondents who do not identify as Cuban live in Florida. One of them is thirty-one years old. She came to this country in 1956, before the larger waves of Cuban migration, and was raised, in her own words, "as an Anglo among Anglos." The other woman who does not identify as Cuban is forty-two years old and came to Miami from Cuba in 1962, when she was twenty. She was the only woman in the group who was in a relationship with a white Anglo woman. Although she came to the United States as an adult and lives in the geographical area where the largest concentration of Cubans in the country is, she strongly rejects Cuban ways. In her words,

> It is great to be able to know and share black beans and rice and talk Spanish, but if we cannot be ourselves, we cannot share with one another if our waves do not click—to what good is Spanish if we cannot communicate? I am afraid black beans and rice are not enough. Latins are provincial, nonworldly, ignorant, superstitious, with no room for individuality, self-expression, nonprogressive, politically oppressive, bound by archaic traditions that enslave people. Come to Miami, see butch/femme still alive and well. Very disturbing. These are 17 to 25 year olds.

Among the descriptions of their process of self-definition as Cuban, two responses seem to express the general sentiment more precisely. A thirty-three-year-old woman who had lived in the United States for twenty-three years describes her process in the following way:

> As a child this self-definition was not conscious, since there was no need for awareness of ethnic identity while I lived in Cuba. Coming to the United States instantly brought to my awareness at the age of 10 what being Cuban meant in this country. I would say that the need to assert that identity was strengthened by the racism of the United States. In my teens, I passed through a period of acculturation in which to some extent I internalized society's view of ethnic groups in a very subtle way. During college, I became active in political and community activities and went through a "militant" phase in which I came to understand the nature of racism and oppression more deeply. Presently, I consider myself to have a more universal or humanistic perspective and I am able to appreciate as well as critically analyze aspects of my cultural heritage.

This woman's description of her process as an ethnic minority person clearly fits Atkinson, Morten, and Sue's model of ethnic minority identity development described earlier When confronted with a culture different from her own, she evolved from a conformity stage as an adolescent to a more synergetic stage at this point in her life.

Another respondent, a forty-five-year-old woman, who had lived in the United States for twelve years, said the following about being Cuban in this country: "It is difficult to be cut off from the Cuban community while not feeling fully understood by Americans and sometimes even by other Latins. Being Cuban at this point in history is not easy!"

The vicissitudes of the process of self-identification as a lesbian woman are described best by the following two responses:

> First, total unawareness. Then, after sleeping with a woman, total rejection of her; as if she was an addiction. I knew this was "sick." I never went to bed with so many men in my life as I did during that period. Then, I started realizing that I was denying my own happiness. Now I am almost totally out. I feel whole.

Although I had been intensely involved with another woman, we both denied it. When I became involved with a woman who defined herself as lesbian, I thought I was not lesbian, only "in love with her." Then, I started feeling attracted to other women, became involved in gay groups. I'm now out at work and to friends. Family is impossible, though.

The internal journeys described by these two women, as well by other respondents, fit the processes involved in developing a homosexual identity as described in Vivienne Cass's model.

Interestingly, one of the respondents did not identify as a lesbian. According to her, "No, my sexual preference does not rule my life. I like women, I love women, that is called being a lesbian, but I don't define myself as one." In spite of these words, this woman, who at forty years old had been out for eighteen years, chose to answer the questionnaire knowing that it was about lesbians.

When asked what was more important for them, being Cuban or being lesbian, twelve women responded that both were equally important. Three women responded that being lesbian was more important and one responded that "being a Latin woman" was most important, because "being a Latin woman gives me a broader perspective—culturally and politically." This person is the same one who said she did not define herself as lesbian.

When confronted with the choice of being among Latinos/Latinas without coming out or living among lesbians who are not Latinas or who are unfamiliar with Latin culture, eleven of the women said they had chosen or would choose the second alternative. However, this choice is not made without ambivalence. A twenty-nine-year-old woman from San Francisco explained her choice in this way: *"Una pregunta muy difícil"* (A very difficult question!) I have done both. I think being able to be a lesbian is too much a part of me for me to repress. I can still be Cuban if I'm around Americans."

A twenty-seven-year-old woman from Miami expressed not only the ambivalence but also the pain and anger associated with choosing between different parts of herself:

I guess that if the choice were absolute, I would choose living among lesbians. This answer may invalidate my answer to question 11 in which I said that being Cuban and being lesbian were both equally important for me. But I want to point out that I would be extremely unhappy if all my Latin culture were taken out of my lesbian life. I had a hard time with all the questions that made me choose between Cuban and lesbian, or at least, made me feel as if I had to choose. It made it real clear to me that I identify myself as a lesbian more intensely than as Cuban/Latin. But it is a very painful question because I feel that I am both, and I don't want to have to choose. Clearly, straight people don't even get asked this question and it is unfair that we have to discuss it, even if it is just a questionnaire.

Two of the respondents said that when confronted with the choice, they prefer to be among Latinos. The reason given by one of them for her choice was, "I feel comfortable with my people—gay or not."

Three women said that they would not choose, without explaining how they have integrated both alternatives in their lives. One woman expressed a strong rejection of the possibility of such a choice: "I would refute that choice and insist on the third alternative of not denying either aspect of myself. This is a false dichotomy as we all know, sort of like saying are you a woman or an ethnic person. Such choices arise out of racism and homophobia and I refuse to even postulate such a possibility for myself."

It is not clear if this woman has in fact answered the question in terms of her own personal choices or if she is primarily making a statement about what she considers to be correct or taking a political position. On the other hand, this woman was the most out person in the group. Perhaps because she was out to parents and family as well as to all the important people in her life, she could actively act out her refusal to choose in a better way than others.

From the responses of this small group, we can conclude that it is impossible to determine that one aspect of the identity of these Cuban lesbians is more important for them than the other. The relative importance given to the different components of their identity does not appear to be related, at least in this group, to factors such as age, years of residence in the United States, place of residence, or any other factors. In fact, the two most extreme and definite positions, that of not wanting to identify as Cuban or as lesbian, are espoused by two women who are more than forty (forty-two and forty, respectively), who have been living in the United States for more than twenty years and out as lesbians for twenty and eighteen years, respectively. The woman who rejects her Cuban identity lives in Miami. The woman who rejects her lesbian identity lives in New York.

Most of the respondents, although regretting their decision, choose behaviorally to be among Anglo lesbians rather than among straight Latinos. The possibility of "passing" or not must be a factor in this decision. Obviously, they cannot hide their Hispanic identity among Anglos as they can hide their lesbian identity among Hispanics. But even when they believe that it is easier to be Cuban among lesbians than it is to be lesbian among Cubans, they do not feel fully comfortable not being both. In fact, what most of them say is that they feel more whole when they can be out both as Cubans and as lesbians. However, because of the realities of racism and heterosexism that they have to confront, they are forced to choose for their lives those alternatives that are more tolerable or less costly to them. Some may choose to live in Miami among Cubans, even if that implies "staying in the closet." Others may choose to live in other areas of the country among Anglo lesbians without feeling fully supported in terms of their Cuban identity.

However, as expressed by one of the women, "eating black beans and rice while speaking in Spanish with other Latina lesbians makes those beans taste like heaven!"

Implications for Psychotherapy

Some implications for the practice of psychotherapy with Latina lesbians can be derived from the discussion of the specific factors influencing the identity development of Latina lesbians and from the results of this brief study. Like all other individuals who seek psychotherapy, Latina lesbians who come to therapy do so for a variety of reasons. As with all other individuals, the formation of their identity occurs in a specific cultural, class, and historical context. For the therapist working with Latina lesbians, it is essential to understand the impact of these specific contextual variables on the individual client. But the understanding of the unique vicissitudes of identity development for Latina lesbians should be tempered by the understanding that certain processes are similar to those encountered by any lesbian woman from any cultural background who is in the process of coming out.

It is essential that the therapist understands the anger, frustration, and pain that the Latina lesbian experiences both as a lesbian and as an ethnic minority member. If the therapist is a white Anglo, it is essential that she develop awareness and understanding of how her own cultural background influences her responses to her Latina lesbian client. If the therapist has a heterosexual orientation, particularly if the therapist is also Hispanic, freedom from heterosexist biases and male-centered cultural values and from Latin stereotypes of homosexuals is essential for effective therapy. Of particular importance is the use of language in therapy when the client's associations to Spanish words that refer to her lesbian identity may all be negative.

As with all clients, it must be remembered that each woman's choices express something about who she is as an individual as well as what her cultural values are. Lesbian choices, like any behavior that violates strict cultural norms, can present a high personal cost to any woman. In the case of Latinas, this high personal cost may additionally involve a loss of support from their ethnic group. Any encouragement of their coming out as Lesbians should be done with sensitivity to the other components of their identity.

The therapist should keep in mind that there is as much danger in explaining individual differences away as culturally determined as there is in ignoring or rejecting the impact of cultural influences on each woman's choices. As always in therapy, validation of each woman's identity and of all the components of her total self is provided through the expansion of feeling states and encouragement to understand their meaning. To understand the multiplicity of tasks involved in identity development for Latina lesbians and to provide the opportunity for the accomplishment of those tasks is the first step in therapy with Latina lesbians.

Notes

Reprinted from Espín, O.M. (1987). Issues of Identity in the Psychology of Latina Lesbian Women. In Boston Lesbian Psychologies Collective (Eds.), *Lesbian Psychologies* (pp.35–55). Urbana: University of Illinois Press.

Lourdes Rodríguez-Nogués helped develop the questionnaire for this study.

References

Amaro, H. (1978, May). *Coming out: Hispanic lesbians, their families and communities.* Paper presented at the meeting of the National Coalition of Hispanic Mental Health and Human Services Organizations (COSSMHO), Austin, Texas.

Atkinson, D.R., Morten, G., & Sue, D.W. (1979). *Counseling American minorities.* Dubuque, IA.: William C. Brown.

Bogdan, R., & Taylor, S.J. (1975). *Introduction to qualitative research methods.* New York: Wiley.

Cass, V.C. (1979). Homosexual identity formation: A theoretical model, *Journal of Homosexuality,* 4, 219–235.

Erikson, E.H. (1975). *Life history and the historical moment.* New York: Norton.

Escaserga, Y.D., Mondaca, E.C., & Torres, V.G. (1975). *Attitudes of Chicana lesbians towards therapy.* Master's thesis, Department of Social Work, University of Southern California, Los Angeles.

Espín, O.M. (1984). Cultural and historical influences on sexuality in Hispanic/Latin women: Implications for psychotherapy. In C. Vance (Ed.) *Pleasure and danger: Exploring female sexuality* (pp.149–163). London: Routledge & Kegan Paul.

Filstead, W.J. (1970). *Qualitative methodology: First hand involvement with the social world.* Chicago: Markham.

Glaser, B.G., & Strauss, A. (1967). *The discovery of grounded theory: Strategies for qualitative research.* Chicago: Aldine.

Hidalgo, H., & Hidalgo-Christensen, E. (1976–1977). The Puerto Rican lesbian and the Puerto Rican community. *Journal of Homosexuality,* 2, 109–121.

Hidalgo, H., & Hidalgo-Christensen, E. (1979). The Puerto Rican cultural response to female homosexuality. In E. Acosta-Belen (Ed.), *The Puerto Rican woman* (pp.110–123) New York: Praeger.

Moraga, C. (1983). *Loving in the war years: Lo que nunca paso por sus labios.* Boston: South End.

Sue, D.W. (1981). *Counseling the culturally different.* New York: Wiley.

Part Four

Immigrant Women and Adolescents

The chapters in the fourth part of this book are focused on the psychology of immigrant women and adolescents. As I discussed in the Preface, I have looked at immigrant and refugee women even when the focus of a particular study was not immigration but another concern of Latinas; the overlap of concerns continues to engage me. The topic of migration becomes even more relevant today in a climate of hostility and anti-immigrant sentiment. It is ironic that the descendants of earlier immigrants reject the likes of their ancestors, frequently holding the illusion that their ancestors were of a different mettle than present-day immigrants and thus deserving of a kinder reception.

Most individuals who are not immigrants understand the process of migration from the naïve assumption that migration consists simply of a geographical relocation followed by a short period of adaptation, a move generally undertaken for the purpose of bettering economic status. Stories about immigrant ancestors always seem to have happy endings. If any reference to hardships is included, the impact of the hardships is minimized. After all, the point of the stories is to tell us that the hardships eventually led to greater happiness. But innumerable examples in the scholarly literature and the newspapers of the time (roughly 1880 to 1930) demonstrate that most of the immigrant ancestors of today's U.S.-born citizens were received with little kindness and perceived as destructive of the culture, language, and traditions of the United States—just like present-day immigrants. Then, as now, the emotional price paid by immigrants was minimized. Yet, migration has a profound psychological impact, and thus a psychological understanding of the process of migration is of utmost importance.

Undoubtedly, my own personal experiences as well as the history of my "nomadic" family inform my professional interest in the psychological impact of migration in women's lives. Even before my personal experience of migration, my ancestors' life stories impressed on me the importance and psychological significance of migration. My maternal grandparents immigrated to Cuba from Spain in the nineteenth century when Cuba was still a colony of Spain. They eventually became successful in business in the early twentieth century. In the mid–1800s, while still children, my paternal grandparents, whose forebears had been Cuban for many generations, moved with their families from Cuba to escape Spain's colonial rule. Eventually ending up in the United States, my paternal grandfather studied medicine at the University of Pennsylvania and then specialized in tropical medicine at Johns Hopkins University. He was part of the medical team that discovered that yellow fever was transmitted by a mosquito. (This occurred under the direction of Cuban physician Carlos Finlay during the U.S. occupation of Cuba at the end of the nineteenth century.) I cherish two artifacts of his life: copies of his articles on the health dangers associated with mosquitoes and a painting of all the main characters in this research project. In the age of AIDS, I feel a profound kinship with an ancestor whose commitment to eradicating a dangerous illness eventually saved many lives. Ironically, he died from a variety of malaria.

My paternal grandparents' fierce Cuban patriotism contrasts with the very different feelings of my maternal grandparents. They decided to stay in Cuba after independence from Spain but always believed that anything originating in Spain was far superior to its Cuban equivalent. Yet, their own social position had been full of hunger and hardships in Spain but relatively comfortable in Cuba. My maternal grandmother nursed her nostalgia by constantly retelling stories about Spain when I was a child. Upon retirement, my grandfather bought himself a small farm, where he tried to recreate as much as possible his idealized memories of his childhood years in Spain. Both of them loved their country of birth and showed me by example how deep love for one's country of birth can last for a lifetime despite distance and length of absence. They also, unknowingly, taught me the emotional limitations that develop when one clings to old memories and dreams that cannot be realized. I have in my dining room a picture of the house in which this grandfather was born. Almost a century later, I visited the house, finding it almost as he had left it, without electricity, running water, or paved road access. Cows and chickens were housed under the same roof, separated only by a thin wall from the family's living quarters. I thought it the quaintest place I had ever seen. Under the picture in my dining room now hangs the old bulky key that opened the door to the house—an apt metaphor for my unlocking my family's past homes and migrations.

I realize I talk more about my grandfathers than my grandmothers. This is because in my family as in so many others it was the men who were considered important. As we know, most cultures devalue the everyday life maintenance and emotional labor that women do. My family's attitudes taught me yet other lessons: the value placed on public life, the thin appreciation accorded to the domestic realm, and how life choices are largely scripted by gender and culture. Thus, I determined to try to broaden the possibilities for myself and for the young immigrant women who were my clients in therapy and my students.

My family's history also presented me with a powerful example of the importance of bilingualism. Once again, through them, I learned of the empowerment and limitations that can result. My father grew up in a household where both parents spoke English better than Spanish. He never learned English because both his parents were fiercely patriotic and wanted their children to speak only Spanish. Ultimately, this was a costly decision. When my father eventually came to the United States half a century later with a minimal knowledge of English, it impaired his adjustment and possibilities considerably.

The stories I heard as a child were all about triumph and success; very little was shared about the pain endured by all of my relatives, although these themes seeped through almost in spite of the storytellers' intentions. Like me, most descendants of immigrants hear more about the successes than about the painful experiences of their ancestors. Memories of migration are colored by the success of descendants; the pain of ancestors tends to be forgotten.

As I mentioned in the introduction to Part 3, the first chapter in this section, "Psychological Impact of Migration on Latinas," is one of the most cited in the literature. This article resulted from years of therapeutic work with immigrant Latinas and women from other regions of the world. It was also inspired by long hours of conversations with friends and close associates who, like me, had lived through the experience of migration to another country. The model presented in this article—which I developed—describes the psychological stages of migration. This model continues to inform and structure my understanding of this process, and it is central in my continued training of service providers who work with this population. Both psychotherapists and immigrant women have told me that the stages and circumstances of the migratory process I describe in this article accurately portray their clients' or their own experiences.

Chapters 9 and 10 afford a dual perspective on a study of letters written by an adolescent immigrant girl. The story of how these two essays came to be is presented in Chapter 1, "Giving Voice to Silence." Chapters 9 and 10 complement one another—in them I look at the same data from different methodological approaches. I regularly use these two articles when teaching to illustrate to students what is gained and lost through the use of quantitative and qualitative methodologies. Both essays rely on Erikson's theory of identity development. If I were to do these studies now, I would rely more heavily on narrative analysis for the qualitative version of the study and I would ground the discussion and analysis of the data on other theoretical conceptualizations beyond identity. All the same, this study makes a very important point: Migration can be a traumatic experience for an adolescent, but it does not have to be destructive. If certain conditions are present, the trauma of migration is not only survivable but also a propelling force for psychological development. This study, significantly, also demonstrates the power and value of women's friendships in traumatic times.

The final chapter in this section is focused on the lives of Latina healers. It is the result of a study done many years ago with funds from the National Institute of

Mental Health while I was a fellow at Harvard University. (A more detailed book-length version was recently published; see Espín, 1996.) In Chapter 11, I explore strategies used by some Latina women for empowerment. This study was my first attempt at using life narrative as a research method. It is also my only study of healers. Entering into this subculture of Latinas taught me some lessons about the difficulties of describing the experiences of others. It also increased my respect for the strengths and resourcefulness of Latinas of different subcultures and social classes. I hope the study has done justice to the experiences of women whose lives are, in many ways, so different from mine.

Together, the chapters in this section present a variety of issues, topics, and perspectives from which to approach the lives of immigrant women. They provide a small window into the richness and variety of immigrant women's and girls' experiences.

References

Espín, O.M. (1996). *Latina healers: Lives of power and tradition.* Encino, CA: Floricanto.

Psychological Impact of Migration on Latinas: Implications for Psychotherapeutic Practice

The unique stresses created by the process of immigration into another country and the need for grieving the loss of the home country and loved ones are important psychological processes confronted by all immigrants and refugees. Frequently, the psychological effects of migration and its specific impact on women will manifest themselves in issues brought to the attention of psychotherapists working with Latinas. There is evidence that the impact of migration on women and their roles is different from the impact of the same process for men (Andizian et al., 1983), and more research is needed in this area.

For both immigrants and refugees, the process of migration implies a certain degree of culture-shock that entails mourning the loss of the old country and of love objects, coupled with the need to confront new situations and interpersonal encounters (Garza-Guerrero, 1973; Grinberg & Grinberg, 1984). Factors such as perceived or real freedom to migrate, relative ease or difficulty of this process, sense of responsibility for those left behind, and conditions in both the home and host countries interact in specific ways with culture-shock for each individual migrant. For example, leaving the home country through illegal means that can be life threatening has a different psychological impact than does arrival in a new country via legal entry.

Some intrapsychic factors such as ego strength; decision-making skills; resolution of feelings of loss; and the ability to tolerate ambiguities, including gender-role ambiguities, also influence migrants' adaptation processes. Shirley (1981) found that these factors actively interact with the joy and hope created by the opening of new doors and opportunities and, in some cases, with the escape from real or perceived life-threatening conditions. Other factors pertaining to the new country such as language proficiency, ability to find a job, losses or gains in status or social class, educational level, degree of similarity between the two cultures, and reception by citizens of the host country also determine and influence the experience of migration and subsequent adaptation (Doran, Satterfield, & Stade, 1988; Taft, 1977). These factors vary substantially for males and females. Thus, the unique interplay of issues pertaining to the psychological make-up of the individual Latina, specifics of the home subculture and social class, and the characteristics of North American culture can facilitate or interfere with the adaptation process.

The purpose of this article is to review and analyze clinical material relating to the psychological correlates of the process of migration in Latina women and girls and to suggest implications for the psychotherapeutic process. Most of the clinical evidence and examples presented in the paper are garnered from my own practice.

The Psychology of Migration and Acculturation

An understanding of the psychological processes involved in adaptation to another culture is essential for the understanding of the psychological implications of migration. Acculturation can be distinguished from assimilation in that acculturation does not imply the disappearance of all values, customs, and behaviors originating in the home culture as implied in the "melting pot" ideology of assimilation. While acculturation is inevitable to some degree for all migrants, it does not need to be disruptive in a negative sense. Healthy acculturation may resolve itself into healthy biculturalism (Szapocznik & Kurtines, 1980).

Regardless of gender and cultural background, the process of immigration involves important psychological changes that take place before and after arrival in the new country. These changes continue to take place throughout the life of the immigrant and include the development of a new identity (Garza-Guerrero, 1973).

Psychological Stages of the Migratory Process

Clinical observations have led me to think of the process of migration as having three stages: (a) the initial decision concerning relocation, (b) the actual geographical move into another country, and (c) the adaptation to a new society and way of life. At each step of the way, men and women will experience the process differently. For instance, at the decision-making stage, women may not be consulted about their preference to leave or stay, whereas most men participate in the family decision to leave or make the decision themselves. At the relocation stage, particularly in situations of escaping dangerous political conditions, women's physical endurance may be questioned and they might not be provided the same opportunities to escape. At the third stage, when acculturation and adaptation are taking place, modifications of women's gender roles may be more dramatic than those experienced by men.

Acculturation and adaptation to a new culture may also follow several stages (Arredondo-Dowd, 1981). These include initial joy and relief, followed by disillusionment with the new country. Finally, if the process is successfully completed, the migrant moves into acceptance of the good and the bad in the host country and thus into adjustment and reorganization coupled with adaptation to a new situation (Garza-Guerrero, 1973; Grinberg & Grinberg, 1984).

The process of adaptation, however, is not linear. The multiple intrapsychic and behavioral changes required for successful acculturation occur at many levels and may proceed at a different pace at each one of them.

If rejection of and distancing from the host culture becomes the preferred mode of coping with the new society and way of life, the adaptation process may never be successfully completed. The traditional expectations for the role of women in Latino culture may even foster the isolation of some women from the mainstream culture. These Latinas will seldom seek psychotherapy on their own because they may be reluctant to do so; unable to afford it; or likely to encounter opposition from family, friends, or husbands who may view psychotherapy as an invasion of family privacy. When traditional Latinas consult a psychotherapist, they may have come into therapy following referral by a medical doctor, as a result of repeated somatic complaints. The high incidence of somatic complaints presented by Latinas with a traditional cultural orientation might be an expression of actual frequency of somatization of conflicts that is prevalent in traditional cultures (Kleinman, 1980).

On the other hand, somatic complaints might be the symptoms of a masked depression or of one of the many types of emotional disorders that frequently are presented with a cluster of somatic complaints. It is possible that traditional Latinas have few other ways to seek help or that generally they are only aware of "feeling bad" without being able to pinpoint the source of those feelings. Perhaps some of the women simply do not know what else to talk about with a "doctor" or do not want to talk with a stranger about their more intimate feelings about themselves and their families and find it easier to continue to discuss physical symptoms instead. The fact that mental health professionals and physicians frequently prescribe tranquilizers and other medication for these patients rather than psychotherapy may also serve to reinforce the belief that they have some kind of physical illness.

Whatever the reason for the high incidence of somatic complaints, the fact is that those complaints are constantly presented by Latino clients (Abad, Ramos, & Boyce,

1974), especially by women. If the therapist does not show in some way that these somatic complaints are being addressed, the woman client who comes from a traditional cultural orientation is likely to see the treatment as irrelevant and may terminate the therapy.

Although some Latinas may choose the traditional role expectations, most Latina immigrants find that these are neither functional nor satisfying. Culturally based conflicts may develop when newly encountered patterns of gender roles combined with greater access to paid employment for women open new economic, social, and emotional options which create an imbalance in the traditional power structure of the family (Torres-Matrullo, 1980). These women may consult a therapist at their own initiative and they may or may not be very explicit about the interrelationship between the migratory process and their feelings of distress.

Gender-Role Conflicts

Women and girls from a Latin background are presently acculturating into North American society at a time when the role of women in this culture is in flux. Sometimes they may come from countries where official government policies or other forces are also fostering a transformation of the role of women or from urban professional environments which have also been affected by the global feminist movement. But in other instances, they may come from very traditional rural environments where adherence to traditional gender roles is considered of primary importance. These factors combine to create some confusion as to what is appropriate behavior for women in the newly found North American culture. Frequently, the contradictions between home and host cultures are stronger for women than for men in terms of what constitutes appropriate gender-role behavior.

Role conflicts in migrant families tend to occur mostly along lines that coincide with age and gender differences (Szapocznik & Kurtines, 1980). It is a common clinical observation that parents tend to be distressed by their children's more rapid pace of acculturation and that husbands tend to become resentful of their wives' apparent new independence and challenge of their patriarchal authority. Research shows that even though the pace of acculturation tends to be slower for females in all other aspects, they tend to acculturate faster than males when it comes to gender roles (Ginorio, 1979). Immigrant families may become entrenched in traditional social and sex-role norms as a defense against the strong pressures to acculturate. The home culture may become idealized and its values, characteristics, and customs may become a symbol of the stable parts of personal identity and probably the strongest defense against any sense of identity loss that might be engendered by acculturation. This attempt to preserve "old ways" tends to increase intergenerational and gender-role conflicts in the family.

In addition to gender, other factors such as age, class, and race affect the process of acculturation and adaptation for migrants. Light-skinned, young, and educated migrants usually encounter a more favorable reception in the United States than dark-skinned, older, and uneducated newcomers. These differences in reception may or may not parallel the migrant's experiences in the home culture. For example, when a migrant comes from a country where she belongs to the racial majority or where, as in Latin countries, racial mixtures are the norm, the experience of turning into a minority in the United States and encountering overt racial discrimination can be disorienting. In addition, economic need combined with lack of fluency in the new language frequently add to the experience of downward mobility in employment, particularly for refugees. This loss of status creates frustration and tensions in the family. Because of the increased employability of women and the loss of status and authority of the father in the family, further conflict related to gender norms often develops.

Psychotherapy with Migrant Latina Women

Seldom will a Latina woman present herself for therapy stating that she has "acculturation problems" or "psychological problems due to immigration." Most typically, an immigrant Latina seeks therapy because of personal problems similar to those presented in therapy by other women: because she is depressed; has trouble in developing relationships; feels disoriented; or has a specific situational problem such as conflicts with her husband, partner, children, parents, or co-workers. However, as does every individual who comes to therapy, she has a unique history that modulates and defines the parameters of her specific problem or problems. In the case of immigrant women, their individual histories are influenced by the experience of migration and by the circumstances surrounding that experience as well as by the vicissitudes of their own personal and family histories.

The specific sociopolitical, economic, and historical circumstances that motivated the migration affect the individual psychological development and the process of therapy. The impact of these circumstances may appear more clearly in Latina women who are refugees than in those women who are voluntary migrants because of the danger surrounding the departure of most refugees and the impossibility of returning regularly to the country of origin. In addition, the problems presented in therapy by women who migrate alone may have different characteristics than those presented by women who migrate with their families.

Latina women who migrate alone have to struggle not only with loneliness but also with feelings of shame and guilt and with the sociocultural expectations about the role of women that present themselves both externally and intrapsychically. On the one hand, they feel freer of family control and have more flexibility in looking for new patterns of behavior in response to acculturation than those who migrate with other family members. Yet, they may continue to have traditional expectations for their own roles and behaviors that may not be realistic in the new context. In addition, they may have to contend with criticism from other immigrants from the same country for not conforming to traditional roles. Because they are alone, they may in fact need to acculturate faster.

These women, even if they constitute a numerical minority among immigrants, present unique challenges for therapeutic work. For example, an adolescent girl or a young woman who left her country without her family may find herself affected by a premature and traumatic separation from her parents that can stall or delay the process of healthy psychological separation in adulthood (Rodríguez-Nogués, 1983). Paris (1978) likens the forced individuation from the parent caused by leaving one's country to the effect of the impossibility of completing the rapprochement period in the life of a child. In order for a child to successfully complete individuation and rec-onciliation with the parents in adulthood, periodic, return to parents is essential for refueling, and yet is impossible for young refugee women. When the rapprochement is interrupted as it is in the case of these refugee women, guilt, frustration, restless-ness, and lowered self-esteem could develop.

The impossibility of contacting parents during the course of therapy may prevent the woman from working out conflicts that may have originated before the separa-tion took place. Although some similarities may be encountered when parents are deceased, major differences are present in the case of migrant women: Dead parents cannot be affected by the woman's present anger or resentment. Living and geo-graphically inaccessible parents, on the other hand, can be affected by anger. The mi-grant woman, particularly if she does not have regular contact with them, frequently feels guilty about her anger toward parents who are geographically distant and per-ceived to be in a situation of more or less danger in the country of origin. A monthly long-distance phone call to an absent mother does not provide the time to address any problematic issues.

Another example of women strongly affected by the inability to work out prob-lematic feelings may be a mother who, at migration time, was forced by her relatives, ex-husband, or situational factors to leave her children behind. This woman's feel-ings of guilt and loss would be exacerbated by the lack of contact with her growing children.

The feelings of guilt and loss usually associated with migration become height-ened by this inaccessibility. Even when the refugee may be allowed to return to her country of origin for brief visits, the time needed for working through issues will not be available in a week or two of family reencounter after many years. And, even if there can be extended visits home, the family does not witness the change experi-enced by the woman in the new country, so they can dismiss or deny the importance of those changes in her life.

Thus, therapy proceeds in a void for many immigrant women and refugees. They have to learn to understand, express, and experience feelings concerning distant fam-ily members without ever fully testing those feelings in the interpersonal context where they originated.

When the migration has been preceded by situations of political persecution that may include experiences of torture or the disappearance of family members, other unique factors may be part of the therapy. Moreover, some of the traumatic events experienced by women refugees are directly associated with their gender. For example, repeated rape or other forms of sexual abuse or harassment may have been used as a means of torture. Or they may have been subjected to rape and harassment at the hands of their "protectors" or "saviors" during their escape from their country of origin.

Persons who have been subjected to these experiences may suffer from post-traumatic stress reactions that may vary in intensity for each individual (Figley, 1985; Molesky, 1986). Post-traumatic stress reactions may manifest themselves through nightmares, numbing of feelings, and overwhelming feelings of guilt. Empirical evidence seems to indicate that sadness, depression, and more serious pathology may recur or develop many years after the actual migration took place. This phenomenon seems to be particularly true of immigrant and refugee women who have suffered traumatic experiences in the process of migration, have lost their networks of female relatives and childhood friends through migration, or did not participate in the decision to migrate (Rumbaut, 1977; Telles, 1980). For the woman suffering from post-traumatic stress, therapy can provide a needed outlet. Because some of the experiences of torture and abuse suffered by refugees are so inconceivable to people who have lived in the United States all their lives, the woman refugee from a Latin American country sometimes has difficulty expressing what she has undergone without feeling she is seen as a liar. Mental health professionals have observed that just the telling of the experiences, the opportunity to speak about what was sometimes felt as unspeakable, may in itself be therapeutic for these women (Cienfuegos & Monelli, 1983; Figley, 1985). To be able to talk about these experiences and be believed provides an enormous relief for the woman who has experienced torture and political persecution before migration.

Young women or adolescent girls who migrate with their families, although accompanied and protected, confront the question of how to "become American" without losing completely their own cultural heritage. Role models of successful bicultural Latinas are scarce. A bicultural Latina therapist can thus provide an invaluable service just by being available to the young woman as a role model.

Girls frequently express their adolescent rebellion against the parental culture by refusing to speak Spanish at home, rejecting cultural customs, and generally reacting negatively toward their parents and native culture. Since American society at large encourages immigrants to deny their cultural heritage, the adolescent Latina finds plenty of support from adults in positions of authority to challenge her parents' values. Often conflicts over authority are played out around issues of appropriate sexual behavior such that dating and other behavior related to sexuality become the focus of conflict between parents and daughters (Espín, 1984). One of the most prevalent myths encountered by Latina immigrants is that all American women are "free" with sex. For the parents and the young woman alike, "to be Americanized" may be equated with becoming sexually promiscuous.

The question of loyalties to the home culture may manifest itself in other ways. For example, the parents of an adolescent Cuban girl became outraged and reacted with apparent unjustified violence to her interest in the new Cuban music, a popular form of song that developed in Cuba after the Revolution. Since she had come to this country when she was two years old, her interest in the music was simply an innocent way of familiarizing herself with something Cuban or simply just listening to music, while for her parents her interest was a political statement that had negative connotations.

Affective and Cognitive Implications of Language Use

Language is an important variable in psychodynamic psychotherapy with Latinas. Extensive discussion of the affective and cognitive implications of bilingualism and language use in therapy is beyond the scope of the paper. However, it is important to address this issue because even for those Latinas who are fluent in English or who have lost fluency in the use of their first language Spanish remains the language of emotions because it was in Spanish that affective meanings were originally encoded (Espín, 1982). To try to decode those affective meanings through the use of another language may be problematic at best. Psychotherapy relies too heavily on language to ignore its psychological implications for the therapeutic process, especially for persons who may constantly be changing between two languages or who are participating in a therapeutic process that is carried on in their second language.

Several authors have commented on the importance of language choice in therapy with bilinguals (Espín, 1982; Krapf, 1955; Marcos, 1976a, 1976b; Rosensky & Gómez, 1983). According to Marcos (1976a), bilinguals may appear to be withdrawn in their second language when they are not fully proficient in it. In this case, the attention paid to how things are said in therapy may distract attention from what is being said, thus impairing the therapeutic process. Conversely, proficient bilinguals may use independence between their two languages as a mechanism for compartmentalizing feelings (Marcos & Alpert, 1976). These mechanisms may render unavailable certain areas of the bilingual's intrapsychic world. Marcos and Urcuyo (1979) also describe the subjective experience of some language-independent bilinguals who experience a dual sense of self as a consequence of using different languages. According to De la Cancela,

> The implications for psychotherapy of these difficulties may be that affects are blocked, hence, the client has difficulty in benefiting from catharsis and abreaction. As such, verbalization of feelings may turn out to be an arduous intellectual task which brings little relief to the client. Additionally both positive and negative transferences may be unsatisfactorily expressed, leading to displacement or acting-out in the therapeutic relationship. (1985, p. 430)

In my own clinical practice I have encountered instances in which the importance of language is expressed directly and those in which it is expressed indirectly. Manifestations of the impact of language in therapy with Latina clients are not clearly understood because the use of language in therapy has always been studied and described from a monolingual point of view (e.g., Havens, 1986). An example of an intuitive sense of the importance of the first language in therapy was provided by a college-age Puerto Rican woman who sought me out for therapy specifically because I could speak Spanish. She was fluently bilingual and did not need Spanish to communicate her feelings with a relative degree of sophistication. However, it was important to be in therapy with a Spanish-speaking therapist because, in her own words, "My problems are with my family and my family speaks Spanish, so my problems are in Spanish." Other clients have approached me as a therapist presenting variations of the same idea.

An indirect example suggesting the importance of the first language in therapy was provided by a professional woman who, having immigrated to the United States at a very young age, preferred to use English for her therapy even though she wanted a therapist who was "culturally sensitive." After two years in therapy conducted in English with minimal interspersed use of some common Spanish words, she came to a session in which she spoke only Spanish. At the end of the session, I pointed out that I had noticed we had used Spanish uninterruptedly during the hour. She stated that there was nothing special in her language change in that particular session, that she just wanted to practice her Spanish more frequently. The content of the session, in fact, had not been particularly deep or cathartic, so I went along with her expressed perception that there was nothing to her change in language. She never came back after that session. I must confess that her abrupt and unanticipated departure from therapy baffles me. But what is clear is that her change to Spanish on that particular day was not innocuous. Perhaps she was developing a negative maternal transference that became suddenly intensified by speaking to me in the only language her mother spoke or perhaps the use of Spanish brought up some other intense feelings that remained unacknowledged while she used English. Needless to say, I have never again treated lightly any shifts in language during therapy with bilingual women.

On the other hand, bilinguals conversing with each other habitually switch from one language to another without any significant psychological pattern being apparent. Speakers may choose expressions in the native or second language depending on the relative applicability of the expression to the context. As a bilingual therapist working with bilingual women, I try to remain alert to their language choice and switches as any therapist would remain alert to a client's choice of words. But, very specifically, I try to remain alert to possible areas of conflict that are being avoided or expressed by sudden shifts in language.

But while the use of English in therapy may act as a barrier and a resistance in dealing with certain components of the psyche, the second language can act as a facilitator for the emergence and discussion of certain topics. Some of these may be taboo topics or words in Spanish while others may refer to the new components of the self acquired through the process of acculturation after English became the primary or most used language. González-Reigosa (1976) has demonstrated that taboo words in the language of origin elicit more anxiety than either taboo words in the second language or indifferent words in the first language.

The facilitative features of the second language become most evident when the topic discussed is sexuality. Latino culture has fairly traditional views of female sexuality (Espín, 1984, 1985a). For Latinas, English provides a vehicle for discussing sexual issues in therapy that may be too embarrassing to initiate with the use of forbidden Spanish words. In my practice I find this is particularly significant for Latina lesbians, who will describe their life situation and choices most frequently using terminology in English and will tend to avoid equivalent words in Spanish.

In addition to the emotional value associated with either the first or second language, an important aspect of language usage for bilinguals is its connection with self-esteem. In the United States, Spanish bilingualism is frequently associated with an inferior social status. Bilingual skills in Latinos are frequently devalued and rejection of bilingual parents as "ignorant" people who are contrasted with "educated" monolingual teachers may be encouraged in schools. The use of Spanish in therapy may be difficult because of these negative connotations but may become an important instrument for reclaiming parts of the self that may have been rejected as negative through the process of acculturation.

Issues of Loss and Grief in Therapy with Immigrant Women

Loss, grief, and mourning are issues of primary importance when working in therapy with immigrants and refugees. Attempts to understand the psychological distress experienced by immigrants and refugees have generally focused on factors in the new environment and the need to cope with them or acculturative stress (Berry & Annis, 1974). However, the loss of home country and loved ones plays a significant role in the immigrant's adjustment. These feelings of loss must be resolved through a grieving process that can be facilitated by the therapy. In its normal form the grieving process involves a moderate level of emotional disorganization which may be manifested by apathy, insomnia, loss of appetite, irritability, angry outbursts, psychosomatic symptoms, and other signs of distress. When grief is delayed or inhibited because the loss is denied or otherwise defended against, the normal signs can take pathological forms by becoming prolonged or exaggerated (Lindemann, 1944). Parkes (1975) suggested several features by which to identify unresolved grief: a gradual process of realization from denial of the grief to recognition and acceptance of it, alarm reactions such as anxiety and other related physiological symptoms, an urge to search for and find the lost object, anger and guilt, feelings of internal loss of self, identification with the lost object, and pathological variants of grief. Telles (1980) has observed the effects of delayed grief on Cuban women who experienced a reactivation of this grieving process at the time of retirement from their jobs after many years of residing in the United States. The depression and emotional distress manifested by these women could be traced directly to the lack of successful mourning for the losses created by the migration in earlier years.

While the grief of the bereaved can be traced to the nature of the relationship to a specific person, in migration the lost object is vague and the loss pervasive. Migrants have lost country, culture, and loved ones—in other words, what Ticho (1971) refers to as the "average expectable environment," which includes everyday patterns of relationships, obligations, networks, familiar food, places and people, and the behaviors that are considered "normal" in the home culture. When all those habitual patterns are disrupted at the same time and new patterns have to be learned, the amount of distress experienced by the migrant can be considerable. The magnitude of this loss is seldom understood by the immigrant or by others. Sometimes it may require returning to the homeland for the immigrant to realize what this loss had entailed (Espín, 1985b). Even supportive friends and social service agencies are more interested in the woman's adaptation to her new life than in her feelings about who or what was left behind in the home country.

Latina immigrants struggle to maintain contact with the home country, either through physical proximity or through food, music, and other immigrants from the home country. In therapy, the effort to recover the lost objects (e.g., mother, country) may be expressed through strong transferential reactions, particularly when the therapist comes from the same country or culture.

Preoccupation with "what could have been" if the woman had not left her country is a central theme in therapy with migrants. This preoccupation is expressed both through concern with what could have happened in a client's life had she stayed in her country of origin and concern with what has been gained by the migration. Not infrequently, the immigrant experiences feelings of guilt in relation to people and relationships left behind. New loyalties to individuals and relationships developed in the host country, including the therapeutic relationship, are frequently experienced as betrayal of the parents or the home country. In other words, "invisible loyalties" may interfere with the course of the therapy and with the process of adaptation to the new country. Boszormenyi-Nagy and Spark (1973) have discussed extensively the impact of "invisible loyalties" in personality development and relationships. "Invisible loyalties" can create powerful paralyzing and compulsive behavioral and emotional effects in individuals and families. They constitute an important aspect of the conflicts presented by immigrant Latinas in psychotherapy.

Conclusions

Because this article is about the stressors created by migration and their implications for psychotherapy with immigrant Latinas, emphasis has been placed on conflictual situations. However, it is important to understand that many of the reactions discussed in this paper are not pathological. It is important that the therapist interpret these reactions as natural consequences of a disturbing process and not as signs of individual pathology. This is not to deny that some Latinas will in fact present pathological manifestations whose sources existed prior to migration.

The therapist working with immigrant Latinas should acquire knowledge and information about each woman's reasons for migration, including the political and economic conditions in her country of origin and the specific circumstances in the woman's life that motivated her migration (Espín, 1985a, 1985b). Because some of the events described by Latinas in therapy are so extreme, it is important for the therapist to be aware of her own countertransferential reactions to the client (Ticho, 1971).

Therapy should provide assistance in the grieving process and with the resolution of "invisible loyalties" that may be hindering adjustment. At the same time, therapy should assist the client in maintaining loyalties and emotional proximity to those people and places that constitute the sources of her identity. Therapy can provide support in managing conflicts in the woman's relationships that might occur as a consequence of changes in her traditional roles and in newly acquired behaviors.

Bilingual/bicultural therapists can be especially helpful in assisting Latinas to resolve some of those concerns and to adapt successfully to their new lives. But the fact that there is a dearth of Latina psychotherapists poses additional problems in the treatment of this population. Anglo therapists who are sensitive and competent in integrating cultural variables in their treatment plan may provide the necessary support and skills needed to assist immigrant Latinas in their process of adaptation. However, the question remains of how cultural sensitivity can be identified or achieved. Lack of research data and information do not allow for clear identification of what requisite experience, background, and communication skills are necessary for competence in the conduct of psychotherapy with immigrant Latinas or with any other ethnic minority population, for that matter.

Until further information from research and clinical practice is available, some of the ideas discussed in this paper can serve to identify stressors present in the lives of immigrant Latinas as well as issues to be addressed in therapy with this population and initial questions for further exploration.

Notes

Reprinted from Espín, O.M. (1987). Psychological Impact of Migration on Latinas: Implications for Psychotherapeutic Practice. *Psychology of Women Quarterly*, 11(4), 489–503.

References

Abad, V., Ramos, J., & Boyce, E. (1974). A model for delivery of mental health services to Spanish-speaking minorities. *American Journal of Orthopsychiatry*, 44, 584–595.
Andizian, S., Catani, M., Cicourel, A., Dittmar, N., Harper, D., Kudat, A., Morokvasic, M., Oriol, M., Parris, R.C., Streiff, J., & Swetland, C. (1983). *Vivir entre dos culturas*. Paris: Serbal/UNESCO.

Arredondo-Dowd, P. (1981). Personal loss and grief as a result of immigration. *Personnel and Guidance Journal*, 59, 376–378.

Berry, J.W., & Annis, R.C., (1974). Acculturative stress: The role of ecology culture and differentiation. *Journal of Cross-Cultural Psychology*, 5, 382–405.

Boszormenyi-Nagy, I., & Spark, C.M. (1973). *Invisible loyalties: Reciprocity in intergenerational family therapy*. New York: Harper & Row.

Cienfuegos, A.I., & Monelli, C. (1983). The testimony of political repression as a therapeutic instrument. *American Journal of Orthopsychiatry*, 53, 43–51.

De la Cancela, V. (1985). Toward a sociocultural psychotherapy for low-income ethnic minorities. *Psychotherapy: Theory, Research and Practice*, 22, 427–435.

Doran, T., Satterfield, I., & Stade, C. (1988). *A road well traveled: Three generations of Cuban-American women*. Newton, MA: WEEA Publishing Center/Educational Development Center.

Espín, O.M., (1982, October). *Language issues in psychotherapy with fluent bilinguals.* Paper presented at a clinical seminar at Wellesley College Stone Center, Wellesley, MA.

Espín, O.M. (1984). Cultural and historical influences on sexuality in Hispanic/Latin women: Implications for psychotherapy. In C. Vance (Ed.), *Pleasure and danger: Exploring female sexuality* (pp.149–164). London: Routledge & Kegan Paul.

Espín, O.M. (1985a). Psychotherapy with Hispanic women: Some considerations. In P. Pedersen (Ed.), *Handbook of cross-cultural counseling and psychotherapy*, (pp.165–171). Westport, CT: Greenwood.

Espín, O.M. (1985b, November). *Roots uprooted: Dealing with historical dislocation.* Paper presented at the Women's Theological Center, Boston. (Abridged version published in *Sojourner*, February 1986, pp.22–23.)

Figley, C.R. (Ed.). (1985). *Trauma and its wake: The study and treatment of post-traumatic stress disorder.* New York: Brunner/Mazel.

Garza-Guerrero, C. (1973). Culture shock: Its mourning and the vicissitudes of identity. *Journal of the American Psychoanalytic Association*, 22, 408–429.

Ginorio, A. (1979). A comparison of Puerto Ricans in New York with native Puerto Ricans and Caucasian- and Black-Americans on two measures of acculturation: Gender role and racial identification (Doctoral dissertation, Fordham University) *Dissertation Abstracts International*, 40, 983B–984B.

González-Reigosa, F. (1976). The anxiety-arousing effect of taboo words in bilinguals. In C.D. Spielberger & R. Diaz-Gurrero (Eds.), *Cross-cultural anxiety* (pp.309–326). Washington, DC: Hemisphere.

Grinberg, L., & Grinberg, R. (1984). *Psicoanálisis de la migración y del exilio.* Madrid: Alianza Editorial.

Havens, L. (1986). *Making contact: Uses of language in psychotherapy.* Cambridge, MA: Harvard University Press.

Kleinman, A. (1980). *Patients and healers in the context of culture.* Berkeley: University of California Press.

Krapf, E. E. (1955). The choice of language in polyglot psychoanalysis. *Psychoanalytic Quarterly*, 24, 343–357.

Lindemann, E. (1944). Symptomatology and management of acute grief. *American Journal of Psychiatry*, 101,141–148.

Marcos, L. (1976a). Bilinguals in psychotherapy: Language as an emotional barrier. *American Journal of Psychotherapy*, 30, 522–560.

Marcos, L. (1976b). Bilingualism and sense of self. *American Journal of Psychoanalysis*, 37, 285–290.

Marcos, L.R., & Alpert, M. (1976). Strategies and risks in psychotherapy with bilingual patients: The phenomena of language independence. *American Journal of Psychiatry*, 133, 1275–1278.

Marcos, L.R., & Urcuyo, L. (1979). Dynamic psychotherapy with the bilingual patient, *American Journal of Psychotherapy*, 33, 331–338.

Molesky, J. (1986). The exiled: Pathology of Central American refugees. *Migration World*, 14(4), 19–23.

Paris, J. (1978). The symbolic return: Psychodynamic aspects of immigration and exile. *Journal of the American Academy of Psychoanalysis*, 6, 51–57.

Parkes, L.M. (1975). *Bereavement: Studies in grief in adult life*. New York: International Universities Press.

Rodríguez-Nogués, L. (1983). Psychological effects of premature separation from parents in Cuban refugee girls: A retrospective study (Doctoral dissertation, Boston University) *Dissertation Abstracts International*, 44, 1619B.

Rosensky, R., & Gómez, M. (1983). Language switch in psychotherapy with bilinguals: Two problems, two models and case examples. *Psychotherapy: Theory, Research and Practice*, 20, 152–160.

Rumbaut, R.D. (1977). Life events, change, migration and depression. In W.E. Fann, I. Karocan, A.D. Pokorny, & R L. Williams (Eds.), *Phenomenology and treatment of depression* (pp.115–126). New York: Spectrum.

Shirley, B. (1981). A study of ego strength: The case of the Latina immigrant woman in the United States (Doctoral dissertation, Boston University). *Dissertation Abstracts International*, 42, 2583A–2584A.

Szapocznik, J., & Kurtines, W. (1980). Acculturation, biculturalism and adjustment among Cuban Americans. In A. Padilla (Ed.), *Acculturation: Theory, models and some new findings* (pp.139–159). Boulder: Westview.

Taft, R. (1977). Coping with unfamiliar cultures. In N. Warren (Ed.), *Studies in cross-cultural psychology* (pp.121–153). New York: Academic Press.

Telles, P. (1980, March). *The psychosocial effects of immigration upon aging Cuban women*. Paper presented at the National Hispanic Feminist Conference, San Jose, CA.

Ticho, G. (1971). Cultural aspects of transference and counter-transference. *Bulletin of the Menninger Clinic*, 35, 313–334.

Torres-Matrullo, C. (1980). Acculturation, sex-role values and mental health among mainland Puerto Ricans. In A. Padilla (Ed.), *Acculturation: Theory, models and some new findings* (pp.111–137). Boulder: Westview.

9

Letters from V.: Adolescent Personality Development in Sociohistorical Context

with ABIGAIL J. STEWART

and CYNTHIA GÓMEZ

This article presents an analysis of 71 letters written over a period of 9 years by a young Latin-American woman, whom we shall call V., to one of her former teachers. The first letter was written in 1961, when she was 13; the last letter included in this study was written in 1970, when she was 22. This period corresponds not only with her adolescence but also with the most traumatic time in her life. At age 13, this young woman was abruptly separated from her parents when they were imprisoned for political reasons in the course of national upheaval in her country. A year later, with both her parents still in prison, she and her two younger brothers were sent to another, distant Latin-American country under the care of a family who had volunteered to be their guardians. When she next saw her parents, she was married and expecting her first child. One of V.'s main outlets for the pain, grief, frustration, and uncertainty of those years was writing letters to her former teacher, who had moved to the United States. Thus, the letters were written at the time the events described were happening and the feelings evoked by those events were being experienced.

The letters, then, provide firsthand information about the internal processes of this young woman as she dealt with traumatic losses from age 13. The analysis of the letters focuses on this young woman's psychological development as she struggled to integrate the traumatic loss of her parents and country and to adjust to the demands of adolescence and early adulthood.

Gordon Allport (1942) provided the framework for the methodology we used in this analysis; he practiced this method in his *Letters from Jenny* (1965). More recently, feminist scholars have encouraged the use of unpublished letters and journals as a valid method for studying and recovering the previously lost experience of women (e.g., Payne, 1983). Although not widely used in psychology (see Haviland, 1983; Sears, Lapidus, & Cozzens, 1978, for exceptions), this method can provide unique access to inner experience.

> Intimate letters, gushing forth from raw personal experience, have a unique fascination. Often better than fiction or biography, even than autobiography, they tell us what a particular concrete human life is like. The fascination is greater if the letters are written over a considerable period of time, presenting consecutively the inner narrative of a life as it unfolds. (Allport, 1965, p.v)

When the writer of letters is an adolescent, the "fascination" might be compounded by the firsthand access to the process of identity formation as it is experienced by the writer. Moreover, it may be that during adolescence journals and letters are more likely to be rich in inner experience precisely because they afford an opportunity for identity development and self-reflection. When, in addition, the writer is undergoing unusual or significant life experiences, psychological material may unfold over a period of time that could produce valuable insights about the particular individual, as well as about the impact of certain events on identity formation.

There are, of course, complexities in interpreting the significance of the psychological experience as recorded in letters.

> The use of letters in research . . . is complicated by the necessity of considering the personality of the recipient as well as that of the sender, the relationship existing between the two, and the topics of thought that comprise the exchange of letters. (Allport, 1942, p.108)

In the case of our analysis, the relationship—that of a former teacher and student—is important because we can assume that it is one in which the writer of the letters felt sufficient safety and acceptance to express strong and anxious feelings. In addition, because the recipient of the letters was older and could be trusted to have a "wiser," more adult perspective, V. could (and did) hope for help and advice in understanding her life situation. Nevertheless, the purpose of the present study is not to analyze the relationship per se but to assess one individual's adolescent personality development in the context of her social and personal situation. The study also provides a test of the applicability of one of the established theories of adolescent development—that of Erik Erikson—to the understanding of the identity development of an adolescent growing up under traumatic political/historical conditions.

According to Erikson (1963, 1968, 1982), the central psychosocial task of adolescence is identity formation; the next task—of young adulthood, but sometimes occurring earlier in women—is the establishment of a capacity for intimate commitment. The formation of identity and development of intimacy in turn prepare the way for the capacity for generativity, which becomes the central preoccupation at some later point in adulthood. Erikson views each developmental stage as the focus of an individual's preoccupations in turn, but he also acknowledges wide cultural and individual variations in the precise ages at which these stages occur. Moreover, he argues that some level of concern with each stage may be present even during periods in which the individual is primarily focused on another main concern.

Stewart, Franz, and Layton (1988) studied the applicability of Erikson's general model using diaries and letters written by Vera Brittain, a feminist pacifist novelist who recorded her traumatic experience of World War I in her autobiography, *Testament of Youth* (1933/1970). Over the course of Brittain's experience of the war, her identity, intimacy, and generativity concerns seemed to reflect both broad psychosocial development and specific reactions to traumatic and other events. Thus, for example, Brittain's concerns with identity were very high (and much higher than her other concerns), but generally decreasing, throughout her late adolescent years. In contrast, her concerns with intimacy and generativity gradually increased during this period. At the same time, her intimacy concerns waxed and waned in response to events in her love life, and her generativity concerns seemed influenced by changes in her work commitments. Finally, the sudden death of her fiancé in the war produced a dramatic increase in identity concerns.

On the basis of this analysis we might anticipate that traumatic loss may generally result in a recurrence of identity concerns or an arrest in psychosocial development. Alternatively, since the subject of our study is much younger than Brittain and had not tied her identity development to a love relationship as had Brittain, traumatic loss might precipitate premature or more rapid personality development. Most generally, then, we expect that, as for all adolescents, identity concerns will predominate over intimacy and generativity concerns throughout adolescence. Second, we expect that the ordinary course of psychosocial development will be evident (first increasing, then decreasing, identity concerns; increasing but lower intimacy, and then generativity, concerns). Third, we expect an accelerated timetable following emigration (i.e., early resolution of the identity crisis and early preoccupation with intimacy and generativity). Since emigration is an event that occurred in the course of development, we must try to assess whether it had effects over and above those attributable to age or the passage of time. Finally, we expect that major life events occurring during the course of adolescence (in this case, marriage and pregnancy) will also influence psychosocial preoccupations.

Method

Measuring Eriksonian Stage Concerns

The 71 letters written by V. were content-analyzed using the coding system developed by Stewart et al. (1988; see their article for full details of coding procedures and derivation of the categories). This coding system for analyzing personal documents was devised to measure personality development based on Erikson's stages of psychological development and specifically focuses on the early adult stages of identity, intimacy, and generativity. Within each broad stage there are subcategories, which include both global references and more specific themes (see Table 9.1 for an outline of the categories associated with each stage). Every expression of a theme in any way related to any of the three stages is coded for one of the subcategories making up the total score.

Broad references to identity are scored when identity concerns are expressed in very general ways. Thus, for example, V. wrote about her identity in this way when she referred to "the temperament I have" or said, "As each day passes, I am more sure of who I am" or "I don't understand myself." More specific themes were also expressed:

I began to doubt God's existence. (Values)

The truth is, nothing saddens me any more; I have changed again. . . . (Lack of sameness and continuity)

I have decided on a career in journalism. (Occupational role)

He is the first in his class and I am so little next to him. (Hero worship)

I am horribly sentimental. (Trait)

Similarly general and specific references to both intimacy and generativity were also reflected in the letters:

I love him too much. (General desire for intimacy)

We understand each other very well. (Shared identity)

In a few days I will be a mother—the thought leaves me dumbfounded. (General generativity)

The feeling that makes me panic is seeing myself not doing anything when the world needs so much. (Negative productivity)

TABLE 9.1   Coding Categories of Identity, Intimacy, and Generativity

Category definitions

I.   Identity
  1. *General concerns.* Preoccupation with broad self-definitional issues not scorable for more specific themes.
  2. *Sameness and continuity.* Expression of concern with one's relative continuity over time within a broader context of change.
  3. *Hero worship as a source of self-definition.* Attempts to define self via hero worship of others.
  4. *Traits. Awareness of stable characteristics.* Awareness of stable identity elements of self and others.
  5. *Integration and restructuring of identifications.* Rejection of some individual group identifications and acceptance of others.
  6. *Occupational role.* Expression of concern about choice of and commitment to an occupational role.
  7. *Preferences and tastes.* Definition of self expressed in terms of tastes and preferences or aversions.
  8. *Values.* Preoccupation with personal values, convictions, beliefs, and ideology.
  9. *Confirmation by intimates.* Discussion of intimate others' recognition and affirmation, or rejection, of aspects of the individual's identity.
  10. *Confirmation by society.* Discussion of affirmations or rejections by the "generalized other" or any nonintimate.
II. Intimacy
  1. *General concerns.* Expressions of concerns about forming close, committed relationships.
  2. *Shared identity.* Expressions of a sense of similarity and/or shared experience in a committed relationship.
  3. *Mutuality of devotion.* Expressions of the capacity for commitment to another person and a relationship.
  4. *Secure identity.* Expressions of concern or conviction about the capacity to retain an individual identity in the context of an intimate relationship.
  5. *"General" sexuality.* Expressions of concern about and/or capacity for a satisfying, full, sexual relationship in the context of intimate sharing.
III. Generativity
  1. *General concerns.* Expressions of concerns about making a lasting contribution, especially to future generations.
  2. *Caring.* Expressions of concern with the capacity to care for others.
  3. *Productivity.* Expressions of concern with developing and growing through creativity and/or productivity.
  4. *Need to be needed.* Expressions of an inner need to be needed by others.

The coding system provides a means of coding self-references but also allows for coding the writer's view of the identity, intimacy, and generativity concerns of another person. In addition, one can code statements the writer presents as others' views of him- or herself. These different types of references are distinguished within the scoring procedure, but all references to these themes are combined in the analyses presented here. In addition, references which are "positive" (expressing certainty or pleasure in these goals) and "negative" (expressing doubt or distaste) are separately coded by combined in these analyses. The vast majority of references to all three stages was positive in this case, and separate analyses of positive and negative subtotals for each stage revealed no difference in the patterns described here.

Coding Letters from V.

The data coded consisted of 71 letters written by V. in Spanish. Between 6 and 14 letters (an average of 10) were available for each year from 1961 through 1966. Twelve letters were available between 1967 and 1970. For purposes of establishing interrater reliability, several letters were randomly selected and translated into English. Two raters coded the English versions of the letters with high reliability; category agreement, which reflects agreement on both identification of the phrase as codable and assignment to a particular subcategory, was .92. In an effort to assess the effects of translation on coding, an additional reliability check was performed: One rater coded the English translation, while the other coded the Spanish version of the same letter. Although agreement was still quite high (above .83), most disagreements were a consequence of translation. In these cases, the meaning of self-descriptive statements was lost in the translated version. To ensure the more accurate coding, all letters were coded by the bilingual coder from the original Spanish. The coding was performed on letters arranged in a random order and blinded to date.

Developmental Analyses

Time-series analyses were performed on the total identity, intimacy, and generativity scores in order to assess overall developmental effects. Although the available data were not ideal, since they were not obtained at equal time intervals, the facts that they were produced over time and in substantial numbers make it reasonable to carry out such analyses. Because all of the letters were written by a single individual, the scores might be expected to be particularly vulnerable to serial dependency, or autocorrelation (see Judd & Kenny, 1981; Kenny & Judd, 1986). If present, autocorrelation can result in biased standard errors and tests of significance in time-series regression models. For each of the three models to be discussed below, we checked for the presence of first-, second-, and third-order autocorrelated residuals; no evidence of autocorrelation was found (autocorrelation estimates were .07, .08, and .05 for identity; .15, −.06, and .08 for intimacy; and −.07, .09, and −.07 for generativity, all not significant at p < .05). Overall, then, the checks we were able to perform for autocorrelated residuals did not indicate a problem and therefore we employed conventional multiple regression techniques to analyze the data (McCleary & Hay, 1980).

Life Event Analyses

The impact of three specific life events (emigration, marriage, new motherhood) was assessed by adding variables dummy-coded to asses time in terms of these events to the regression models (0 = pre-event, 1 = post-event). In this way, possible effects of those events over and above effects associated with time (or development) could be assessed.

Results

To compare the overall prevalence of each type of theme, we performed a one-way repeated measures analysis of variance (ANOVA) with type of theme as a repeated measures factor. Overall, it is clear that identity themes predominate, $\bar{x}$ = 7.46, SD = 4.86, with intimacy themes next most frequent, $\bar{x}$ = 5.41, SD = 4.33, and generativity themes least, $\bar{x}$ = 1.34, SD = 1.84; $F(2,70)$ = 56.49, $p < .001$.

Developmental Analysis

In separate hierarchical regression analyses for identity, intimacy, and generativity, we tested whether the effects of time, or development could best be captured by a linear, quadratic, or cubic regression equation. In all three cases, a quadratic equation provided the best fit to the data.

Identity. The best-fitting regression equation was as follows: Identity = 2.96 + .20 (Time)–0016 (Time Squared), where the significant tests for the linear and quadratic terms were $t(67)$ = 3.16, $p < .01$, and $t(67)$ = 2.83, $p < .01$, respectively. The R^2 for the model was .14, $p < .005$. The regression equation is plotted in Figure 9.1, which shows the predicted pattern of first increasing, then decreasing, preoccupation with identity themes.

Intimacy. The best fitting regression equation was: Intimacy = −.51 + .19 (Time).0009 (Time Squared), where the significant tests for the linear and quadratic terms were $t(67)$ = 4.32, $p < .001$, and $t(67)$ = 2.36, $p < .05$, respectively. The R^2 for the model = .48, $p < .001$. The equation for intimacy is plotted in Figure 9.2, which shows the predicted increase in these themes over the course of this period.

Generativity. The equation providing the best fit to the generativity scores was: Generativity = .73–.02 (Time) + .0006 (Time Squared). The linear term was not significant, $t(67)$ = −.28, *ns,* but the quadratic effect was $t(67)$ = 3.57, $p < .001$. The R^2 for the model was .53, $p < .001$. Results are plotted in Figure 9.3 and show the predicted low level of scores in the early period, with a sharp rise later.

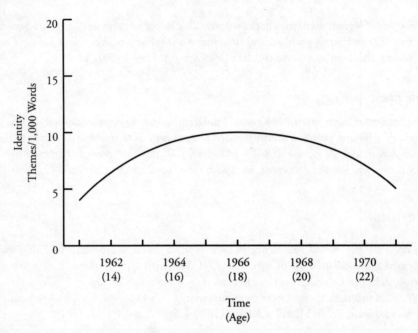

FIGURE 9.1   Identity Themes/1000 Words Expressed in V.'s Letters over Time (months)

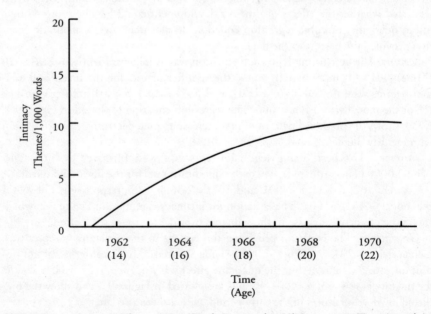

FIGURE 9.2   Intimacy Themes/1000 Words Expressed in V.'s Letters over Time (months)

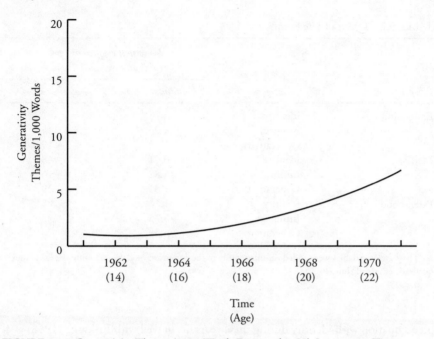

FIGURE 9.3   Generativity Themes/1000 Words Expressed in V.'s Letters over Time (months)

Impact of Life Events

In order to assess the separate impact of three important life events occurring during this period, each event was dummy-coded and the resulting three variables were added to the model including the linear and quadratic effects of time. These analyses provide an estimate of the impact of these three events over and above their association with age or the passage of time.

As seen in Table 9.2, emigration precipitated increased intimacy concerns, while parenthood acted to reduce those concerns from the level aroused by emigration. Marriage reduced concerns with identity and precipitated generativity concerns.

Discussion

V.'s Psychosocial Development

The letters V. wrote to her teacher and friend beginning at age 13 and continuing until age 22 included many themes which were codable for the three psychosocial preoccupations under study. Of these, identity preoccupations dominated most of the period, though they were most pronounced around ages 16 to 18. This primary

TABLE 9.2　Effects of Life Events

Life events	Category	Regression coefficients[a] for events on psychosocial scores	
		Unstandardized	*Standardized*
Emigration	Identity	.75	.07
	Intimacy	4.03	.43[**]
	Generativity	−.52	−.13
Marriage	Identity	−6.01	−.48[*]
	Intimacy	−1.82	−.16
	Generativity	−1.84	.39[*]
Parenthood	Identity	1.16	.05
	Intimacy	−5.75	−.27[*]
	Generativity	.53	.06

[a]These event variables were added simultaneously to the regression models, including the linear and quadratic effects of time.

[*]$p < .05$.

[**]$p < .01$.

preoccupation with identity during these years fits in well with Erikson's (1968) general description of the process of psychosocial development in adolescence. It should be noted, though, that Erikson has expressed conflicting views about the modal and ideal course of psychosocial development for women (Erikson, 1968, 1974). In some places he has suggested that identity formation is less an adolescent preoccupation for females and that instead females either do or should establish identities after the choice of an intimate life partner.

V. did express increasing preoccupation with intimacy issues over the course of the same period, and in the period between ages 17 and 22 she expressed nearly equal preoccupation with identity and intimacy issues. Finally, V. expressed little concern with generativity issues throughout the period, though she was clearly more interested in such issues in the later part of this period.

Overall, the pattern of V.'s scores suggests broad support for Erikson's theory that identity preoccupations are the focus of psychosocial development for adolescents, and that as they are resolved, and a secure identity established, they gradually give way to increasing intimacy concerns. However, it is interesting that the developmental trends are much stronger for intimacy and generativity than for identity. Perhaps the intensification of the identity preoccupation associated with emigration also resulted in an early resolution of the issue, permitting early development of intimacy concerns. Similarly, the increasing expression of generativity is consistent with Erikson's view that generativity will be the focus of psychosocial development once intimacy concerns have fully developed. Thus, despite the severity of her losses and her uprooting at the beginning of adolescence, V. (like Vera Brittain in Stewart et al.'s [1988] earlier analysis) seems to have experienced Erikson's hypothesized normal course of psychosocial development in terms of both individuation (identity) and connection with others (intimacy and generativity).

It is important to note, though, that V. may have expressed somewhat premature concerns with identity (high levels of concerns at least by age 14) and expressed an unexpectedly high level of preoccupation with intimacy—and even with generativity—a little later (by age 17 or so). Both in Vera Brittain's case and in present-day U.S. culture, identity concerns would be expected to dominate psychosocial development throughout much of the early 20s. Perhaps the particularities of V.'s cultural/historical situation would lead to her different pattern. For example, as an emigré, separated from her family, she was probably forced to define her identity more fully at an earlier age than contemporary U.S. adolescents. Alternatively, perhaps her early intense preoccupation with identity was one mechanism she used to cope with her loss of family and home country. This early identity preoccupation may in turn have prepared the way for an early resolution of the identity crisis and early concern with intimacy. Finally, given the extreme demands for adaptation V. faced, perhaps she drew—in the sheer fact of her extensive correspondence as well as in the themes she expressed—on her capacity for relationship and connection (intimacy and generativity) as a source of strength, even though they would more typically be less well developed at these ages. In any case, it seems likely that V.'s psychosocial development was importantly affected by her special situation even though this effect was not strong enough to derail the course of normal development.

Links Between Life Experiences and Psychosocial Development

One way to assess the likelihood that the course of V.'s psychosocial development was tied to her situation is to examine the patterns of preoccupation as a function of important life events. Analyses aimed at assessing the effect of life events over and above their association with time (or age) did suggest that both emigration and marriage had specific effects on the course of V.'s personality development. Emigration seems to have precipitated a concern with intimacy issues at an early point; this early preoccupation with intimacy may have encouraged V. to resolve—or foreclose—identity concerns very rapidly. V. herself viewed emigration as having had that effect:

I know that you know that I am only a child in body, that in the last few months there has been a radical change in me. It is not my choice, but I am not the same. I have been forced to become a grown woman at fourteen. (August 25, 1962)

Both loneliness and a sudden freedom from earlier fear that expressions of love and concern for others might endanger them (both of which were associated with her emigration) may partially account for the increase in intimacy themes.

V.'s marriage seems to have reduced her concerns with identity issues and increased her concerns with generativity, though it did not precipitate an increase in intimacy concerns. In fact, the biggest increase in intimacy seems to have substantially predated the marriage; perhaps the formal marriage reflected a resolution of this issue, with an earlier courtship period more reflective of an intimacy "crisis." It is unclear whether her reduced preoccupation with identity after her marriage should be understood as a reflection of her identity resolution (hence, no need to express the theme) or as a reflection on her marriage (as precluding further identity development, for the moment). It is interesting that V.'s increased generativity concerns were associated with her marriage and predated her motherhood (much as her intimacy concerns rose before her marriage, in association with her emigration), perhaps suggesting that this marriage provided a vehicle for generativity.

Finally, V.'s pregnancy and new motherhood were associated with relatively reduced preoccupation with intimacy but not with any changes in the age-related patterns for identity or generativity. Since V.'s early preoccupation with intimacy seems to have resulted from the extreme relational losses and loneliness associated with emigration, it is possible that she was less preoccupied with intimacy concerns after the birth of her first child because her needs for intimacy were gratified during that period by her small new family. Alternatively, V. may have experienced the demands of the motherhood role as inconsistent with intimacy concerns that might have been more centrally expressed in the marriage relationship.

Using Case Study Methods to Study Personality Development

In this study of a single individual, a long time-series involving one type of personal document (letters to a mentor) was available for analysis. We were fortunate to have a large number of letters that were relatively frank and open, covered a psychologically significant period (adolescence), and coincided with a number of important life events for this individual (emigration, marriage, motherhood). In an analysis like this in which we tried to separate the effects of age or psychological development from the effects of events, time-series designs can be very helpful. Such designs are particularly easy to interpret when, as here, we have more than one dependent variable (identity, intimacy, and generativity themes) expected to show different patterns. Thus, this design builds in "control" or "comparison" series.

There are, however, a number of difficulties with and limitations to the design we employed. For example, it is difficult to know whether emigration, marriage, and parenthood were in fact the psychologically significant life events for V. during this period. Perhaps engagement, completion of high school, or other unmeasured events were more important. The design also might be stronger if more than one type of document were available. Confirmation of the same pattern in diaries or letters to another recipient would provide a within-subject replication. Even more powerfully, identification of more than one individual with comparable time-series data available would build in a cross-subject replication. Finally, the ideal set of time-series analyses would include several different people who had experienced the same relevant events (in this case emigration, marriage, parenthood) at different ages or at the same ages but in different sequences (see discussions in Judd & Kenny, 1981; Higginbotham, West, & Forsyth, 1988).

Conclusion

Although the field of psychology as a whole has paid little attention to the impact of social events on psychological development (see, however, Elder, 1974; Stewart & Healy, 1989), the psychological effects of traumatic historical events manifest themselves in the lives of many individuals. Refugees from oppressive political regimes and survivors of the Holocaust are obvious examples. Psychologists' increased involvement in studying and trying to alleviate posttraumatic stress disorder in Vietnam veterans and the effects of international terrorism and the torture of political prisoners indicate a growing awareness of the importance of these issues for our field (see, e.g., Figley, 1978; Figley & McCubbin, 1983; Kelly, 1985; Rothblum & Cole, 1986). Our study sheds light on some of the experiences of an adolescent whose life was dramatically affected by a personally traumatic, politically motivated event.

Systematic content analysis of letters written in the course of adolescence and in the context of an open, accepting relationship seemed to have provided a valuable perspective on one young woman's personality development in this context. Overall, the analysis suggests that despite substantial challenges to adaptation and many personal losses V. experienced the normal sequence of adolescent psychosocial preoccupations and in that sense may be viewed as possessed of great "ego strength." Specifically, there are suggestions that V. drew on her capacity for relationships in making adaptations to both her losses and her development.

Our study sheds light on the process of identity development of one adolescent; as such, the results cannot be generalized to other children and adolescents developing under similar conditions. However, it is clear from this analysis that, at least for V. (as for one other adolescent, Vera Brittain, raised in a very different context), the traumatic events created by the political/historical circumstances under which she developed, while producing a definite impact on her psychosocial development, did not produce the destructive psychological effects that could have been anticipated (e.g., arrested psychological development, absence of preoccupation with developmentally appropriate issues, etc.). In future work it will be important to identify the personal and circumstantial factors that facilitate maintenance of normal personality development in the face of traumatic loss.

In this particular case, having a mentor and friend to correspond with may have played an important role. An additional feature of this study is that V. as well as her correspondent participated in its interpretation. They both reacted to the interpretations suggested by the quantitative analyses as presented in Discussion, and they both provided general information about the meaning of events in V.'s life. The interpretations presented were viewed by both women as consistent with their view of that period in V.'s life. No idea we felt was suggested by the data was rejected by either woman; moreover, both were able to offer supporting evidence from V.'s later life which increased our confidence in our conclusions. V. told us that she has never been in therapy. However, now in mid-adulthood, she believes that the writing of these letters and the presence of this woman correspondent were essential factors in her survival and psychological development at the time of crisis. The importance of friendships between women, and of mentors and role models for healthy psychological development, have been discussed in the literature (e.g.; Berzoff, 1985; Rubin, 1985).

Considering the importance given in Latin culture to relationships among women, and considering the intensity of political turmoil in Latin America, the notion that friendship between women can be valuable in enhancing psychological survival of traumatic events has implications for the psychology of Latin-American women, as well as for psychotherapy with women who have experienced traumatic losses due to historical events, as many Latin-American women have (e.g., Rodríguez-Nogués, 1983). The historical events relevant to V.'s life took place years ago, but similar events are still happening all over the world. Further study of the lives and personal documents of other children and adolescents developing under traumatic political conditions will clarify which aspects of V.'s development were unique to her and which may be more general. It is through studies like this, of resilience and survival, that we may identify the sorts of interventions which may prevent unnecessary pain and suffering in the lives of children and adolescents whose development is severely challenged by the sociopolitical world they inhabit.

Notes

Reprinted from Espín, O.M., Stewart, A.J., & Gómez, C. (1990). Letters from V.: Adolescent Personality Development in Sociohistorical Context. *Journal of Personality*, 58(2), 347–364.

In an effort to protect V.'s privacy, as well as that of her correspondent, only general information about her life situation and experience is presented, but all information given is accurate.

References

Allport, G. (1942). *The use of personal documents in psychological science*. New York: Social Science Research Council.

Allport, G. (1965). *Letters from Jenny*. New York: Harcourt Brace Jovanovich.

Berzoff, J. (1985). *Valued female friendships: Their functions in female adult development*. Doctoral dissertation, Boston University.

Brittain, V. (1970). *Testament of youth*. New York: Wideview. (Original work published in 1933)

Elder, G. (1974). *Children of the great depression.* Chicago: University of Chicago Press.

Erikson, E.H. (1963). *Childhood and society.* New York: Norton.

Erikson, E.H. (1968). *Identity: Youth and crisis.* New York: Norton.

Erikson, E.H. (1974). *Once more the inner space: Letter to a former student.* In J. Strouse (Ed.), *Women and analysis: Dialogues on psychoanalytic views of femininity* (pp.365–387). New York: Dell.

Erikson, E.H. (1982). *The life cycle completed: A review.* New York: Norton.

Figley, C.R. (Ed.). (1978). *Stress disorders among Vietnam veterans.* New York: Brunner/Mazel.

Figley, C.R., & McCubbin, H.I. (Eds.). (1983). *Stress and the family: 2. Coping with catastrophe.* New York: Brunner/Mazel.

Haviland, J. (1983). Thinking and feeling in Woolf's writing: From childhood to adulthood. In C. Izard, J. Kagan, & R. Zajonc (Eds.), *Emotions, cognitions, and behavior* (pp. 515–546). New York: Cambridge University Press.

Higginbotham, H.N., West, S.G., & Forsyth, D.R. (1988). *Psychotherapy and behavior change: Social, cultural, and methodological perspectives.* New York: Pergamon.

Judd, C.M., & Kenny, D.A. (1981). *Estimating the effects of social interventions.* Cambridge, UK: Cambridge University Press.

Kelly, W.E. (Ed.). (1985). *Post-traumatic stress disorder and the war veteran patient.* New York: Brunner/Mazel.

Kenny, D.A., & Judd, C.M. (1986). Consequences of violating the independent assumption in analysis of variance. *Psychological Bulletin, 99,* 422–431.

McCleary, R., & Hay, R.A. (1980). *Applied time series analysis.* Beverly Hills, CA: Sage.

Payne, K. (Ed.). (1983). *Between ourselves: Letters between mothers and daughters.* Boston: Houghton Mifflin.

Rodríguez-Nogués, L. (1983). Psychological effects of premature separation from parents in Cuban refugee girls: A retrospective study (Doctoral dissertation, Boston University, 1983). *Dissertation Abstracts International, 44,* 1619B.

Rothblum, E., & Cole, E. (Eds.). (1986). *Another silenced trauma: Twelve feminist therapists and activists respond to one woman's recovery from war.* New York: Harrington Park Press.

Rubin, L. (1985). *Just friends.* New York: Harper & Row.

Sears, R. R., Lapidus, D., & Cozzens, C. (1978). Content analysis of Mark Twain's novels and letters as a biographical method. *Poetics, 7,* 155–175.

Stewart, A.J., Franz, C., & Layton, L. (1988). The changing self: Using personal documents to study lives. *Journal of Personality, 56,* 41–74.

Stewart, A.J., & Healy, J.M., Jr. (1989). Linking individual development and social change. *American Psychologist, 44,* 30–42.

10

Traumatic Historical Events and Adolescent Psychosocial Development: Letters from V.

In this chapter I present and analyze the experience of a Latin American adolescent who was separated from her parents because of her country's political circumstances. The study is based on the data provided by seventy-one letters written by this young woman, here called V. These letters span the period of nine years, while V. was between the ages of thirteen and twenty-two, covering not only her adolescence but also the most traumatic period in her life. At age thirteen, V. was abruptly separated from her parents when they were imprisoned as political dissidents. A year later, while both her parents were still in prison, they decided to send their children to another country. There she was cared for by a family who had volunteered to be her guardians. Thus, to the trauma created by political events and her parents' imprisonment, the traumas of uprooting, migration, and adaptation to foster parents were added. After nearly a decade of separation, when she next saw her parents, V. was married and expecting her first child. Her primary outlet for the pain, grief, frustration, and uncertainty of those years was writing letters to one of her former teachers who had also emigrated. This teacher was herself a young twenty-two-year-old woman at the time this correspondence started.

A previous study of these letters (Espín, Stewart, & Gómez, 1990) focused on the applicability of Erikson's (1963, 1968) general model of psychosocial development to this adolescent's development. That study employed a coding system for analyzing personal documents based on Erikson's stages of psychosocial development devised by Stewart, Franz, and Layton (1988). A time-series analysis of the data provided by the coded letters showed that "despite the severity of her losses and her uprooting at the beginning of adolescence, V. . . . seems to have experienced Erikson's hypothesized normal course of psychosocial development" (Espín et al., 1990. p.358) while, simultaneously, some unique features, such as "an unexpectedly high level of preoccupation with intimacy—and even with generativity" (p.358) were present.

In that study, my coauthors and I concluded that "in future work it will be important to identify the personal and circumstantial factors that facilitate maintenance of normal personality development in the face of traumatic loss" (Espín et al., 1990, p.362). This chapter is an attempt at identifying those factors, using a qualitative approach to the data, thus allowing V.'s words to present the reader with her process as she described it. My analysis focuses on themes of coping and resilience in addition to references to Erikson's theory.

Reading these letters we witness the writer's development process as she experienced it. Her description of and reflections about her life experiences provide firsthand understanding of the impact of historical/political events on her life.

As Allport (1942) argued, "In the analysis of letters, the psychological an historical methods fuse" (p.109). Reading these letters, it is difficult to disentangle the effects of historical/political events on V.'s life course from her individual psychological development. Indeed, is it impossible to understand individual psychological development without considering the specific historical circumstances in which that individual is immersed. It is also problematic to determine the interplay between the two because it is difficult to "specify the process by which historical events are manifested in the life course, [although it is evident that] psychological questions are posed by knowledge of the particular historical situation and its life course effects" (Elder, 1981, p.97). That is why research on individuals who have experienced traumatic historical/political events

can yield knowledge unlikely to be gained from more traditional samples—knowledge about psychosocial development under conditions of concentrated and chronic adversity, knowledge about the factors that influence whether adversity will or will not be overcome, and finally, knowledge that is not only important for developmental theory but essential for the formulation of social policy. (Jessor, 1993, p.119)

V.'s individual experience, then, is invaluable. Although it cannot help us disentangle the effect of historical/political events on all individuals, it does provide a concrete case through which to describe the lived experience of one adolescent.

V.'s adult psychological make up most probably would not have been the same without the attendant cultural/political/ historical events that framed her life. As a thirteen-year-old, before the events that transformed the course of her life, V. was bright, vivacious, and slightly shy. Through her childhood and early adolescence she appeared to be reasonably adjusted, did well in school, and was well liked by her peers. Most probably, her ability to withstand the traumatic events of her life was related to her previous adjustment and maturity. As an adult V. has had a productive, apparently healthy life. She has been successful in both her personal and professional life. Yet the question remains: How did historical conditions interact with her biography to create her individual psychology? Moreover, is there any "biography" outside of historical events for V. or anyone else? Most people are not aware that they are immersed in a particular historical context. For most of us it is only when that context becomes traumatic or in other ways "unusual" that we start questioning its psychological effects (Espín, 1992). In this chapter, I probe the interplay between history and psychology by focusing on the experience of one individual.

The Impact of History

From V.'s letters we know that during her adolescence, when the upheaval was most intense, she was acutely aware of her historical circumstances. Her letters include regular reference to the effects of political/historical events on her everyday life and on her relationships with people. She writes frequently of the fear and anxiety created by those events, both directly and through veiled and "encoded" allusions that she trusts her correspondent to interpret. From her first letters, references to the relationship between events in her life and political upheaval are constant. As she presents, describes, and interprets those events, she reveals her unique mixture of unusual maturity and childish expression. Simultaneously, she exposes her internal anguish and concern for the well-being of the adults no longer able to provide her with protection because of their own helplessness.

In her first letter, written before her emigration, she tells her correspondent:

> I would love to be with you, but I would not judge myself to be a good person if I left my parents now when they need me the most. Also I have been very agitated these days because my grandfather was taken to a farm for vacation. It was short, but I was terrified as hell. (July 15, 1961)

This story about a "farm" her grandfather is "taken to for vacation" is, in fact, a veiled description of his recent brief arrest and unexpected release. It terrifies her because with her parents already in prison, she fears for her fate if her grandparents are also imprisoned for an extended period of time.

The depth of her terror and the intensity of her anxiety come through in words that seem almost unlike a thirteen-year-old's:

> We are OK, but my parents are still in the hospital and I am really desperate and cannot take it anymore. Only belief in God sustains me.(October 6, 1961)

This time "hospital" represents the prison. In this letter, as in many others, God is seen as the only source of consolation, strength, and meaning to mitigate the traumatic experience. The situation was indeed terrifying for a thirteen-year-old living in a context where rumors were the only source of information:

> I went to see my father on Wednesday. But I am very nervous because under each section of [the small island where the men's prison is located] they have placed 25,000 pounds of dynamite. So there are 100,000 pounds under the place. You can imagine what it is for, so that makes me very nervous. (June 11, 1961)

In the first letter she writes after leaving her country she explicitly articulates her fears and the events' impact on her life. In this letter, the psychological transformation that resulted from her early losses begins to manifesting itself:

> I have decided to leave my country and come to this country only because my parents were desperate for me to do so. However, it makes me feel like a coward. I feel bad not being able to do anything. My hands are tied, although I would be willing to give my life for my country and for God. That is why I feel desperate not being able to do anything about the horrible political regime in our country. I have wanted to say this to you for a long time, but I could not do it while I was there: I could have endangered my parents . . . I know you understand that I am serious about these words that I need so much to say to someone. I know you know that I am only a child in body, that in the last few months there has been a radical change in me. It is not my choice, but I am not the same as I was: I have been forced to become a grown woman at fourteen. (August 24, 1962)

Indeed, her letters reveal unusual maturity for her age. She perceives that the traumatic events have pushed her development beyond what was expected at her age for other adolescents of her culture and social class. This letter, perhaps more than any other, illustrates her uncanny ability to analyze her experience. It also presents with clarity one of the themes that reappear constantly in the letters: The wishes of others and the will of God are at the center of her life decisions and inform the acceptance of her fate.

During nine years of letter writing, V. never met her correspondent face to face. Their eventual meeting was cathartic for V. As is common for trauma victims, reviewing the experiences after several years fosters a sense of integration and healing of the painful memories (e.g., Herman, 1992). The encounter with her correspondent facilitated this process and fostered a sense of reconciliation with the past. This process may or may not have happened without this visit, but if nothing else, the visit and long hours of conversation after so many years of letter writing facilitated the opportunity for the reviewing and integration of the painful events.

Immediately after their first visit, V. reflected on the impact of these historical/political events on her life course:

I believe that today I have hated [all those events and the political leaders who have created them] the most. It is terrible to have to live away from someone who can understand us just because events beyond our control have determined our fate and where we
are to live. (February 13, 1970)

She differentiated between positive and negative results of her experiences. Not
everything in the forced migration and loss of country was destructive to her:

I guess that I can also thank [the political leaders I hate] for good things in my life and
even my happiness. If I had met my husband in our country, he probably would have
never talked to me. Not only because I had more money than him but also because I
would not have lowered my social status for his sake. In fact, thanks to these horrible
events I have learned that money is not worth much and neither are social position and
family name. As you can see, I seem to owe [those political leaders] more than one thing
in spite of everything else. (March 4, 1970)

Yet her pain cannot be forgotten that easily. As often happens with grief, any event
may trigger it again. Years after her emigration, a few months after the visit of her
correspondent, V. wrote:

I am watching a film that takes place in our country about forty years ago. I am seeing
familiar views of that all too familiar land. It seems impossible that such simple things
after so many years can move us so much. It is as if I had left only yesterday. The pain
and the memories are there all over again. (May 8, 1970)

V.'s Psychosocial Development

Many theories have been proposed for the study of adolescent psychosocial development. Of these Erikson's (1963, 1968) is probably the best known and provided a
valuable theoretical frame for an earlier study (Espín et al., 1990) of these letters.
"Overall the pattern of V.'s [development] suggests broad support for Erikson's theory that identity preoccupations are the focus of psychosocial development for adolescents, and that as they are resolved, and a secure identity established, they gradually give way to increasing intimacy concerns" (Espín et al., 1990, p.358). However,
in V.'s case, "it is interesting that the developmental trends are much stronger for intimacy and generativity than for identity" (Espín et al., 1990, p.358). Yet overall,
"despite the severity of her losses and her uprooting at the beginning of adolescence,
V. . . . seems to have experienced Erikson's hypothesized normal course of psychosocial development in terms of both individuation (identity) and connection with others (intimacy and generativity)" (Espín et al., 1990, p.358).

Themes of *identity* appear consistently in V.'s letters. She expresses these concerns
in several ways. As with other adolescents, career concerns emerge as an expression of
her search for identity.

You may think that I change my mind easily because in a recent letter I told you that I wanted to study Psychology. But it is my worse subject this year, so I have realized that God does not want me there and I have decided for journalism . . . Something in writing has a powerful attraction for me. I think writing about things that are important is something that fulfills me. (March 25, 1965)

Her career concerns intermingle with considerations about how best to be of service to God and others. In the same letter, she says:

Let's see if I can find in a newspaper the most effective place to work for Christ . . . To help others see the injustice in which some people live is also something that does not let me remain silent. And I think a newspaper is the best means to help others see things. (March 25, 1965)

She also expressed concerns about her identity through statements about herself, often portrayed in a negative light. References to her personal deficiencies serve as running commentary throughout the letters:

I am so stupid! The truth is that I deserve everything that is happening to me (February 5, 1963); I am intolerable, nothing comes out right because of my own fault. I am boring, silly, and stupid and you must be tired of this ridiculous friend (June 10, 1966).

Only once in a while does a positive comment slip through, but not without being immediately followed by some of the usual negative comments about herself:

At this point I am beginning to believe (please don't think I am vain) that I am pretty, even though I continue to be shy and easily embarrassed. (December 5, 1965)

It is possible that some of this self-criticism may have been a normal part of adolescent identity testing, an initially awkward and exaggerated effort at gaining a sense of perspective on aspects of her own character. At the same time, V.'s comments appear to have been part of a maneuver to achieve mastery over a chaotic, painful, and confusing situation by attributing all difficulties to personal deficiencies that could be more or less easily overcome. As conflicts and difficulties arose, it was easier for V. to blame herself and her deficiencies rather than blame others or confront the reality that she was immersed in a situation completely beyond her control.

In spite of these negative self-appraisals, she was sensitive to nuances of feelings, to her own internal states, and to others. Statements about who she is and who she is in relation to others appear more frequently in the letters than any other theme, revealing her adolescent overriding concern with identity, and to a lesser degree, intimacy. At times her "self-analysis" helps her avoid acknowledging further losses. For example, when her correspondent leaves their country, she wrote:

You know I am stupid . . . like when I didn't want to go to the airport to say good-by to you, just because I was embarrassed. I don't know how to express my feelings, I never do. (July 7, 1961)

Oftentimes, her "self-analysis" comforts her in the face of loss, as when she left her country:

> I am perfectly ok and I haven't even cried. I don't even know myself; I am surprised because I have never been strong . . . I feel completely mature and I am not just saying this to say something . . . I have had to become a grown woman at 14. (August 25, 1962)

V.'s concerns with *intimacy* are expressed in her letters in reference to boyfriends, classmates, and other friends. Her first mention of a boyfriend has a young adolescent's characteristic naïvete:

> What's happening is that I am in love even if I am too young for that. But I guess this is something that cannot be avoided or resisted. (January 5, 1963)

Three years later, in letters where she mentions her future husband, she shows increased maturity in her understanding of the meaning of love and commitment. She has become a young woman making significant life decisions on the basis of relationships:

> I have made the decision to get married a few months after I finish high school. He is good and intelligent. But I am scared. I am scared of confronting life, but this is the decision. I already bought the graduation shoes that will be my wedding shoes too. (June 10, 1966)

Throughout the letters, V. expresses intimacy concerns vividly in the context of her relationship with her correspondent. Their friendship, through correspondence, provides a very important source of strength and emotional support for V.:

> If you only knew how much I would like to be with you, because I love you and miss you more than you can believe it. I never really considered you as a teacher but as a friend even if I never said it because I was embarrassed to say so. (July 15, 1961)

Generativity issues are also present in her early letters as she reveals her concern for her parents. Later, this theme reemerges when she talks about her children. Through their years of correspondence, she also expressed care for her correspondent and for others mentioned in the letters:

> You are living alone in that place and that makes me upset. It is not fair that you have to be alone. I would give anything to be there with you for a while. I don't know if I am conceited but I think that you would be happy to have me bugging you for a couple of months. (February 26, 1965)

Throughout the letters V.'s constant concern for others, and her minimizing of her own feelings, fits a very typical "female pattern." Miller (1986) and Gilligan (1982) among others have described this pattern. They identified it as one of women's strengths, but clearly this pattern also has significant drawbacks for women (e.g., Kaschak, 1992).

Coping with Loss

For persons like V., as for others in traumatic and catastrophic social situations, a variety of protective mechanisms prevent the individual from realizing the gravity of the occasion (Allport, 1942; Rodríguez-Nogués, 1983). They may show little or no reaction for weeks, even years, (Herman, 1992; Parkes, 1972; Rodríguez-Nogués, 1983) if the bereavement occurs at a time when they are confronted with important tasks. The same pattern is present when there is a need for maintaining the morale of others.

Research suggests this can be a positive form of adjustment to a traumatic situation. Rodríguez-Nogués (1983) studied Cuban girls who emigrated to the United States as unaccompanied minors. She found they usually denied their actual losses and concomitant psychological pain at the time of the events. This tended to create a delayed grief reaction and posttraumatic effects but also facilitated their functioning at the time of the events. Similarly, as events transformed the course of V.'s life, she suffered a few minor psychosomatic reactions. Yet, on the whole she seems to have coped with the situation without further complications.

Clearly, V. experienced an acute sense of loss in early adolescence when her parents were imprisoned and she left them and her country. When confronted with loss, children, adolescents, or adults may progress though psychosocial stages by developing new bonds to special individuals. This is one of the most effective strategies for coping with the loss of significant relationships and familiar places and the threats to identity imposed by migration (Espín, 1987). V.'s early capacity for intimacy served her well. It provided her with skills to establish new bonds. Demonstrably, her relationship with her teacher/correspondent/long-term friend, flourished. This bond is particularly noteworthy because maintaining friendship through letters is not a highly valued skill in the modern world. The relationship V. established with the nuns and classmates at school also contributed to her emotional survival. It is interesting to note that, with the exception of her future husband, it appears that all her significant relationships were with women.

Loss and grief affect one's image of oneself (Parkes, 1972), as V.'s letters well illustrate. Yet, her attribution of all negative events to herself, despite the pain and self-negation involved, paradoxically provided her with a sense of control over the situation. Attributing negative events to herself was preferable to a total sense of helplessness in the face of uncontrollable events. Thus in the letters she actively denies her suffering or copes with her losses by attributing her painful feelings and experiences to personal deficiencies or to the privilege of having been especially chosen by God. She never faults the reality of the situation or others' wrongdoing.

Her interactions with her foster mother vividly illustrate how she coped with the loss of her mother's love:

> I am really intolerable today and I am about to cry because something simple happened. I asked my "aunt" to fix some clothes for me because they were hand outs from others and very old fashioned and she told me I was too proud. I might be wrong to take her

rejection too much at heart but you know I am too sensitive and easily hurt. Please don't feel sorry for me. What happens is that I am only 15 years old and even if my situation is not so bad, sometimes I explode. (January 18, 1963)

A few months later she wrote in a similar vein:

I don't talk about feeling bad because everything is only in my nervous system. Besides, I am embarrassed to ask them for help. For example, last night I was throwing up in the bathroom. My "aunt" came to the door and when she found out that it was me and not her daughter, she just left. I felt bad. It is horrible to miss your mother's love. But, on the other hand, perhaps my aunt did not think it was important. And you know that I am extremely sentimental and extremely proud. Don't think that it is I am depressed, it is just how I am. (May 3, 1965)

Significantly, V.'s pejorative self-descriptions and negative self-evaluations contradict her actual accomplishments and positive relationships with others. For example, her school grades were always high, her classmates elected her "queen" of the class, the nuns in her school were fond of her and treated her with great kindness, and she had several boyfriends during adolescence. She also belonged to a theater group and was accepted and loved by friends. Other positive events occurred in her life. However, she consistently uses negative self statements, apparently to deny the intensity of her pain and losses. Alternatively, her denial of her true feelings may have fueled her negative self-perception. Even when she is unable to deny the felt impact of her experiences she still tries to explain those feelings away:

I don't know what is happening to me but I feel empty regardless of what I do. I know that I have a normal life, but I am just tired of this. (August 9, 1966)

V. has yet another positive interpretation for her pain. She identifies it as God's will, even God's special choosing of her. Her intense belief in God is the only relief from a pain that cannot be explained in everyday terms by an adolescent. Her spirituality seems to afford her another nurturing and wise "parent" in God, through whom she feels "chosen" and uniquely loved.

I know that God doesn't want me to be a coward, but I have terrible moments and today is one of them. (March 29, 1964)

Many months later she reasons similarly:

These problems are killing me but without problems I would not consider myself happy, because if God is sending me this it must be because he trusts that I am going to respond in a good way. (November 19, 1965)

Yet another way she expresses her difficulties is through recounting some of her peers' experiences. She refers to a girl mentioned by her correspondent whose mother has recently died. Her empathy is all the more striking as she does not know this girl:

You don't know how much she must be suffering even though she may not have told you. (May 3, 1965)

Likely, V. is talking about herself and letting her correspondent know that she has not fully revealed the hardest parts of her experience.

In another instance, V. refers to a friend who may marry to escape a painful home situation. V. insists that she will never fall into this trap, no matter how difficult her own situation with her foster parents might become. She describes in great detail what this girl's feelings and doubts must be and expounds on why it is wrong for this girl to marry despite the chance of resolution for immediate tensions. In fact, V.'s long description of this girl's situation is a clear description of her own temptation to marry her boyfriend too soon in order to escape her foster home.

The Resolution Phase

Despite rationalizations to the contrary, V. married a few months after finishing high school. Although this early marriage may have foreclosed some possibilities, it certainly was an adaptive solution to her problems at that point in time. Indeed, it allowed her to start a new life with someone who loved her after all those years of feeling unloved and barely tolerated by her foster parents. Almost a year later, when she was ready to give birth to her first child, her parents were released from prison and joined her in exile.

As previously mentioned, her correspondent visited her for the first time several years later. This two-week visit served to reaffirm their long-distance friendship and to reintegrate memories of V.'s traumatic adolescent years. At the same time, the additional separation after this visit prompted an intense reactivation of V.'s feelings of loss.

Upon their reunion, V. experienced a clear and direct acknowledgement of what the initial separation had meant for her. She realized the significance the correspondence had in sustaining her through her adolescence and traumatic losses and separation from her parents. In other words, it became evident that the validation of her pain provided by this friendship had been an essential and sustaining factor during V.'s adolescence.

> One of the most disconcerting effects of your visit is that I have realized how influential you have been in my life without even knowing it. I realize now that I started changing my ways of being with people the moment you started to be concerned about my things. I think that has been decisive in my life. Do you realize what that means? I have reached the conclusion that a lot of what is good in me I owe to you. (February 21, 1970)

Clearly, writing these letters and receiving support and comfort through them was a saving grace in V.'s development. Yet her own capacity for deep interaction at a very early age made this relationship possible, for just as clearly, the sustaining power of this relationship cannot only be attributed to the efforts of her correspondent.

Implications of this Case Study

The established theories of psychological development presume an environment characterized by political stability, in which "environment" is equated with parental behavior. These theories do not take into consideration the eventuality of disruptive sociohistorical events and their impact on "normal" development. Obviously, dealing with the common tasks of psychological development while dealing with traumatic sociopolitical events complicates these tasks for children and adolescents. As Erikson (1964) argued, "The danger of any period of large-scale uprooting and transmigration is that exterior crises will, in too many individuals and generations, upset the hierarchy of developmental crises and their built-in correctives; and [make the developing individual] lose those roots that must be planted firmly in meaningful life cycles" (p.96).

Violent or abrupt political events produce traumatic experiences that psychologically affect the lives of children and adolescents who undergo them. Ironically, the focus on the physical safety of both children and adults may divert attention from considerations about their psychological well-being. Usually, psychological services or research studies tailored to these populations focus on victims or survivors who manifest serious emotional maladjustment. Survivors who are reasonably adjusted, like those who remain relatively psychologically unscathed, seldom attract the attention of psychologists and are frequently left to their own devices.

The friendship between V. and her correspondent may have buffered the impact of her losses and may have protected V. from the additional trauma that could have been created by surrounding her experience with silence. The historical events relevant to V.'s life took place years ago, but similar events are still happening all over the world. The notion that friendship with a trusted adult can be valuable in enhancing psychological survival has implications for the lives of children and adolescents whose development is severely challenged by the sociopolitical world they inhabit.

This chapter has presented the case of one individual who found her own path through a series of traumatic events precipitated by historical/political conditions. In constructing that path, her correspondence with another woman a few years older, a former teacher turned lifelong friend, acted as an anchoring force. This ongoing conversation, together with V.'s previous psychological health and spiritual groundedness, provided her with the strength to cope with the traumatic events of her adolescence.

It is apparent that for V., as for other individuals under her circumstances, the encounter between individual and society involved a transformation in subjectivity. Her understanding of who she is has been forever marked by those traumatic events. However, it is almost impossible to disentangle what the pure effect of those events may have been. The person who could have been without those events never came to be. Paradoxically, because we are dealing with the absence of any evident pathology or posttraumatic stress disorder, it is hard to determine what the consequences of the traumatic events were for V. But we do know that "the self is the sum of an individual's changing internal conversations, the forecastings, the recollections and the wishes, the voices that make up our intrapsychic life" (Gagnon, 1992, p.239) and "self-understanding is always shaped by culture. The tales we tell each other about who we are and might yet become are individual variations on the narrative templates our culture deems intelligible" (Ochberg, 1992, p.214) and on the limitations that historical events force upon us. V.'s narrative of the events of her life as transmitted through her adolescent letters is but one individual's conversation with herself through her conversation with a trusted friend. Because she was a gifted and unusually mature adolescent, she was able to make sense of her experiences in her own way and avail herself of the friendship and support provided by this correspondence.

V.'s normal life and adjustment in adulthood conceal a difficult route and reveal her strength. Other less fortunate children and adolescents subjected to similar traumatic events may respond differently or resort to other strategies to cope with trauma. But although only a single individual's story, V.'s story as presented through her correspondence is a tribute to human strength and resilience.

Notes

Reprinted from Espín, O.M. (1994). Traumatic Historical Events and Adolescent Psychosocial Development: Letters from V. In C.E. Franz & A.J. Stewart (Eds.), *Women Creating Lives: Identities, Resilience, and Resistance* (pp.187–198). Boulder: Westview.

References

Allport, G. (1942). *The use of personal documents in psychological science.* New York: Social Science Research Council.

Elder, G.H. (1981). History and the life course. In D. Bertaux (Ed.), *Biography and the life course: The life history approach in the social sciences* (pp.77–115) Beverly Hills, CA: Sage.

Erikson, E.H. (1963). *Childhood and society.* New York: Norton.

Erikson, E.H. (1964). *Insight and responsibility.* New York: Norton.

Erikson, E.H. (1968). *Identity, youth, and crisis.* New York: Norton.

Espín, O.M. (1987) Psychological impact of migration on Latinas: Implications for psychotherapeutic practice. *Psychology of Women Quarterly,* 11, 489–503.

Espín, O.M. (1992). Roots uprooted: The psychological impact of historical/political dislocation. In E. Cole, O.M. Espín, & E. Rothblum (Eds.), *Refugee women and their mental health: Shattered societies, shattered lives* (pp.9–20). New York: Haworth.

Espín, O.M., Stewart, A.J., & Gómez, C. (1990). Letters from V.: Adolescent personality development in socio-historical context. *Journal of Personality,* 58, 347–364.

Gagnon, J.H. (1992). The self, its voices, and their discord. In C. Ellis & M. Flagerty (Eds.), *Investigating subjectivity: Research on lived experience* (pp.221–243). Newbury Park, CA: Sage.

Gilligan, C. (1982). *In a different voice.* Cambridge, MA: Harvard University Press.

Herman, J. (1992). *Trauma and recovery.* New York: Basic Books.

Jessor, R. (1993). Successful adolescent development among youth in high-risk settings. *American Psychologist, 48,* 117–126.

Kaschak, E. (1992). *Engendered lives: A new psychology of women's experience.* New York: Basic Books.

Miller, J.B. (1986). *Toward a new psychology of women* (2nd ed.). Boston: Beacon.

Ochberg, R.L. (1992). Social insight and psychological liberation. In G. Rosenwald & R. Ochberg (Eds.), *Storied lives: The cultural politics of self-understanding* (pp.214–230). New Haven, CT: Yale University Press.

Parkes, C. M. (1972). *Bereavement: Studies of grief in adult life.* New York: International University Press.

Rodríguez-Nogués, L. (1983). Psychological effects of premature separation from parents in Cuban refugee girls: A retrospective study (Doctoral dissertation, Boston University, 1983). *Dissertation Abstracts International, 44,* 1619B.

Stewart, A.J., Franz, C., & Layton, L. (1988). The changing self: Using personal documents to study lives. *Journal of Personality, 56,* 41–74.

11

Spiritual Power and the Mundane World: Hispanic Female Healers in Urban U.S. Communities

Both men and women exercise the role of healer in Hispanic communities, and many recognized healers are women (Garrison, 1977, 1982; Harwood, 1977; Trotter, 1982). But to my knowledge, the development, role, and status of Hispanic women healers have not been studied. The prominence of women as healers suggests that the relationship of the Hispanic woman healer to her community should be a focus of such a study. How does a woman become a healer in the Hispanic community in the United States? Does her new role contradict her status as a Hispanic woman? Does a woman healer transcend cultural definitions of her feminine role without actually challenging them? How does each woman make sense of the supernatural in her own life?

This study is based on life history interviews and participant observation I conducted in 1983 of ten Hispanic women identified as healers and currently living in urban centers in the continental United States (Espín, 1983). The data consist of participants' self-perceptions and personal process. Factors not directly related to their lives (such as the characteristics or needs of their clients) were not explored. The interviews were transcribed and I sought patterns in the group that were revealed in the analysis of the transcripts. All interviews were conducted in Spanish.

Of the ten women interviewed, eight are Cuban-born, one is Peruvian, and one is Venezuelan. The predominance of Cubans in my sample reflects the fact that most of the interviews took place in Miami, Florida, where most of the Latin community is Cuban. In fact, one of the non-Cuban interviewees volunteered that she had made a conscious effort to change her accent and vocabulary to approximate those of her Cuban clientele.

The healers of this study subscribe either to *santería* or to charismatic Catholicism. Of the two non-Cubans interviewed, one is a *santera* and the other is a Catholic charismatic healer. *Santería* is a syncretic belief system based on Yoruba religion and Catholicism. It developed in Cuba for several centuries among the black slaves and has spread throughout the general population in the past three centuries (González-Wippler, 1975; Sandoval, 1975, 1979; Halifax & Weidman, 1973). Charismatic Catholicism is a form of Pentecostalism, with Catholic dogmatic content and institutional allegiance to Catholicism (McGuire, 1982; McDonnell, 1976). It has spread among Roman Catholics in the past few years.

The healers of this study ranged from twenty-two to ninety years of age, with a mean age of fifty-two. Four are married, two are divorced, one is a widow, and three have never been married. Five have adult children, three have grandchildren, and one has several great-grandchildren. Four have received formal education in the United States: one has a master's degree, one has a bachelor's degree, one has a few years of college education, and another is in the process of obtaining a bachelor's degree. Questions about formal education were not included in the interviews, but information on this topic was volunteered by the interviewees.

I compensated the healers for participating in this study by engaging their services on my behalf (e.g., oracle reading, prayers). Since I could not pay them for the interviews, I purchased a "consultation" to demonstrate respect for their skills and to pay them indirectly for their collaboration. Needless to say, these *consultas* provided additional opportunities for participant observation and thus an additional source of data.

Selection of Hispanic Female Healers

In response to my questions about how these women became healers, three main factors emerge from their life histories: the "calling" to a healing role by events that are interpreted as manifestations of the supernatural; the unique opportunities for empowerment provided to women by the role of healers; and stresses on the participants created by the process of acculturation to U.S. society. The rest of this paper will discuss the impact of these factors on the selection and development of Hispanic female healers presently living in urban centers in the United States.

The "Calling"

Regardless of her preferred belief system each healer attributed her vocation to a special choosing by a supernatural being or beings. This "calling" was manifested through one of three circumstances: an illness, a message, or role modeling. The most frequently mentioned way of being chosen was an experience of illness or other dire suffering from which the woman was miraculously saved. The extraordinary help she received at the time of crisis usually came from practitioners or adherents to a belief system with which she had had some previous association either directly or through friends or relatives. In a few instances this experience was her first real contact with the particular belief system. The miraculous healing was interpreted as a "calling" to the role of healer.

For example, Rosa's initial involvement in *santería* came about because of a serious disease. As she tells the story, she became very ill eleven years ago while living in New Jersey. A friend took her to see a doctor who in turn referred Rosa to a famous orthopedic surgeon in New York. She was told that she had cancer in her back and needed surgery. Even surgery was not a guarantee that she would live, since her cancer was very advanced. When she heard this, Rosa was in despair, but her friend suggested that she try other approaches. Other friends took Rosa to a healer. This woman, who was a *santera*, performed an oracle reading through the use of ceremonial shells and told Rosa that somebody was trying to kill her ("*Te han tirado a matar*") and that her only protection was to become a *santera* as soon as possible; not to do so would be certain death. Other suggestions were made, such as purifying baths, but a crucial thing was that she become a *santera* herself. Rosa did not have the money to pay for the initiation ceremony, but she remembered that she knew a *santero* who had previously suggested that she get involved in *santería*. She had never wanted to follow that advice, but at this point she decided to seek this help. Through this *santero* she again received the oracular message that someone was trying to kill her and that her only salvation lay in becoming a healer. He told her that she had been born to help people in need. Eventually Rosa was initiated as a *santera*. Her illness never recurred and she has worked full time as a healer ever since.

The second impetus to becoming a healer for some of the interviewees was a message or command received through an oracle, through the words of a trusted person, or even from a knowledgeable stranger. These messages informed some of the women in my study that healing was their mission in life or that they needed to heal others in order to protect their own health and that of their families. These "supernatural" commands did not seem to be related to any specific events in the women's lives.

For example, Magdalena's involvement with healing began almost by chance. Her daughter Carmen went with a couple of friends to consult an *espiritista* (a person who contacts the spirit world for advice) when she was an adolescent. The *consulta* cost five cents then, and they decided to just go for fun. The *espiritista* told Carmen that her mother was the one who should be consulted because she really had powers (*vista*). Magdalena was at the time earning a living by sewing doll clothes. Prompted by curiosity or need, she decided to go and see the woman. Apparently the *espiritista* not only convinced Magdalena that she had powers but even helped her to set up her own spiritual center. After several years of working "spiritually" (*lo espiritual*) Magdalena was told by an oracle that she should become a *santera*. She was initiated thirty-two years ago and has practiced *santería* ever since.

A third factor women mentioned as part of their decision to become healers was role modeling by their older female family members who were already initiated. Sometimes this would combine with one or both of the other factors cited—an illness or a command—to determine a woman's involvement as healer. For example, Magdalena's daughter Carmen was initiated both because of her mother's influence and because she was told to do so by a trusted stranger. However, even when human influence on their decision to become healers was acknowledged, the source of the "calling" is always considered to be supernatural.

In fact, the ten women interviewed all consider the source of their ability to heal or to perform unusual activities to be the supernatural beings who have called each of them to the healing role. The Holy Spirit, *el santo*, or another supernatural being controls the woman's abilities, directly or indirectly. A perplexing question, however, is why other women did not respond to an illness, command, or role modeling in this way. The literature (e.g., Garrison, 1977) and the interviews on which this study is based provide examples of Hispanic women who, though they were miraculously healed or were told that they "had to" become healers, never followed through with initiation. These women who did not become healers were not the focus of my study. Nevertheless, the existence of a second set of factors relating to power, discussed in the next section, might help to explain what was special about the women who did become healers.

Empowerment and the Woman Healer

A woman's acceptance of the healing role may be associated with the consciously or subconsciously perceived opportunities for empowerment or financial independence. These opportunities satisfy needs. But in no way do these opportunities negate or contradict the belief in a supernatural calling to the role of healer.

The healer's role provides women with an opportunity for empowerment in areas of their lives that seem independent from the supernatural level. Their power manifests itself in intrapersonal ways such as self-esteem and self-assurance. In addition, interpersonal relations are changed as the healer gains influence. For example, Josefina, who was only twenty-two at the time of the interview, travels across the United States without her husband or relatives, exercising her healing ministry at charismatic meetings with no objection from her husband. Sometimes the healer also attains financial power either through prescribed fees (*derechos*) or through valuable gifts offered by thankful clients. This was the case of Consuelo, Rosa, and Magdalena.

Most of the healers I interviewed did not articulate these other forms of empowerment. They do not view themselves as transcending the role expectations of Hispanic women. However, they all dare to behave in certain ways and to express certain opinions *because* they believe they have special supernatural powers. Precisely because these powers are given to the healer by external forces without her consent and even against her will, she is freed from many of the normative restraints on women and is able to exercise more control over her life. We know from anthropological sources that the role of women can be drastically modified by their role as healers.

> The supernatural provides the legitimacy that enables them to leave the domestic sphere. Furthermore, this legitimacy is not amenable to human intervention. The woman's husband and/or family who protest are liable to find that they have little or no control. . . . Women who are able to obtain supernatural legitimacy through ritual often have much power. (Hoch-Smith & Spring, 1978, pp.15–16)

By surrendering her will to the supernatural the woman healer is able to make decisions and interpretations about the will of the supernatural in her life. Many times she challenges male authority in ways that would not be accepted except for their source in supernatural commands. I observed, particularly in the families of Consuelo and Angela, how husbands, adult children, siblings, and other relatives tolerate, accept, or even encourage behavior that would not be tolerated under other circumstances. Thus, the belief that they have supernatural powers appears to be for some women a source of rebellion against established norms and an expression of strength. Consciously, though, they continue to see the source of "special powers" or "the gift of healing" as external (e.g., the spirits) rather than internal (i.e., herself).

A few of the healers were quite explicit about using their "supernatural" power and were very aware of its effect in transforming their lives. For example, Consuelo spoke about her power to harm those who hurt her and her relatives as a source of strength in interpersonal interactions. Interestingly, the healers who did *not* report a painful experience as their motivation for becoming healers, such as Consuelo, seemed to speak about their own power more clearly and openly than the others, who emphasized to a greater degree their debt to the supernatural intervention in their lives. Nevertheless, all the women interviewed transform their "supernatural" power into concrete activities. All of them participate in processes by which they convert this "supernatural" power into strengths manifested in interpersonal relations. The most important change for all the women interviewed appears to be the increase in self-determination, manifested in their relationships with their families, particularly their decision to exercise their healing and religious beliefs in spite of relatives' opposition, mockery, or other negative reactions. The financial independence from male relatives that the practice of healing provides for some women is an additional incentive to self-determination mentioned by Consuelo, Rosa, and Magdalena.

The power provided by the healing function can work in two different ways. It may compensate a woman for her lack of other resources such as status and self-esteem or it may be an expression of the personal strength she had before becoming a healer.

Two of the women interviewed, Consuelo and Angela, illustrate these contrasting situations as well as some of the individual factors that may be at play in the selection process. Each woman has a sister who shares her religious beliefs but does not have healing powers. Consuelo is the least-educated member of her family and was considered duller than her sisters when she was growing up. Having become a healer, she is consulted and acknowledged by all her relatives, including those still living in Cuba. She tells her adult children what is best for them, and they listen because what she says comes from a supernatural source. One of her sisters, a highly educated and independent woman, who is also a believer in *santería* but has never felt any desire to become a healer, also receives advice from her. Thus, by virtue of her healing ability, Consuelo has been transformed from a powerless member of the family to its most powerful member. It seems evident that for this woman healing has been a way of acquiring what she lacked as well as compensation for her previously low status. Moreover, her healing practice has provided her with a substantial income that she probably could not have earned otherwise and so has enabled her to be financially independent.

By contrast, Angela is a strong, well-educated woman who has always been financially independent and commanded the respect of her family and friends. She became involved with the charismatic movement and almost immediately began to take an informal leadership role in prayer groups, became able to transmit the Holy Spirit, and has had several experiences of healing others. One of her sisters has been involved in the charismatic movement for several years but this sister has never claimed to have special powers. In Angela's case, her healing powers constitute more an expression of strength than a source of it. Healing has become a legitimate way of expressing power in the context of her family, and it frees her from the guilt that could result from pursuing her own interests and neglecting her family duties. Although the two women described have been empowered interpersonally by their healing, this empowerment appeared to serve different psychological functions for them.

Even though I argue that the healing powers of these women become the source of empowerment for them, it is possible that the "unusual" behavior manifested by these women healers reinforces the norms of patriarchy. In their apparent rebellion against culturally prescribed sex roles, the healers may be simply "letting off steam." Without such an outlet, the pressure of women's frustrations with their sex role could mount to the point of bringing about actual social change. Viewed from this perspective, the role of healer seems to be part of an established system of sex roles and power allocations within the culture. It could be that by accepting them as healers, the culture accounts for and accommodates those women who do not fit the general mold without disturbing the status quo. In the end, women healers' deviations from the norm may promote compliance rather than change.

The findings of this study suggest, however, that at least for the participants, the role of healer leads to personal empowerment. It constitutes, for some, the expression of a sense of self that is strong and competent but cannot be fully communicated in all spheres of life without breaking cultural norms, as in Angela's case. For others, healing becomes an opportunity to be considered strong and important, as in Consuelo's case.

While the magical or supernatural form of power involves *power over* illness, misfortune, enemies, sin, evil spirits, or whatever, the other manifestations of the healers' power that we are referring to are mostly expressed through the *power to* exercise more self-determination. The financial independence from their husbands or male relatives, which the practice of healing provides for some of them, is an obvious factor in their self-determination, but not the only one.

This capacity for self-determination provided or facilitated by the power derived from the role of healer is particularly relevant for women. The empowerment of women, or the development of their own personal power, involves the development of skills and attitudes which enhance a woman's ability to exercise maximum control over her own life (Barnett, 1981). This process of empowerment involves a variety of dynamics: increased self-esteem, competence, and sense of self-worth; access to concrete resources and opportunities; challenging sex role constraints; and increased risk-taking. All of these dynamics seem to be manifested in different degrees by the women healers interviewed.

The conceptualization of the empowerment of women as involving *power to* rather than *power over* is in accordance with the most important goals of female psychological development as understood by Miller (1976) and other authors. Miller speaks of power as "the capacity to implement" (p.116), referring to the capacity for women to implement their own goals in life rather than those of someone else. The empowerment provided by the healer's role is not power as it is conventionally thought of: adversarial, hierarchical, finite. It is rather a felt state of being, potentially accessible to all women, defined as the sense of having or being able to attain control over one's life. It is true that some of the healers interviewed may use their powers in adversarial ways and that the ability to do so may enhance their interpersonal and financial power. Nevertheless, the sense of empowerment provided by adopting the healer's role is manifested also in those women who do not use their special powers in an adversarial way. In other words, the empowerment of women healers is not dependent on these expressions of adversarial power.

Self-Healing

Several studies (Langner, 1965; Soto & Shaver, 1982; Torres-Matrullo, 1976) show that Latina women who exhibit psychological and psychophysiological symptoms are less assertive, hold less power or status, or otherwise have less control of their lives than Latina women without these symptoms. Since the healer role provides an opportunity for empowerment, it is probably a source of healing for the woman herself. This may be related to the experience of being healed from illness or pain described by some of the interviewees as a sign of their "calling." They were relieved of their suffering when they became healers and consider the continued exercise of that role essential to their well-being. It can be argued that by empowering them and giving them more control over their lives, their role as healers, in fact, helped relieve their symptoms. A case can also be made that those Hispanic women who are ready to take charge of their lives but not equipped to be successful in the mainstream of society may find it easier than others to respond to the calling of supernatural forces.

The women interviewed continue to perceive themselves as very traditional. They have not "found themselves" through consciousness raising or feminist ideology. In fact, many would repudiate and condemn such ideas. However, most of them are ready to behave in ways usually associated with women who espouse feminism: they would be willing to leave their families or move to another city if they believed they were being "called" to it, and they take their work as healers very seriously and would not abandon it at the request of any man. In many ways they are living in accordance with feminist ideology while interpreting their behavior in very different terms.

Traditional Healing and Acculturation

In addition to the experience of a calling and the opportunities provided by the healer's role, the acculturative stress to which Latinos are subjected in the United States may also be a factor influencing the selection of Hispanic female healers in urban centers in the United States.

Paradoxically, for some Hispanic immigrants, there is an increased adherence to traditional systems of healing after migration. This increased traditionalism can be seen in many ways: the experiences of the healers interviewed; the spread to other subgroups of beliefs previously confined to only one segment of Hispanic culture; and the observation that the practice of healing is on the increase among some Latinos in the United States. Halifax and Weidman (1973) believe that "'*santería*' is proliferating in Florida more than it did in Cuba" (p.317), and Sandoval (1975), referring specifically to the practice of *santería* among Cubans in Miami, attributes the increase to several factors that may apply to other belief systems as well, including the need for sources of strength in order to deal with the threat, stress, and anxiety created by economic insecurity and unfamiliar experiences. In addition, the current interest in healing practices and esoteric religious systems among educated elites in the United States creates a climate of acceptance for practices and beliefs that would have been considered inappropriate by mainstream American society only a few years ago.

Alternative healing systems may symbolize the newcomer's struggle and represent a way of coping in a situation of change that might otherwise be too threatening. The healer uses her faith to help other newcomers cope with their anxiety. According to Halifax and Weidman (1973), *santería* provides an ego-integrative mechanism by defining the individual as more acted upon than as actor, and thus provides "the reason" for the Cuban's increased sense of powerlessness—a powerlessness which accompanies the fact that traditional behavioral "keys" do not always fit a new social "locks." . . . It defines sources of responsibility as lying within the supernatural realm and, therefore, supports the "transfer" of guilt in the individual to loci outside the self. . . . Such psychological processes serve to enhance the individual's sense of mastery by separating the acceptable "me." (pp.325–327)

The sense of mastery is also enhanced because "the client is always advised to perform certain rituals, harmless in themselves but usually involving sacrifice of some sort" (Halifax & Weidman, 1973, p.327) that convey a message of control over the external and internal worlds.

Charismatic Catholicism also expresses metaphorically the immigrant's helplessness and offers empowerment through the supernatural and the externalization of responsibility. "'The baptism of the Spirit' is specifically an act of empowerment" (McDonnell, 1976, p.36) that offsets the immigrant's impotence against external forces.

Newly arrived immigrants find themselves discriminated against and oppressed in all areas of their lives, including access to health services. The system of health care and specifically of mental health care prevalent in the United States reinforces their feelings of helplessness by emphasizing the individual, intrapsychic responsibility (even if unconscious) for all personal problems. Most psychotherapeutic approaches involve talking with someone who "knows better" than the sufferer and takes control over treatment but frequently refuses to give specific direct advice or suggestions on how to behave or to get better. Because mental health professionals may consider mental distress and illness to originate in unconscious processes beyond the client's control, there is nothing the client can do except collaborate in the uncovering of the unconscious. It is practically impossible to understand the connection between talking about one's childhood or other seemingly irrelevant topics and one's presenting problems, which might be a persistent headache or the behavior of an unruly child.

In the traditional healing systems such as *santería* or *espiritismo,* and even in charismatic Catholicism, the cause of a personal problem is considered to be outside the sufferer. This coincides with the client's intuitive experience of daily life. Satan, the offending spirit, or an enemy's destructive hex can be overcome through certain prescribed activities that have a clear relationship to the problem. Most traditional healers use simple forms of homeopathic and/or contact magic (González-Wippler, 1975; Trotter, 1982; Trotter & Chavira, 1981) that seek to provide immediate understanding and relief.

The traditional healing system thus places responsibility outside clients and helps them recover an internal locus of control. The prevailing psychodynamic psychotherapeutic approaches, in contrast, make clients responsible for their difficulties but externalize their control. Traditional healing practices help Hispanics deal with stress by providing a cognitive structuring of problems that approximates their personal experience. The externalization of responsibility corresponds with the client's sense of powerlessness, and the prescription of concrete rituals and behaviors returns a sense of mastery.

Healers "provide a valuable counseling service to their clients, if absolutely nothing else" (Trotter & Chavira, 1981, p.165). It is no surprise, then, that when people are experiencing little control and enormous responsibility, they increase their use of traditional healing practices. Such practices are culturally relevant not only in historical terms but especially in the psychohistorical situation of Latinos in the modern-day United States.

Surprisingly, Janeway (1981) in her discussion of the "powers of the weak" considers magic and religion only as another form of control of the powerful over the powerless or as a metaphor for the uncontrollable power of the powerful. De la Cancela and Zavala (1983) seem to take a similar position. The literature, however, provides innumerable examples of magic and religion as instruments for the empowerment of the powerless and expression of the "powers of the weak" (Turner, 1974). As Turner asserts, the "power of the weak" is often assigned to the female symbols and the "'liminal' and the 'inferior' conditions are often associated with ritual power" (Turner, 1977, p.100).

In fact, women of all cultures have traditionally resorted to religion and its variations as a source of strength and empowerment. "Religious laws and bureaucrats can dictate that only men shall be priests, but the gods choose whom they will" (Falk & Gross, 1980, p.39). The belief in this divine choosing, usually shared by both women and men of a given culture, can sometimes provide women healers with the power to balance the inequality of sex roles for themselves as well as for others (Lerch, 1979; Pressel, 1979). This power to balance inequality may be important for the healers as women and as Hispanics in the United States.

The healers interviewed are involved in a process that is affected by many factors. From one perspective they are insiders in the religious traditions characteristic of their cultural background, but they are at the same time outsiders in their own culture because their role as healers brands them as different. In addition, they, like all Hispanics, are outsiders in U.S. mainstream culture, both in the sense of being foreigners and in their belief systems. Healers and clients alike espouse a world view that differs from and even contradicts that of U.S. middle-class culture.

It is very possible that Hispanic women healers and their clients are seeking to order their lives in a social context foreign to them by adapting in ways that can create new roles for themselves and for other women. Conversely, they may be rejecting the forces of acculturation by behaving in ways that do not fit into American culture at all. At worst, they may even be choosing to express their needs through a regressive element in Hispanic culture, as De la Cancela and Zavala (1983) suggest.

The discussion of the empowering effect of the healer's role and of the possible influence of acculturative stress on this role provides clues to the social and psychological processes underlying the development of the healer. Ironically the empowerment of some Hispanic women in this way may undermine the empowerment of the whole group by delaying the acculturation process or by divesting to the religious sphere some energies that might be best applied to efforts directed at changing social conditions.

There are several implications of the explanatory task attempted in this paper. Explaining the insights of one world view in the vocabulary of another distinctly different paradigm creates practically insurmountable difficulties. The participants' own explanations of their psychological processes are coherent and clear from their vantage point. From the vantage point of the outsider, however, these explanations may not be sufficient. Women's studies scholars need to explore the wider meaning of women's experiences in this realm to understand how cultural elements that could not be considered as partaking of feminist ideology can, in fact, contribute to the development of attitudes and behaviors in individual women that embody the best consequences of feminist ideology.

This study is but one attempt at understanding the process involved in the development of the female healer in one particular group living in specific psychohistorical circumstances. Perhaps it also sheds some light on the process of empowerment for women who conceptualize their development with a frame of reference different from extant feminist conceptualizations and yet achieve parallel results in their lives.

Notes

Reprinted from Espín, O.M. (1988). Spiritual Power and the Mundane World: Hispanic Female Healers in Urban U.S. Communities. *Women Studies Quarterly*, 16(3–4), 33–47.

References

Barnett, E.H. (1981). *The development of personal power for women.* Doctoral dissertation, Boston University.

De la Cancela, V., & Zavala, I.M. (1983). An analysis of culturalism in Latino mental health: Folk medicine as a case in point. *Hispanic Journal of Behavioral Sciences*, 5(3), 251–274.

Espín, O.M. (1983). *Hispanic female healers in urban centers in the United States.* Unpublished manuscript.

Falk, N.A., & Gross, R.M. (Eds.). (1980). *Unspoken worlds: Women's religious lives in non-western culture.* San Francisco: Harper & Row.

Garrison, V. (1977). The "Puerto Rican syndrome" in psychiatry and espiritismo. In V. Crapanzano & V. Garrison (Eds.), *Case studies in spirit possession* (pp.383–449). New York: Wiley.

Garrison, V. (1982). Folk healing systems as elements in the community support systems of psychiatric patients. In U. Rueveni, R. Speck, & J. Speck (Eds.), *Innovative interventions* (pp.58–95). New York: Human Science Press.

González-Wippler, M. (1975). *Santería: African magic in Latin America.* New York: Anchor.

Halifax, J., & Weidman, H.H. (1973). Religion as a mediating institution in acculturation: The case of *santería* in greater Miami. In. R.H. Cox (Ed.), *Religious systems and psychotherapy* (pp.316–330). Springfield, IL: Charles C. Thomas.

Harwood, A. (1977). *Rx: Spiritists as needed.* New York: Wiley.

Hoch-Smith, J., & Spring, A. (Eds.). (1978). *Women in ritual and symbolic roles.* New York: Plenum.

Janeway, E. (1981). *Powers of the weak.* New York: Morrow Quill Paperbacks.

Langner, T.S. (1965). Psychophysiological symptoms and the status of women in two Mexican communities. In J.L. Murphy &. A.H. Leighton (Eds.), *Approaches to cross-cultural psychiatry* (pp.360–392). Ithaca, NY: Cornell University Press.

Lerch, P.B. (1979). Spirit mediums in *Umbanda Evangelizada* of Porto Alegre, Brazil: Dimensions of power and authority. In. E. Bourguignon, (Ed.), *A world of women: Anthropological studies of women in the societies of the world* (pp.129–160). New York: Praeger.

McDonnell, K. (1976). *Charismatic renewal and the churches.* New York: Seabury.

McGuire, M. (1982). *Pentecostal Catholics: Power, charisma and order in a religious movement.* Philadelphia: Temple University Press.

Miller, J.B. (1976). *Towards a new psychology of women.* Boston: Beacon.

Pressel, E. (1979). Spirit magic in the social relations between men and women (São Paulo, Brazil). In E. Bourguignon, (Ed.), *A world of women: Anthropological studies of women in the societies of the world* (pp.107–128). New York: Praeger.

Sandoval, M. (1975). *La religión Afro-Cubana.* Madrid: Playor.

Sandoval, M. (1979). *Santería* as a mental health care system: A historical overview. *Social Science and Medicine,* 13(3), 137–152.

Soto, F., & Shaver, P. (1982). Sex-role traditionalism, assertiveness and symptoms of Puerto Rican women living in the United States. *Hispanic Journal of Behavioral Sciences,* 4(1), 1–19.

Torres-Matrullo, C. (1976). Acculturation and psychopathology among Puerto Rican women in mainland United States. *American Journal of Orthopsychiatry,* 46, 710–719.

Trotter, R.T. (1982). Contrasting models of the healer's role: South Texas case samples. *Hispanic Journal of Behavioral Sciences,* 4(3), 315–327.

Trotter, R.T., & Chavira, J.A. (1981). *Curaderismo: Mexican-American folk healing.* Athens: University of Georgia Press.

Turner, V. (1974). *Dramas, fields and metaphors: Symbolic action in human society.* Ithaca, NY: Cornell University Press.

Turner, V. (1977). *The ritual process: Structure and anti-structure.* Ithaca, NY: Cornell University Press.

Part Five

The Interplay of Migration and Sexuality in Women's Lives

The two chapters in this section were written quite recently. They emerge from a book-length study in which I explore immigrant women's sexuality and gender roles. That study—and the two essays presented here—merge the two topics in women's psychology that consistently interest me: the impact of the experience of migration and the role of sexuality in women's lives. The two essays in this section incorporate these two topics explicitly. I include them in a separate section because they represent an integration of these two topics not yet developed in the essays on sexuality and immigration presented in the previous sections of this book. These two pieces also embody a coming together of my professional interests, career, and personal life. The issues presented in these essays elaborate, expand, and deepen my previous work.

Emphasized in this work is the significance of language for women who have developed their identities in the context of multiple linguistic communities. As I note in Chapter 12, language is more than vocabulary and grammar rules. Sociolinguistic studies of bilingualism as well as firsthand accounts from bilingual individuals illustrate the evocative power of the use of one or another language. Eva Hoffman's (1989) *Lost in Translation* is a fascinating autobiographical account of the impact of language on the life of the immigrant. Hoffman poignantly describes feeling split between her Polish-speaking and her English-speaking selves. According to her, only after narrating in therapy, in English, the events that had happened to her in Polish did she feel herself to be an integrated person. Thus, she offers another example of the role of psychotherapy in constructing a meaningful story out of disjointed, painful events and unintegrated, contradictory fragments of the life story. The immigrant women interviewed for my study provide a rich texture from which to understand the significance of language for sexuality. Their ability to speak more than one language brings this significance to the fore in a very dramatic way.

Chapter 12, which was first presented in London during a trip sponsored through a fellowship of the British Psychological Society, is also focused on the impact of "racial" differences and other cultural factors on the experiences of women immigrants. I also discuss the methodology of my study. Together, Chapters 12 and 13 reiterate the importance of cultures and their transformations for the development of women's sexual desire and expression. The particular implications of these transformations for lesbian and adolescent immigrants are the focus of Chapter 13 "Leaving the Nation and Joining the Tribe," which also interrogates parallels in identity transformations experienced in the processes of migration and coming out. Thus, I approach the issue of lesbian identity from a new angle. I also focus on issues confronted by lesbians who are immigrants.

The life stories of the women interviewed for the study on which these two essays are based confirm some concepts, question presuppositions, and open new possibilities for the exploration of women's sexualities. The women interviewed demonstrate that similar acts do not have the same meaning across historical and geographical planes. Arguably, the one common characteristic of sexuality across these variables is that the sex women have with men is not the same sex men have with women and certainly not the same that women have with women—a reality across nations and ethnic groups if one is to listen to the women interviewed for the study. These life narratives demonstrate the variety of paths taken by women on the road toward integrating the contradictory messages provided in diverse cultural backgrounds about sexuality and gender roles. The women's narratives illustrate a process of transformation that is both enriching and challenging. These women are witnesses to a particular set of historical and cultural circumstances. They are also witnesses to the process of transformation in which so many women all over the world are engaged.

This transformation is, after all, what this book is about.

References

Hoffman, E. (1989). *Lost in translation*. New York: Dutton.

12

"Race," Racism, and Sexuality in the Life Narratives of Immigrant Women

In March 1994 a new exhibition, *Becoming American Women: Clothing and the Jewish Immigrant Experience, 1880–1920,* opened at the Chicago Historical Society. In the book that accompanies the exhibition, Barbara Schreier (1994), its conceptualizer and curator, recounts her early interest in this study of clothing and acculturation. When she interviewed first- and second-generation immigrants about the years of adjustment to U.S. society, "everyone had a clothing story" (p.2). She concluded that clothing and acculturation mirror each other closely and that "clothing [is] an identifiable symbol of a changing consciousness" (p.5). As she wrote:

> The decision to focus [the exhibition] on women was based on the long-standing relationship women have had with their appearance. . . . Issues of dress unified women and framed their experience of life separate from men. . . . Even though men considered issues [of clothing], they did not record them with the same iconographic vocabulary as did women. (p.8) . . . Female immigrants discuss clothing in their memoirs, oral histories, and correspondence as pivotal markers of their journey and remembered objects of desire. (p.9)

Referring to a population vastly different in cultural background and immersed in different historical circumstances a century later, Anne Woollett and her collaborators (Woollett, Marshall, Nicholson, & Dosanjh, 1994), reporting on their research on present-day Asian women's ethnic identity, noted "frequent associations of dress with ethnic identity" (p.124) and observed that

> while dress is seen as an important aspect of ethnic identity by almost all the women interviewed . . . men's choice of clothing was rarely mentioned in the interviews. . . . Clothes would appear to have different significance for women as compared with men, and given that most studies have not focused upon women, may explain why dress is rarely used as a measure of ethnic identity in much of the literature. (p.125)

They state that because "the impact of gender on the representations of ethnic identity is not frequently or adequately considered" (p.120), aspects of the acculturation process that are expressed through women's clothing choices are usually ignored.

While these authors astutely observe the importance women assign to their clothing and appearance as a statement of their relation to acculturation, they do not question why it is so. Yet we know that women, in Western culture as well as in other cultures, are defined and define themselves through physical appearance. Women are their bodies. Connections and disconnections between mothers and daughters, even without the tensions created by acculturation, are mediated by clothing, fashion, weight and other issues related to appearance (Kaschak, 1992).

Interestingly, the historical period on which the Chicago Historical Society exhibition focuses coincides with a period of intense public preoccupation with young women's sexuality, not coincidentally a period when large numbers of young immigrant unmarried women living in American cities were gainfully employed (Nathanson, 1991). According to Schreier (1994), the Jewish press admonished young women at the time in lengthy editorials not to use their savings to buy frivolous items of clothing. Similarly, many a family conflict had its source in parental anger with daughters who spent money from their meager wages buying coveted clothing rather than contributing further to the family's resources. Immigrant women's identity conflicts and identity transformations continue to be expressed in our time through clothing and sexuality. For parents and young women alike, acculturation and sexuality are seen as closely connected (Espín, 1984, 1987b). For parents and young women alike, "dressing Western" or preserving traditional clothing styles can be grounds for intergenerational conflict.

Obviously, women's preoccupation with clothing and appearance is closely associated with sexuality. (Let me say in parentheses here that heterosexual standards of sexual attractiveness are not the only ones expressed through clothing. Lesbian preoccupation with dress codes, whether the "politically correct" jeans and sneakers or "lipstick lesbians'" fashion outfits, are an expression of concern with sexual attractiveness. Standards of attractiveness vary among different groups and generations of lesbians but, in any case, clothes and sexual attractiveness are connected for lesbians too.)

The self-appointed "guardians of morality and tradition" that are ever-present among immigrant "communities" are very concerned with women's roles and sexual behavior. It is no secret that religious leaders are rather preoccupied with women's sexuality. Indeed, the great religions of the world uphold similar principles in so far as the submission of women to men is concerned (el Saadawi, 1980).

We are witnessing how "women, their role and, above all their control, become central to the fundamentalist agenda" (Yuval-Davis, 1992, p.278) of Protestants, Catholics, Muslims and others. When immigrant communities are besieged with rejection, racism and scorn, those self-appointed leaders have always found fertile ground from which to control women's sexuality in the name of preserving "tradition." Women's subservience is advocated as a type of "steadying influence."

It is significant that groups that are transforming their way of life through a vast and deep process of acculturation focus on preserving "tradition" almost exclusively through the gender roles and lives of women. Women's roles become the "bastion" of traditions.

> The "proper" behaviour of women is used to signify the difference between those who belong to the collectivity and those who do not. Women are also seen as "cultural carriers" of the collectivity who transmit it to the future generation. The "proper" control of women in terms of marriage and divorce ensures that children who are born to those women are not only biologically but also symbolically within the boundaries of the collectivity. (Yuval-Davis, 1992, p.285)

Schreier (1994) tells us that in the case of Jewish immigrants to the U.S. the beginning of the century, "contemporary observers did not pay as much attention to male plumage; even when they did, their words lack the moralistic beseeching, and condemnatory tones with which they addressed women" (p.9). Conversely, women resisted domination from both the larger society and their own communities through the use of clothing and other forms of resistance. The new freedom young immigrant women from diverse ethnic backgrounds acquired from being wage earners expressed itself through the clothes they wore and through the refusal to accept chaperons and other forms of parental control over their sexuality (Ruiz, 1992).

Although understudied, the role of women in international migration has begun to draw attention from researchers, policy-makers and service providers (e.g., Andizian et al., 1983; Cole, Espín, & Rothblum, 1992; Gabaccia, 1992; Phizacklea, 1983). However, little is known about experiences considered to be private, such as sexuality.

Referring specifically to women in the Middle East, the Lebanese author Evelyne Accad (1991) asserts that

> sexuality seems to have a revolutionary potential so strong that many political women and men are afraid of it. They prefer, therefore, to dismiss its importance by arguing that it is not as central as other factors, such as economic and political determination. . . . [However] . . . sexuality is much more central to social and political problems . . . than previously thought, and . . . unless a sexual revolution is incorporated into political revolution, there will be no real transformation of social relations. (p. 239)

Not coincidentally, women's clothing has been one of the core issues in the Iranian revolution (Tohidi, 1991).

Indeed, sexuality is not private (Foucault, 1981). This explains why so many cultures and countries try to control and legislate it (Brettell & Sargent, 1993; di Leonardo, 1991). Many immigrant women have experienced restrictions on their sexuality before migration as well as in the context of their communities after migration. And, among political refugees, some may have experienced sexualized torture.

We know that the sexual behavior of women serves a larger social function beyond the personal. It is used by enemies and friends alike as "proof" of the moral fiber or decay of nations or other social groups. Worldwide, women are enculturated and socialized to embody their sexual desire or lack thereof through their particular culture's ideals of virtue. Women's reproductive capacities are appropriated by the state to establish its control over citizens and territories alike. Thus the social group's expectations are inscribed in women's individual desire and expressed through their sexuality (Jaggar & Bordo, 1989). Historically, warriors have celebrated victories and consoled the frustrations of defeat through the forceful possession of women's bodies: war and rape are deeply connected. The present situation in the former Yugoslavia brings this reality to the forefront in a tragic and dramatic way.

Sexuality may be a universal component of human experience, yet how it is embodied and expressed is not (see, for example, Laqueur, 1990). As anthropological, historical and literary studies contend, "sexuality is culturally variable rather than a timeless, immutable essence" (Parker, Russo, Sommer, & Yaegar, 1992, p.4). Indigenous interpretations of seemingly similar sexual practices (or even what is considered to be sexual or not) is often strikingly different for people in different cultural environments. The study of women's experiences reveal a varied representation of sexual/gender differences among cultures. These cultural constructs inextricably inform the expression of female sexuality. Cultural traditions, colonial and other forms of social oppression, national identity and the vicissitudes of the historical process inform the development and perception of female sexuality. The development of women's sexuality is affected by the eroticization of power differentials and the links between power and sexual violence (e.g., Valverde, 1985). Worldwide definitions of what constitutes appropriate sexual behavior are strongly influenced by male sexual pleasure. These definitions are justified in the name of prevalent values in a given society—nationalism, religion, morality, health, science, etc. Too often women's expressions and experiences of their own sexuality are silenced and/or condemned (e.g., Ruiz, 1992).

The acculturation process opens up different possibilities for women the men, particularly with reference to gender roles and sexual behavior (Espín 1984, 1987a, 1987b; Espín, Cavanaugh, Paydarfar, & Wood, 1990; Espín, Stewart, & Gómez, 1990; Goodenow & Espín, 1993). Among immigrant women in the USA who come from traditional societies, sexuality is frequently associated with "becoming Americanized". One of the most prevalent myths about American women in other countries is that they are very "free" with sex. For immigrant parents and the young woman herself, "to become Americanized" may be equated with becoming sexually promiscuous. Thus, in some cases, during the acculturation process sexuality becomes the focus of the parents' fears and the girls' desires (Espín, 1984). As expressed by Bhavnani and Haraway (1994) "These young women, in their embodiment, are the points of collision of all these powerful forces, including forces of their own" (p.33).

Conversely, newly encountered sex role patterns, combined with greater access to paid employment for women, may create possibilities to live a new life-style. This way of life may have been previously unavailable in the home culture. In this scenario, the traditional power structure of the family may be changed (Espín, 1987b). Transmitted through words and silences that pass between women of different generations are values and beliefs about what constitutes appropriate sexual behavior. These include ideas about pregnancy, male/female relationships, women's reproductive health and so forth (Marín, Marín, Juárez, & Sorensen, 1992; Marín, Tscham, Gómez, & Kegeles, 1993). Mothers provide the core of cultural messages for women through what they say about men and other women, and what is allowed and what is forbidden to a "good woman" in the culture of origin. These messages continue to be powerful injunctions for first-, second- and even third-generation immigrant women (Espín, Cavanaugh, et al., 1990).

All pressures on immigrant women's sexuality do not come from inside their own culture. The host society also imposes its own burdens and desires through prejudices and racism. Women immigrants, particularly those who are not white experience degrees of "gendered racism" (Essed, 1991, 1994). Although racism may be expressed subtly, the immigrant woman finds herself between the racism of the dominant society and the sexist expectations of her own community. Paraphrasing Nigerian poet and professor 'Molara Ogundipe-Leslie (1993) we could say that immigrant women have several mountains on their back, the two most obvious ones being "the heritage of tradition" and "the oppression from outside." The racism of the dominant society makes the retrenchment into "tradition" appear to be justifiable, while the rigidities of "tradition" appear to justify the racist/prejudicial treatment of the dominant society. Paradoxically, the two "mountains" reinforce and encourage each other. Needless to say, the effect of racism and sexism is not only felt as pressure from the outside, but it also becomes internalized, as all forms of oppression are. Women exposed to more direct contact with the dominant society experience the contradictions more dramatically although perhaps less consciously than those who do not confront the dominant society on a regular basis (e.g., Essed, 1991, 1994; Gold, 1992). As Essed (1994) argues,

> From a macro point of view, the massive and systematic reproduction of belief systems which legitimate certain dominant group positions predispose individuals to internalize these ideas, whether or not they themselves occupy these dominant positions. From a micro point of view, however, individuals do not necessarily and unthinkingly accept "dominant" ideologies. Moreover, the cognitive domain of individuals is a fundamental area where new and critical knowledge can generate change. . . . The study of individual motivation and sense-making in the process of resistance against confining race and gender boundaries is still, however, largely unexplored. (p.101)

In the past year I have been engaged in a study that seeks to increase knowledge and understanding of sexuality and gender related issues among immigrant/refugee women. The study is still in its preliminary stages. It focuses on the expression and experience of women's sexuality in different cultures as they are created by disparate social forces. I would like to share some of the preliminary results with you today. I am collecting narratives from mothers and daughters about their experiences as immigrant women. These narratives are obtained through individual interviews and focus groups.

"The focus group interview is a qualitative research technique used to obtain data about feelings and opinions of small groups of participants about a given problem, experience or other phenomenon" (Basch, 1987, p.414). The narratives explore immigrant women's understanding of sexuality and their internalization of cultural norms. Their open-ended narratives allow for the expression of thoughts and feelings while inviting participants to introduce their own themes and concerns. Narratives are a particularly valuable research method when the concepts being explored are "new territory" for participants and/or researcher (Mishler, 1986; Riessman, 1993). In addition to its value as a research tool (e.g., Denzin, 1989; Josselson & Lieblich, 1993; Riessman, 1993), retelling the life story, including the migration (particularly if it was motivated by some form of persecution), has been shown to have a healing effect (Aron, 1992). Focus groups provide opportunities for in-depth interviewing of a group concerning a particular topic. This form of in-depth interviewing is effective and economical in terms of both time and money; thus it is a pragmatic approach for any study done with limited funds and limited personnel—in this case, only one researcher Focus groups follow basic principles of qualitative research and take advantage of the additional information generated by the group interaction. They provide the researcher with the additional flexibility of probing unanticipated areas when initially designing the discussion questions (see, for example, Krueger, 1994; Morgan, 1988, 1993; Stewart & Shamdasani, 1990).

By the end of the study, focus groups will have been held in several cities in the United States of America, probably San Diego, Chicago, and Miami. (Thus far, all data have been collected in San Diego.) Individual narratives will also be collected from immigrant/refugee women in these cities. The choice of these cities has been determined by two factors. One is the possibility of accessing a wider variety of cultures/countries of origin and population recruiting prospective participants in three regions of the United States. The three cities chosen for the study have a rich ethnic and racially mixed population of immigrants/refugees. These sites complement one another because they represent geographical, national origin and ethnic diversity within the United States. The second is pragmatic: personal plans and professional connections facilitate my travel and access to these three cities.

Immigrant/refugee women have been recruited in the chosen cities through personal contacts and friendship pyramiding. They have been asked to participate voluntarily in small groups of five to ten women from the same cultural background (i.e., country, social class, first language). The women recruited so far range in age from early twenties to mid-forties and they are all college-educated. A few are still in the process of completing their higher education. These women have been chosen on the basis of their being particularly articulate about the research topic and fluent in both English and the language of origin. The interviews have focused in depth on respondents' individual life stories and experiences.

In the focus groups and individual interviews conducted so far, I explored ways in which women's sexual behavior signifies the family's system; this entails exploring ways in which the struggles surrounding acculturation in immigrant/refugee families center around issues of daughters' sexual behaviors and women's sex roles in general. An important aspect of the focus groups has been to explore the vocabulary of sex in different languages: specifically, what is permissible to say about it. I have explored variations in speakers' comfort (or discomfort) when addressing sexuality in the mother tongue or in English.

The focus groups explore what mothers, as transmitters of cultural norms, tell their daughters (or don't tell them) about what they should (or shouldn't do) as women. They explore "protective" behaviors that silently express prescriptive sexual ideology for women. Generational differences among women that are usually associated with gender role differences and sexual behavior are also discussed. They explore how generational differences are associated with acculturation and how differential access to the host culture may circumscribe sexual behavior. Younger women talk about how they perceive their mothers' expression of and comfort with sexuality issues. Women who are mothers address how they relate to their daughters concerning sexuality issues. I am giving primary importance to the messages transmitted between mothers and daughters concerning sexuality and its related issues.

So far, I have conducted three focus groups and five individual interviews. Two of the groups have been constituted by native speakers of the same language (in one case, German; in the other, Spanish). A third group included women from several different countries. The Spanish-speakers group was conducted in English and Spanish; the other two groups were conducted in English.

All focus groups and interviews have been facilitated and conducted by me. For Spanish-speaking participants, the possibility of conducting the groups or individual interviews in their mother tongue has been offered. When participants who speak Spanish preferred to be interviewed in English their request has been honored and the request itself will be considered data. For participants whose first language is not English, Spanish or French, careful questioning about vocabulary in their language and questions about the effect of conducting the interview in English have been incorporated into the session. In addition to Mexican-American and German, participants have been Cuban, Korean, South Asian and Austrian.

Topics discussed in the focus groups and in the individual interviews cover a wide range of concerns. The issues discussed include menstruation, arranged marriages versus dating, marrying outside one's ethnic group, sex and violence, lesbianism and bisexuality, sex education in the schools and at home, mothers' passivity versus active involvement in their daughters' lives from the point of view of both mothers and daughters, silences about sex in their families, sex and romance and sexual behavior and heterosexual intercourse.

Interviews and focus groups have been taped, transcribed and analyzed following accepted techniques for the analysis of qualitative data (e.g., Strauss, 1987; Silverman, 1993). The possibility of using a computer package for the analysis of the data is being investigated; the availability of resources and applicability of existing computer packages for data analysis will determine its feasibility.

The study emphasizes the geographical and psychological borders and boundaries crossed in the process of migration. This process is central to the life experiences of women who have migrated from their country of origin. The crossing of borders through migration may provide for women the space and "permission" to cross boundaries and transform their sexuality and sex roles. For lesbians, an additional border/boundary crossing takes place in relation to the "coming out" process. "Coming out" may have occurred after the migration, as part of the acculturation process, or it may have been the motivating force behind the migration. However, for most women, issues of sexuality may not have been part of the conscious decision to migrate.

Through this study, I would like to ascertain the main issues and consequences entailed in crossing both geographical and emotional boundaries for both lesbians heterosexual women. For example, one of the participants reported trying to escape the constraints imposed by society on her lesbianism was the force that inspired and fostered her migration. In other cases, the migration provides the space and permission to come out at a later date, although the awareness of lesbianism may not have been present when the decision to migrate was made.

I am particularly interested in how this internal process develops for lesbian immigrants because obviously their life choices add further dimensions to the process of identity formation (Espín, 1987a). Lesbian immigrants illustrate vividly the notion that "identity is not one thing for any individual; rather, each individual is both located in, and opts for a number of differing and, at times conflictual, identities, depending on the social, political, economic and ideological aspects of their situation" (Bhavnani & Phoenix, 1994, p.9).

In short, I am exploring how questions of national identity/sexual identity are determined and negotiated for immigrant and refugee women. Throughout, I will highlight two important aspects of these boundary and border crossings: geography/place and language. Both are invaluable and central to understanding immigrant women's experiences in general and sexuality in particular.

Immigrants are preoccupied with "geography"; with the place in which events occur. This preoccupation is connected with life events and how they have been and still are being affected by the vicissitudes of place and geography (Espín, 1992, 1994). This phenomenon/preoccupation has two components. First, vicissitudes of the actual country of origin give that place almost a sense of unreality in spite of its constant psychological presence in the immigrant's life. The other is what I call a preoccupation with "what could have been." This translates into ruminations about what life might have been (and other "what ifs") had the immigrant remained in the country of origin or migrated to a different country or if the immigration had taken place at another life stage.

Bandura's (1982) discussion on the importance of chance encounters in the course of human development addresses the impact that chance has in determining one's life path. For some, chance encounters and other life events are, additionally, influenced by uncontrollable historical and political events. While all human beings experience life transitions, people who have been subjected to historical dislocations feel more drastic and dramatic crossroads in their lives. The experience of uprootedness and migration is frequently compounded by two factors: one's status as an ethnic minority person in the host country and/or new gender role patterns that contradict the norms of the home culture.

Even among immigrants who are fluent in English, the first language often remains the language of emotions. Thus, speaking in a second language may "distance" the immigrant woman from important parts of herself. Conversely, a second language may provide a vehicle to express the inexpressible in the first language (either because the first language does not have the vocabulary or because the person censors herself from saying certain "taboo" things in the first language) (Espín, 1984, 1987b). I contend that the language in which messages about sexuality are conveyed and encoded impacts the language chosen to express sexual thoughts, feelings and ideas. Among the participants in the study two apparently contradictory patterns concerning language have emerged. In several cases, after the completion of an interview or group session conducted in English, participants said that they could have expressed themselves and answered my questions and comments easier had they done so in their first language. However, the same participants believed that although it would have been easier to use their first language in terms of vocabulary, they felt it was easier to talk about these topics in English. They believed that feelings of shame would have prevented them from addressing these topics in the same depth had they been talking in their first language. Other participants, on the other hand, said that they could not have had this conversation in their first language because they actually did not know words or were not used to talking about sexuality in their native language. These women had migrated at an earlier age, usually before or during early adolescence, and had developed their knowledge of sex while immersed in English. The women who manifested this second pattern explained that they could not conceive of "making love in their first language" while those in the first case thought they were unable to "make love in English."

Is the immigrant woman's preference for English when discussing sexuality—as I have clinically observed and the participants in this study express—motivated by characteristics of English as a language or is it that a second language offers a vehicle to express thoughts and feelings that cannot be expressed in the first language? Or does the new cultural context, in which English is spoken, allow more expression of the woman's feelings? Acquired in English, these experiences and expressions may become inextricably associated with the language (as happens with professional terminology acquired in a second language).

*   *   *

I would like to spend the rest of the article describing some of the participants' stories to illustrate the findings thus far.

I have first chosen two life stories, in some ways very similar and yet quite different, to illustrate two disparate adaptations to migration. Of course, names and other identifying information have been changed, although significant facts have been preserved.

Maritza and Olga are both Cuban. Both migrated to the USA when they were twenty-two years of age, during the 1970s. Olga comes from a middle-class family, Maritza from a poor working-class family. Maritza had come out as a lesbian in Cuba, when she was 14. She had (and still has) considerable artistic talent as a musician and poet. From a very early age she identified her lesbianism as a consequence of her artistic talent. In Cuba and other Latin American countries there is widespread association between artists and homosexuality that is more or less accepted. She was rebellious as an adolescent, frequently came back home drunk in the middle of the night and, more or less openly, displayed her preference for girls. At the age of twenty-two she decided that staying in Cuba, considering the government's position in relation to homosexuality, was impossible for her. Although she was completely in favor of the Revolution, and precisely because of her connections with it, she masterminded an escape during a trip sponsored by the Cuban government for young artists to Eastern Europe. Her family continues to live in Cuba. Even after all these years, they strongly disagree with her decision to leave the country. In the United States, Maritza refuses to participate in anything having to do with gay/lesbian activism and lives a very private life, although she makes no secret about her sexual orientation. Although she still writes poetry and composes music, she decided that "poems and songs were not going to feed her" and she actively pursued other professional endeavors. The fact that writing in Spanish did not provide her with a significant audience in an English-speaking country, and that writing creatively in English was next to impossible for her, were not minor factors in her decision to enter another career. Her love relationships, with very few exceptions, have been with Spanish-speaking women. She is one of those who "cannot make love in English."

Olga left Cuba because of her disagreement with the Revolution. She came to the United States with her family in one of the "Freedom Flights" instituted after 1968. Although she was aware of having had feelings for other girls during her childhood and adolescence, those feelings were never acknowledged then because lesbianism was "sinful" and she was deeply Catholic. She came out as a lesbian two years after arriving in the United States and was rather torn by the feeling that what she was doing was "sinful." On the other hand, she was very much in love with another Cuban woman she had met in Los Angeles, and they both decided to start attending religious services at Dignity, a group of gay Catholics that had just started. Through her involvement in Dignity, Olga started becoming politically active in gay/lesbian issues, mostly inside the lesbian community, and she continues to be active. She is convinced that she would never have come out as a lesbian had she stayed in Cuba and believes that the process of acculturation to the United States made it possible for her to come out. She has a Masters in Social Work and works in a government agency mostly serving a Latino population. She remains mostly "closeted" in the Latino community out of concern about the impact that revelation of her lesbianism could have for her clients and colleagues alike.

For both of these women, clearly their migration offered certain freedoms that fostered the development of a lesbian life. Their political, religious and social affiliations with the lesbian community vary greatly. Their shared experience is the link between migration and sexual self-expression. Both Maritza and Olga are out to their families and don't find any particular conflict with their family members concerning their lesbianism.

A heterosexual perspective is provided by Jazmin, a serious and reflective Korean woman in her mid-thirties, and Sudha, a second-generation South Asian woman. Jazmin came to the United States with her family in her early adolescence and moved away from her parents a few years later to attend college. Jazmin finds sex education in the United States cold and unromantic, while finding her mother's sex explanations, mumbled in Korean, rather irritating. Her mother's position is that men should never be trusted, particularly Korean men—advice that Jazmin has taken rather seriously in never dating Korean men, much to the paradoxical disgust of her mother. Her mother keeps talking to her daughters about not having sex before marriage and never marrying a white man. For this reason, she has not dared to introduce her boyfriend to her parents. According to Jazmin, for a Korean woman to date a man outside her ethnic group is seen as proof that she is a whore. Recently, while visiting some friends of her family, an old woman turned her back on her for shaming her mother by not being married to a Korean man yet, when she is already old enough to have several children.

Jazmin is keenly aware of the racist stereotype of Asian women as whores and worries about how she is perceived by strangers when she is affectionate in public with her Caucasian boyfriend. She knows that her race is part of her attractiveness for some white men. She finds it hard to believe that race is not always part of sexuality and vice versa. Although she loves her boyfriend, she believes their racial difference gives him additional power in the relationship besides the power he already has by being a man. Because all of Jazmin's lovers have been white men and because she learned about sex in the United States and acquired her vocabulary about sex in English, she believes that she cannot use Korean words when talking about sex. Jazmin believes that her growing up in the United States rather than Korea has made her more assertive and able to enjoy sex more than both Korean and white American women. She says many Caucasian women who are rather promiscuous in their sexual behavior confess in private that they do not enjoy sex. Korean women living in Korea, on the other hand, do not enjoy sex either and frequently feel "dirty" because of complying with their husbands' sexual demands.

Sudha, on the other hand, could not imagine dating a man who was not of Indian parentage. In fact, the only reason she has succeeded in convincing her parents to let her date while going to college, rather than arranging a marriage for her, is that she has had only one boyfriend and his parents come from the same social class and region of India as hers. In her words, she intends to have a career and not live a life dedicated to a man, like her silent, passive mother. On the other hand, she finds great pleasure in cooking for her boyfriend and taking care of him in a "traditional way." Sudha dresses in Western clothes and so does her mother, although her mother would much rather wear a *sari*. Sudha's father, however, does not permit his wife to wear a *sari*. He believes *saris* are too sexually revealing for Western eyes and, besides, it will make his wife look too traditional and this will contradict his professional status and his image as a "modern" Indian man. Never mind that in this process he is behaving like a traditional husband ordering his wife around. Sudha feels a lot of compassion for her mother and believes that religion has been her only support in all these long years as an immigrant. Her mother's experience is one of the reasons she will try to avoid an arranged marriage. On the other hand, she believes that arranged marriages are not necessarily bad.

Both Jazmin and Sudha appear to be openly conflicted about loyalty to their families and cultural traditions while feeling that those same traditions are frustrating and limiting for them as women. They act "very American" while expressing feelings of alienation in the midst of a racist society. Probably their immersion in North American society at an earlier age than Olga and Maritza plays a part in their greater internal conflict concerning adaptation to this society.

Regardless of their differences, these four women are in agreement about the difficulties of acculturating to American society. The four of them mention encounters with racism. Jazmin and Sudha, in particular, remember being stereotyped by teachers and classmates alike during their high school years. At the same time, they believe that living in the United States has opened economic opportunities for them and their families and has opened doors for them as women as well.

Talking to them, and to the other women I have interviewed, has been exciting and enlightening. At this point, I am looking forward to the continuation of this study. I hope that it will help me clarify an important aspect of immigrant women's lives.

I also hope (and have already witnessed) that the focus groups and individual interviews can become a tool to encourage participants to get in touch with their own sexuality and their own erotic power. Speaking of the power of the erotic in women's lives, the late poet Audre Lorde (1984), who was also an immigrant, said that

> Our erotic knowledge empowers us, becomes a lens through which we scrutinize all aspects of our existence, forcing us to evaluate those aspects honestly in terms of their relative meaning within our lives. And this is grave responsibility, projected from within each of us, not to settle for the convenient, the shoddy, the conventionally expected, nor the merely safe. (p.57)

She warns us that "in order to perpetuate itself, every oppression must corrupt or distort those various sources within the culture of the oppressed that can provide energy for change" (p 53). One such source is women's erotic energy. She encourages all "women . . . to examine the ways in which our world can be truly different" (p.55) and not to be afraid of "the power of the erotic." "Once we know the extent to which we are capable of feeling that sense of satisfaction and completion, we can then observe which of our various life endeavors bring us closest to that fullest" (p.54). This is, indeed, a necessary endeavor for immigrant women in the essential process of developing our identities and struggling against the racisms we encounter.

Notes

Reprinted from Espín, O.M. (1995). "Race," Racism, and Sexuality in the Life Narratives of Immigrant Women. *Feminism and Psychology*, 5(2), 223–238. (Based on the keynote address to the Feminism and Psychology Day Conference "Challenging Racisms" held at the London Women's Centre, London, May 1994.)

References

Accad, E. (1991). Sexuality and sexual politics: Conflicts and contradictions for contemporary women in the Middle East. In C.T. Mohanty, A. Russo, & L. Torres (Eds.), *Third World women and the politics of feminism* (pp.237–250). Bloomington: Indiana University Press.

Andizian, S., Catani, M., Cicourel, A., Dinmar, N., Harper, D., Kudat, A., Morokvasic, M., Oriol, M., Parris, R.G., Streiff, J., & Setland, C. (1983). *Vivir entre dos culturas*. Paris: Serbal/UNESCO.

Aron, A. (1992). *"Testimonio,"* a bridge between psychotherapy and sociotherapy. In E. Cole, O.M. Espín, & E. Rothblum (Eds.) *Refugee women and their mental health: Shattered societies, shattered lives* (pp.173–189). New York: Haworth.

Bandura, A. (1982). The psychology of chance encounters and life paths. *American Psychologist*, 37, 747–755.

Basch, C.E. (1987). Focus group interview: An underutilized research technique for improving theory and practice in health education. *Health Education Quarterly*, 14, 411–448.

Bhavnani, K.-K., & Haraway, D. (1994). Shifting the subject: A conversation between Kum-Kum Bhavnani and Donna Haraway, 12 April 1993, Santa Cruz, California. *Feminism & Psychology*, 4(1), 19–39.

Bhavnani, K.-K., & Phoenix, A. (1994). Editorial introduction. Shifting identities shifting racisms. *Feminism & Psychology*, 4(1), 5–18.

Brettell, C.B., & Sargent, C.F. (Eds.). (1993). *Gender in crosscultural perspective*. Englewood Cliffs, NJ: Prentice Hall.

Cole, E., Espín, O.M., & Rothblum, E. (Eds.). (1992). *Refugee women and their mental health: Shattered societies, shattered lives*. New York: Haworth.

Denzin, N.K. (1989). *Interpretive biography*. Newbury Park, CA: Sage.

di Leonardo, M. (Ed.). (1991). *Gender at the crossroads of knowledge: Feminist anthropology in the post-modern era*. Berkeley: University of California Press.

el Saadawi, N. (1980). *The hidden face of Eve: Women in the Arab world*. London: Zed Press.

Espín, O.M. (1984). Cultural and historical influences on sexuality in Hispanic/Latin women. In C. Vance (Ed.), *Pleasure and danger: Exploring female sexuality* (pp.149–164). London: Routledge & Kegan Paul.

Espín, O.M. (1987a). Issues of identity in the psychology of Latina lesbians. In Boston Lesbian Psychologies Collective (Eds), *Lesbian psychologies: Explorations and challenges* (pp.35–55). Urbana: University of Illinois Press.

Espín, O.M. (1987b). Psychological impact of migration on Latinas: Implications for psychotherapeutic practice. *Psychology of Women Quarterly*, 11(4), 489–503.

Espín, O.M. (1992). Roots uprooted: The psychological impact of historical/political dislocation. In E. Cole, O.M. Espín, & E. Rothblum (Eds.), *Refugee women and their mental health: Shattered societies, shattered lives*(pp.9–20). New York: Haworth.

Espín, O.M. (1994). Traumatic historical events and adolescent psychosocial development: Letters from V. In C. Franz & A.J. Stewart (Eds.), *Women creating lives: Identities, resilience, and resistance* (pp.187–198). Boulder: Westview.

Espín, O.M., Cavanaugh, A., Paydarfar, N., & Wood, R. (1990, March) *Mothers, daughters and migration: A new look at the psychology of separation*. Presented at the Annual Meeting of the Association for Women in Psychology, Tempe, AZ.

Espín, O.M., Stewart, A.J., & Gómez, C. (1990) Letters from V.: Adolescent personality development in socio-historical context. *Journal of Personality*, 58, 347–364.

Essed, P. (1991). *Understanding everyday racism*. Newbury Park, CA: Sage.

Essed, P. (1994). Contradictory positions. Ambivalent perceptions: A case study of a black woman entrepreneur. *Feminism & Psychology*, 4(1), 99–118.

Foucault, M. (1981). *The history of sexuality*. Harmondsworth, UK: Penguin.

Gabaccia, D. (Ed.). (1992). *Seeking common ground: Multidisciplinary studies of immigrant women in the United States*. Westport, CT: Praeger.

Gold, S.J. (1992). *Refugee communities: A comparative field study*. Newbury Park, CA: Sage.

Goodenow, C., & Espín, O.M. (1993). Identity choices in immigrant female adolescents. *Adolescence*, 28, 173–184.

Jaggar, A., & Bordo, S. (Eds.). (1989). *Gender/body/knowledge*. New Brunswick, NJ: Rutgers University Press.

Josselson, R., & Lieblich, A. (Eds.). (1993). *The narrative study of lives*. Newbury Park, CA: Sage.

Kaschak, E. (1992). *Engendered lives*. New York: Basic Books.

Krueger, R.A. (1994). *Focus groups: A practical guide for applied research* (2nd ed.). Thousand Oaks, CA: Sage.

Laqueur, T. (1990). *Making sex: Body and gender from the Greeks to Freud*. Cambridge, MA: Harvard University Press.

Lorde, A. (1984). *Sister outsider*. Freedom, CA: Crossing Press.

Marín, B.V., Marín, G., Juárez, R., & Sorensen, J.L. (1992). Interventions from family members as a strategy for preventing HIV among intravenous drug users. *Journal of Community Psychology*, 20, 90–97.

Marín, B.V., Tscham, J.M., Gómez, C.A., & Kegeles, S.M. (1993). Acculturation and gender differences in sexual attitudes and behaviors: Hispanic versus non-Hispanic white unmarried adults. *American Journal of Public Health*, 83, 1759–1761.

Mishler, E.G. (1986). *Research interviewing: Context and narrative*. Cambridge, MA: Harvard University Press.

Morgan, D.L. (1988). *Focus groups as qualitative research*. Newbury Park, CA: Sage.

Morgan, D.L. (Ed.). (1993). *Successful focus groups*. Newbury Park, CA: Sage.

Nathanson, C.A. (1991). *Dangerous passage: The social control of sexuality in women's adolescence*. Philadelphia: Temple University Press.

Ogundipe-Leslie, 'M. (1993). African women, culture and another development. In S.M. James & A.P.A. Busia (Eds.), *Theorizing Black feminisms* (pp.102–117). London: Routledge.

Parker, A., Russo, M., Sommer, D., & Yaegar, P. (Eds.). (1992). *Nationalisms and sexualities.* New York: Routledge.

Phizacklea, A. (Ed.). (1983). *One way ticket: Migration and female labour.* London: Routledge & Kegan Paul.

Riessman, C. (1993). *Narrative analysis.* Newbury Park, CA: Sage.

Ruiz, V.L. (1992). The flapper and the chaperone: Historical memory among Mexican-American women. In D. Gabaccia (Ed.), *Seeking common ground: Multidisciplinary studies of immigrant women in the United States* (pp.141–157). Westport, CT: Praeger.

Schreier, B.A. (1994). *Becoming American women: Clothing and the Jewish immigrant experience 1880–1920.* Chicago: Chicago Historical Society.

Silverman, D. (1993). *Interpreting qualitative data: Methods for analysing talk, text, and interaction.* London: Sage.

Stewart, D.W., & Shamdasani, P.N. (1990). *Focus groups: Theory and practice.* Newbury Park, CA: Sage.

Strauss, A L. (1987). *Qualitative analysis for social scientists.* Cambridge, UK: Cambridge University Press.

Tohidi, N. (1991). Gender and Islamic fundamentalism: Feminist politics in Iran. In C.T. Mohanty, A. Russo, & L. Torres (Eds.), *Third World women and the politics of feminism* (pp.251–270). Bloomington, IN: Indiana University Press.

Valverde, M. (1985). *Sex, power, and pleasure.* Toronto, Ontario: The Women's Press.

Woollett, A., Marshall, H., Nicholson, P., & Dosanjh, N. (1994). Asian Women's ethnic identity: The impact of gender and context in the accounts of women bringing up children in East London. *Feminism & Psychology,* 4(1), 119–132.

Yuval-Davis, N. (1992). Fundamentalism, multiculturalism and women in Britain. In J. Donald & A. Rattansi (Eds.), *"Race," culture and difference* (pp.278–291). London: Sage.

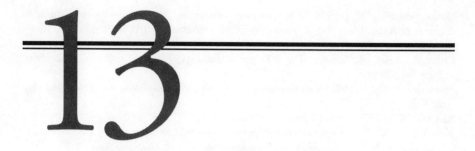

Leaving the Nation and Joining the Tribe: Lesbian Immigrants Crossing Geographical and Identity Borders

Maritza and Olga are both Cuban. They both migrated to the United States when they were 22 years of age, during the 1970s. Maritza from a poor working-class family, Olga from a middle-class family. The stories of these two women exemplify some of the connections between migration and lesbian life choices. They serve to illustrate how the experience of crossing borders through migration evokes the border crossing lesbians undergo as they shed their heterosexual identities and embrace new identities as lesbians.

Maritza had come out as a lesbian in Cuba, when she was 14. From a very early age she identified her lesbianism as a consequence of her artistic talent. (In Cuba and other Latin American countries there is a widespread association between artists and homosexuality.) She was rebellious as an adolescent, and more or less openly displayed her preference for girls. At the age of 22 she decided that staying in Cuba, considering the government's position on homosexuality, was impossible for her. Although she was otherwise completely in favor of the Revolution, and precisely because of her connections with it, she masterminded an escape during a trip sponsored by the Cuban government for young artists to Eastern Europe. Her family continues to live in Cuba. Despite the passage of time, they strongly disagree with her decision to leave the country. In the United States, Maritza lives a very private life and refuses to participate in any form of lesbian activism.

Olga left Cuba because of her disagreement with the Revolution. She came to the United States with her family in one of the "freedom flights" instituted after 1968. Although she was aware of having feelings for girls during her childhood and adolescence, those feelings were not acknowledged then because she was devotedly Catholic and lesbianism was "sinful." She came out as a lesbian two years after arriving in the United States, and for some years after her coming out she remained tormented by feelings that what she was doing was "sinful." However, she was very much in love with another Cuban woman she had met in Los Angeles, where she lived with her family. They both became involved in Dignity, a newly formed group of gay Catholics. It was through Dignity that Olga began her political activism in gay/lesbian issues. She is convinced that she would have never come out as a lesbian had she stayed in Cuba and believes that immigration to the United States made it possible for her to come out.

I believe the transitions demanded in the migratory process provide insights into the process of coming out for all lesbians. These transitions could be seen to represent the metaphorical crossing of borders and boundaries that all lesbians confront when refusing to continue living in "old countries," even if those old countries exist only in their minds. In other words, the dislocations caused by the migration seem to mirror the discontinuities that are characteristic of the coming out process. In addition, learning how women from a variety of social groups negotiate lesbian identity and the coming out process expands our understanding of lesbianism and makes it more inclusive.

Culture and history are powerful forces in human development. What, then, happens to the individual life, sense of self and life story when the cultural narrative changes abruptly with migration? The process of rewriting one's life story is further problematized when in addition to the physical relocation, the narrator begins to redefine herself as a lesbian. Although, as Polkinghorne (1988) writes, "the story about life is open to editing and revision" (p.154), some editing and revision may require more work than others. He goes on to say that "rewriting one's story involves major life changes" (p.182). But what happens when events that are not "personal events" in the usual way "invade" the life story? Some of these events transform the "plots" provided by the culture and social context either because they transform the culture itself or because the individual finds herself in a new cultural context that allows a different kind of story. The process of coming out also demands a rewriting of the life story and, almost always, a migration to another cultural context even though the person may not actually move. I believe that migration and coming out are "historical events" that disrupt and detour the life course. Personal narratives provide the threads to reweave one's own life after migration and coming out. National identity and sexual identity are determined, negotiated, and intertwined in the lives of women immigrants and lesbians whether they are immigrants or not. In fact, perhaps exploring the connections between migration and coming out could illuminate why so many non-immigrant lesbians move away from their hometowns and established network of friends while in the process of searching for a new identity.

Immigration, even when willingly chosen and eagerly sought, produces a variety of experiences with significant consequences for the individual. No matter how glad the immigrant might be to be in a new country, the transitions created by immigration often result in profound dysphoria. These feelings include: loneliness due to the absence of people with shared experiences; strain and fatigue from the effort to adapt and cope with cognitive overload; feelings of rejection from the new society which affect self-esteem and may lead to alienation; confusion in terms of role expectations, values, and identity; "shock" resulting from the differences between the two cultures; and a sense of uprootedness and impotence resulting from an inability to function competently in the new culture.

The immigrant's acculturation into a new society is first and foremost a process of disassembling and reassembling social networks (Rogler, 1994). The process of coming out involves also a disassembling and reassembling of one's life and social networks. Coming out as a lesbian, even inside one's own country of birth, demands a certain "acculturation"—an adaptation to new norms and expectations of one's roles and relationships. There is an element of loss in coming out as a lesbian in the context of a heterosexist society, no matter how joyful and self-affirming the new identity might otherwise be. The new perspectives developed in the coming out process involve risks and joys that, though unique, evoke some of the risks and possibilities created by geographic migration.

When immigrants cross borders, they also cross emotional and behavioral boundaries. Becoming a member of a new society stretches the boundaries of what is possible in several ways. When one's life changes, roles and identities change as well. In the new culture, new societal expectations lead to transformations in identity. The identities expected and permitted in the home culture may not be those expected or permitted in the host society. Boundaries are crossed when new identities and roles are incorporated into life. Most immigrants who, either eagerly or reluctantly, cross geographical borders do not fully suspect the breadth of emotional and behavioral boundaries they are about to cross.

For lesbians who are immigrants, such as Maritza and Olga, the crossing of geographical borders and the subsequent crossing of lifestyle and sexual identity boundaries provide opportunities for developing new identities. This also generates new challenges and new life options (Espín, 1984, 1987a, 1987b, 1990, 1994). Frequently, newly encountered sex role patterns combined with greater access to paid employment for women create possibilities for a new lifestyle that was previously unavailable.

Although the experiences of women in international migration have begun to draw the attention of researchers, policy makers, and service providers (e.g., Andizian et al., 1983; Cole, Espín, & Rothblum, 1992; Gabaccia, 1992; Phizacklea,

1983), the lesbian experience is largely invisible in these studies. Women comprise a large proportion of the world's immigrant and refugee population. The United Nations estimates that 80% of all refugees in the world are women and their children (U.S. Committee for Refugees, 1990). The current estimate of the foreign-born population in the United States is about 20 million (Rogler, 1994). Demographic studies have demonstrated that the composition of the gay and lesbian population in North America resembles the entire population (Tremble, Schneider, & Appathurai, 1989). In other words, the ethnic, racial, and religious characteristics of the general population are represented in the same proportion among gays and lesbians. As it is true for all other groups of women, one can assume that lesbians are present in significant numbers among immigrants.

Specific difficulties exist, however, in obtaining adequate statistics on gay and lesbian populations among immigrants and refugees. In fact, little is known about the experiences of both heterosexual and lesbian immigrant women in such "private" realms as sexuality, sexual orientation, and identity. Yet, as scholarship has demonstrated (e.g., Parker, Russo, Sommer, & Yaeger, 1992), sexuality and related issues instead of being private matters are present in the public domain as expressions of societal values. This illuminates why so many cultures and countries try to control and legislate sexuality. Indeed, as one historian observed, "sexual behavior (perhaps more than religion) is the most highly symbolic activity in any society. To penetrate the symbolic system implicit in any society's sexual behavior is therefore to come closest to the heart of its uniqueness" (Trumbach, 1977, p.24).

We know that the sexual and gender role behaviors assigned to women serve a larger social function beyond the personal in all societies. It is used by enemies and friends alike as "proof" of the moral fiber or decay of social groups or nations. In most societies, women's sexual behavior and their conformity to traditional gender roles signifies the family's value system. Thus, in many societies, a lesbian daughter, like a heterosexual daughter who does not conform to traditional morality, can be seen as "proof" of the lax morals of a family. This is why struggles surrounding acculturation in immigrant and refugee families frequently center around issues of daughters' sexual behaviors—and women's sex roles in general. For parents and young women alike, acculturation and sexuality are closely connected; in many immigrant communities, being "Americanized" is derogatorily synonymous with being sexually promiscuous (Espín, 1984, 1987b).

Girls and women are more often than not forced to embody cultural continuity amidst cultural dislocation. While young men are allowed and encouraged to develop new identities in the new country, girls and women are expected to continue living as if they were still in the old country. Groups that are transforming their way of life through a vast and deep process of acculturation focus on preserving "tradition" almost exclusively through the gender roles of women. The traditional role of women becomes the repository of traditions. The "proper" behavior of women is used to signify the difference between those who belong to the collectivity and those who do not (Yuval-Davis, 1992, p.285).

Although lesbianism is not only about "sex," it is, obviously, closely connected with sexual behavior/identity. Sexuality is a universal component of human experience, yet how it is embodied and expressed is not. Even the definition of what is sexual changes among cultural contexts. These cultural constructs inextricably entwine with the expression of lesbian sexuality. Many women who identified as lesbian before the migration have to learn to be lesbian in their new cultural context.

The immigrant lesbian acculturates as an immigrant and sometimes as a lesbian at the same time. If she comes to the United States from a non-European background, she also has to acculturate as a (so-called) "minority" person. As I argued in my earlier work,

> Identity development for persons of ethnic or racial minority groups (or immigrants) involves not only the acceptance of an external reality that can rarely be changed (e.g., being Black, Puerto Rican, Vietnamese, Jewish), but also an intrapsychic "embracing" of that reality as a positive component of one's self. By definition, in the context of a heterosexist and sexist society, the process of identity development for . . . [immigrant lesbians] entails the embracing of "stigmatized" or "negative" identities. Coming out to self and others in the context of a sexist and heterosexist American society is compounded by coming out in the context of what is usually a sexist and heterosexist . . . [culture of origin] immersed in racist society. (Espín, 1987a, p.35)

Needless to say, lesbians present unique challenges to immigrant communities while, at the same time, their communities' expectations create enormous pressures on them. This is particularly true for girls who "come out" as adolescents. As the authors of a study on Canadian youth remind us,

> Every adolescent, regardless of ethnic affiliation, must resolve a number of issues as part of the coming-out process. These include: (a) deciding whether or not to disclose to the family, (b) finding a niche among gay and lesbian peers, and (c) reconciling sexual orientation with other aspects of identity. For the child of immigrant parents, the coming-out process takes place against the backdrop of ethnic traditions, values, and social networks. For some, this adds a dimension of complexity to the issues. Homosexuality, often in conflict with North American religious and cultural mores, seems even more incongruous and unacceptable in the context of conservative, Old World values. Furthermore, the rift that occurs between parent and child over sexual orientation is set in the context of an existing conflict as the child pulls away from the Old World culture to espouse the North American way of life. (Tremble, Schneider, & Appathurai, 1989, p.255)
>
> Paradoxically, these values also provide the pathway to reconciliation between homosexual children and parents. When the love of children and the value of family ties are strong, nothing, including homosexuality, will permanently split the family. Ultimately, when the family system is bound by love and respect, a way is found to embrace the homosexual member. (p.257).

Whether adolescent or adult, being a lesbian in the midst of an immigrant community involves choice about one's own life. It also affects the community's perception of itself and attitudes towards the lesbian's family of origin. Coming out may jeopardize not only family ties but also the possibility of serving the community in which the skills and energy of all members are such important assets. For example, many lesbian immigrants are single and self-supporting and take advantage of the opportunities for employment and education in the United States (Espín, 1987a). They are frequently involved in services and advocacy in their communities. At the same time, they feel constrained by the possibility of serving their community for fear of being "discovered" and rejected by that same community (Espín, 1987a, 1990).

Pressures on immigrant women's sexuality, however, come from the host society as well. The host culture imposes its own burdens and desires through prejudices and racism. Even though racism may be subtle, the immigrant woman finds herself caught between the racism of the dominant society and the sexist and heterosexist expectations of her own community. The racism of the dominant society makes the retrenchment into "tradition" appear to be justifiable. Conversely, the rigidities of "tradition" appear to justify the racist/prejudicial treatment doled by the dominant society. Moreover, the effect of racism and sexism is not only felt as pressure from "the outside", but it also becomes internalized, as are all forms of oppression. Immigrant women who are lesbian develop their identity against the backdrop of these contradictions.

Immigrants are preoccupied with "geography," with the place in which events occur (Espín, 1992). This phenomenon has two components. One is preoccupation with the country of origin; the other is a fixation on "what could have been." This translates into ruminations about life's crossroads. According to Rogler (1994), "The migration experience creates an emergent phenomenology of incessant reference group comparisons and trade-offs between the benefits of the host society and the losses incurred in departing from the society of origin" (p.704). The immigrant often reflects about life's possibilities: What if she remained in the country of birth? or the immigration had taken place at this or that stage of life? and other similar preoccupations.

The immigrant's ruminations about "what could have been" are paralleled by lesbians' concerns about past events that are seen in a new light after coming out. Some lesbians are preoccupied with the relationship between childhood events and having become a lesbian. To this, the immigrant lesbian adds thoughts/concerns and general "what could have been" ideas concerning her lesbianism. These are often concentrated around a basic question: Would I have become a lesbian if I had not emigrated? The Cuban-American lesbian writer Achy Obejas illustrates these concerns in a recent story, when she ponders,

> What if we'd stayed? What if we'd never left Cuba? . . . What if we'd never left. . . . I wonder, if we'd stayed then who, if anyone . . . would have been my blond lovers, or any kind of lovers at all. . . . I try to imagine who I would have been if Fidel had never come into Havana sitting triumphantly on top of that tank, but I can't. I can only think of variations of who I am, not who I might have been. (1994, p.124–125)

For lesbian immigrants, identity develops in the context of these questions and contradictions. For lesbians who are not immigrants, the process of coming out requires a transformation that parallels the acculturation process of those who migrate.

For everyone, identity is neither singular nor static. As the feminist social scientists Bhavnani and Phoenix tell us, each person "is both located in, and opts for a number of differing and at times conflictual identities, depending on the social, political, economic and ideological aspects of their situation" (1994, p.9). This notion of identity is particularly significant when studying the experiences of lesbian immigrants.

Notes

Reprinted from Espín, O.M. (1996). Leaving the Nation and Joining the Tribe: Lesbian Immigrants Crossing Geographical and Identity Boundaries. *Women and Therapy*, 19(4), 99–107. Copublished simultaneously in M. Hall (Ed.), *Sexualities* (pp.99–107). New York: Harrington Park Press.

References

Andizian, S., Catani, M., Cicourel, A., Dittmar, N., Harper, D., Kudat, A., Morokvasic, M., Oriol, M., Parris, R.G., Streiff, J., & Setland, C. (1983). *Vivir entre dos culturas*. Paris: Serbal/UNESCO.

Bhavnani, K.-K., & Phoenix, A. (1994). Editorial introduction. Shifting identities shifting racisms. *Feminism & Psychology,* 4(1), 5–18.

Cole, E., Espín, O.M., & Rothblum, E. (Eds.). (1992). *Shattered societies, shattered lives: Refugee women and their mental health.* New York: Haworth.

Espín, O.M. (1984). Cultural and historical influences on sexuality in Hispanic/Latin women. In C. Vance (Ed.), *Pleasure and danger: Exploring female sexuality* (pp.149–164). London: Routledge & Kegan Paul. (2nd ed., London: Pandora, 1994)

Espín, O.M. (1987a) Issues of identity in the psychology of Latina lesbians. In Boston Lesbian Psychologies Collective (Eds.), *Lesbian psychologies: Explorations and challenges* (pp.35–55). Urbana: University of Illinois Press.

Espín, O.M. (1987b). Psychological impact of migration on Latinas: Implications for psychotherapeutic practice. *Psychology of Women Quarterly,* 11(4), 489–503.

Espín, O.M. (1990, August). *Ethnic and cultural issues in the "coming out" process among Latina lesbians.* Presented at the 98th Annual Convention of the American Psychological Association, Boston.

Espín, O.M. (1992). Roots uprooted: The psychological impact of historical/Political dislocation. In E. Cole, O.M. Espín, & E. Rothblum (Eds.), *Refugee women and their mental health: Shattered societies, shattered lives* (pp.9–20). New York: Haworth.

Espín, O.M. (1994, August). *Crossing borders and boundaries: The life narratives of immigrant lesbians.* Presented at the 102nd Convention of the American Psychological Association, Los Angeles.

Gabaccia, D. (Ed.). (1992). *Seeking common ground: Multidisciplinary studies of immigrant women in the United States.* Westport, CT: Praeger.

Obejas, A. (1994). *We came all the way from Cuba so you could dress like this?* Pittsburgh: Cleis.

Parker, A., Russo, M., Sommer, D., & Yaeger, P. (Eds.).(1992). *Nationalisms and sexualities.* New York: Routledge.

Phizacklea, A. (Ed.). (1983). *One way ticket: Migration and female labour.* London: Routledge & Kegan Paul.

Polkinghorne, D.E. (1988). *Narrative knowing and the human sciences.* Albany, NY: State University of New York Press.

Rogler, L.H. (1994). International migrations: A framework for directing research. *American Psychologist, 49*(8), 701–708.

Tremble, B., Schneider, M., & Appathurai, C. (1989). Growing up gay or lesbian in multicultural context. In G. Herdt (Ed.), *Gay and lesbian youth* (pp.253–267). New York: Harrington Park Press.

Trumbach, R. (1977). London's sodomites. *Journal of Social History,* 11, 1–33.

U.S. Committee for Refugees. (1990). *World refugee survey: 1989 in review.* Washington, DC: American Council for Nationalities.

Yuval-Davis, N. (1992). Fundamentalism, multiculturalism and women in Britain. In J. Donald & A. Rattansi (Eds.), *"Race," culture and difference* (pp.278–291). London: Sage.

About the Author

Oliva M. Espín is professor of women's studies at San Diego State University and part-time core faculty at the California School of Professional Psychology–San Diego. She received an Award for Distinguished Professional Contribution from the American Psychological Association and is a fellow of five divisions of the APA.